THE GREATEST PLOT
in
HISTORY

THE GREATEST PLOT
in
HISTORY

by

RALPH de TOLEDANO 1916

ARLINGTON HOUSE·PUBLISHERS
NEW ROCHELLE, NEW YORK

Selections from *Men and Decisions* by Lewis L. Strauss, copyright © 1962 by Lewis L. Strauss and the Lewis L. Strauss Literary Trust, are reprinted by permission of Doubleday & Company, Inc.

Library of Congress Cataloging in Publication Data

De Toledano, Ralph, 1916–
    The greatest plot in history.

    Includes index.
    1. Espionage, Russian—United States. 2. Atomic bomb. I. Title.
UB271.R9D38 1977   327'.12'0947   76–54290
ISBN: 0–87000–371–2

Preface to the New Edition

In a recent book,* a minor playwright and storyteller now turned pundit delivers himself of some opinions on the case of atom spies Julius and Ethel Rosenberg. With a great show of impartiality—he casually admits that the *Death House Letters* written by the Rosenbergs to each other during their incarceration at Sing Sing were doctored by the Communist Party—and with the expertise he no doubt gained at New York's Stage Delicatessen, David Zane Mairowitz dismisses the charges against them:

Even if the Rosenbergs were guilty in some degree, the massive frame-up, railroading, and sentencing they suffered was out of all proportion to their alleged spy operation. The idea that the Soviets would entrust a big-time network to such obvious small-fry as these taxes credibility. The A-Bomb sketches made by [David] Greenglass and produced as damaging evidence were primitive and could not give any idea of the bomb's mechanism. Julius's use of two halves of a Jell-O box to link agent to agent was the gesture of a thorough amateur . . . Finally master spies are rarely caught.

Because the writer of that paragraph is a dilettante in matters of espionage and nuclear science, it may seem like attacking a gnat with a howitzer to rebut them. But since those words reflect perfectly the knee-jerk reaction of certain citizens to the Rosenberg Case, they warrant analysis.

* David Zane Mairowitz, *The Radical Soap Opera*. Avon Books, New York.

v

The facts then:

1. The trial of the Rosenbergs was conducted under an incandescent illumination provided by the media and by the international Communist apparatus. The conviction of the Rosenbergs was reviewed by a U.S. Court of Appeals in New York known for its meticulous devotion to the Bill of Rights. It was further sustained by the Supreme Court. The trial was debated *ad infinitum* and, in the views of some, *ad nauseam*. Books were written and polemics launched, but none of them adduced one iota of evidence to prove that the Rosenbergs were "framed" or "railroaded." The finality of the death sentence can be challenged, but it in no wise impinges on the guilt or innocence of the Rosenbergs. And to argue that there was a conspiracy against the Rosenbergs requires the indictment of President Truman and the entire federal establishment. By now, certainly one of the conspirators would have spoken out.

2. An innocent man does not hide behind the Fifth Amendment when his life is at stake, as both the Rosenbergs did when they were on trial.

3. The A-Bomb sketches produced by David Greenglass may have seemed "primitive" to those with but a high school knowledge of physics. But expert witnesses at the trial demonstrated that they were invaluable in any attempt to reproduce American nuclear weapons.

4. The use of halves of a Jell-O box, or any similar piece of cardboard irregularly cut, was not the "gesture of a thorough amateur" but standard operating procedure for identification among espionage agents—as anyone but an amateur would know. At the time of the Rosenberg trial, I questioned American and foreign intelligence agents on this subject, and they all agreed that it was a telling piece of evidence.

5. Master spies are frequently caught. The Japanese arrested and executed Richard Sorge, one of the greatest Soviet spies of World War II. Ronald Seth's *Encyclopedia of Espionage* cites case after case of the arrest of master spies.

6. Julius Rosenberg was not the "obvious small-fry" or the little man caught in the vortex of war that propagandists have attempted to portray. A 1955 report of the Senate Permanent Investigations Subcommittee, prepared by chief counsel Robert F. Kennedy, stated:

The Rosenberg spy ring successfully penetrated the Army Signal Corps and related private establishments [doing classified work for the Army]. This espionage ring took and obtained secrets from the Army Signal Corps and transmitted them to the Soviet Union.

According to the Kennedy report, the Rosenberg spy ring had wide ramifications and was, two years after the execution of Ethel and Julius, "on the basis of available evidence" probably still operating. One of the top Soviet agents in the scientific field was Harry Gold, Klaus Fuchs' "contact," who worked directly and closely with the Rosenbergs, an index of their importance to the Soviet apparatus.

And the evidence is still coming in. When Scotland Yard and MI-5 arrested master spies Gordon Lonsdale and the Krogers, Peter and Helen, in London, they discovered that all three had worked with the Rosenbergs in past years. The Lonsdale apparatus was uncovered in 1961, however, eight years after the execution of the Rosenbergs. What MI-5 learned of the Rosenberg complicity in the Lonsdale master group was turned over to the FBI where it simply went into the file of closed cases.

Since then, the FBI has opened up the many thousands of pages of the Rosenberg file, under the compulsion of a Freedom of Information Act suit filed by friends of the couple. Though these friends had argued for years that this disclosure would give them the proof of a frame-up, it has resulted in just the opposite. A minute study of the file disclosed only that David Greenglass, when first questioned by the FBI, attempted to shield his wife and the Rosenbergs.

Klaus Fuchs led the way to Harry Gold, though reluctantly. Gold led the way to Greenglass. Greenglass led the way to the

Rosenbergs. That is how an espionage apparatus is apprehended and broken up. Had the Rosenbergs talked, as small-fry spies always do, more of the cancer of Communist espionage would have been cut out. But the Rosenbergs were too important to be allowed to speak—and too fanatically devoted to Communism— and the Soviets made sure that they remained silent. There was enough of that fanatical devotion to make the task relatively simple, although once or twice Julius seemed to be on the verge of cracking.

Whether or not the Rosenbergs were "small-fry" has little to do with the deadliness of their contribution. David Greenglass was a small cog in both the A-Bomb project and the espionage apparatus. Yet he added significantly to the Soviet Union's store of knowledge and saved the Russians time and money in the construction of their own bomb. The master spy would be ineffectual if he did not have his agents, important and otherwise, funneling information to him. The record of the Rosenberg contribution is there, and nothing has surfaced, despite the prodigious efforts of their defenders, to cast doubt on the testimony of witnesses who testified in open court—and suffered long prison sentences for their pains—about the activities of Ethel and Julius.

The orchestrated protests, the books and articles depicting the Rosenbergs as idealistic victims of the cold war, and all the paraphernalia of international propaganda have little to do with the thrust of this book. The Rosenbergs were but part of one of the greatest espionage campaigns ever mounted by the Soviet Union. It ranged from New York to Chicago, from Philadelphia to Tennessee, from Los Alamos to the Cal Tech radiation laboratory in Berkeley, from Canada to England. It took in famous scientists, academicians, Army lieutenants, the most skilled of Stalin's spies in the United States, small-fry and big fish—a cross section of all those who worked on the A-bomb.

The Soviets penetrated every major scientific installation working on the bomb. Through the courtesy of the Lend-Lease Administration, they were able to channel to their own laboratories scarce materials needed for the American war effort. After the explosion of the Hiroshima and Nagasaki bombs, a tremendous campaign was launched to convince the Congress and the American people that what little information had not been stolen should be delivered to them. The bomb the Soviets finally built was a carbon copy of ours.

It would require more than a layman's knowledge of human motivation to understand why so many rational people, confronted by clouds of witnesses and mountains of evidence, should close their eyes to the obvious. In the abstract, they can admit to the fact of Soviet espionage—military, political, scientific, and industrial. But when the specifics are presented to them, they enter into a state of "controlled schizophrenia"—Klaus Fuchs' phrase. This is not a retreat from reality but a bifurcation of reality. The out-croppings of Soviet nuclear espionage were everywhere, so it became necessary to explain them away.

The specific man brought to book, whether for outright espionage or for shutting his eyes to it, could not be guilty but must be the victim of governmental devils. Why? Because the Soviet Union did not need America's nuclear secrets.* If some high-minded individuals had, in fact, turned over a few of those secrets to the Kremlin, they were merely doing what their government should have done since Russia was an "ally" and suspicious of American "imperialism."

The idea that the Soviets did not need to rely on American nuclear research persists to this day. In the spring of 1976, the *Washington Post* reported:

The Soviet Union exploded a hydrogen bomb six months before the United States conducted its first H-bomb test in 1954, according

---

* The Soviet secret police went through the highly hazardous exercise of breaking into the German Foreign Ministry in Berlin, led by General Walter Krivitsky, in order to photograph a copy of the Anti-Comintern Pact—even though Stalin had received the text from Richard Sorge in Tokyo.

to the authors of a new book. . . . U.S. Intelligence made a "dangerously inept" mistake in not telling [Edward] Teller, a developer of the H-bomb, about the Soviet experimentation.

Now an H-bomb is not exploded in a shoe box. Such an explosion would have been detected by British or French scientists, even if their American counterparts were living in a selective coma. The story, moreover, had the Soviets testing their first thermonuclear device, presumably built by a war-devastated country, in 1950!

The truth is that the Russians had the theoretical knowledge that must precede the construction of the H-bomb at the same time as the Americans, the Germans, the French, and the British. What they lacked was the technology to translate the theory into military hardware. The Soviets have always had excellent theoretical scientists, but they are short on technological know-how, as their backwardness in computers demonstrates. The Manhattan Engineering District experimented long and expensively, mobilizing all our technological resources, before it found the one way that would work. The "primitive" drawing of an implosion lens provided by David Greenglass was sufficient to show them the way in which we had moved—and this was of incalculable value.

Before this decade has ended, there will be more books and articles accusing the FBI—which had no part in protecting the security of our atomic installations—of "framing" this or that participant in the greatest plot in history. The Rosenberg children have been dragged from their obscurity to become pawns in this endless propaganda game.

The purpose of this book is to substitute facts for crocodile tears, and to point out the voluminous record for those truly interested in learning what happened while America was at war.

Preface

IN the more than two decades since the Kremlin ordered its many-pronged attack on the West's nuclear secrets, millions of words have been written on atomic espionage. When I began work on this book, however, I realized why much of the story remained untold. Many of the salient facts jutted out of newspaper accounts, but they were isolated. Reporters, under the pressure of deadlines, could only take a brief look at the peaks. Magazine writers tried to encompass too much material within the limits of their assigned space. Two excellent books—*The Atom Spies* by Oliver Pilat and *The Traitors* by Alan Moorehead—were written before the returns were in.

Those who tried to tell the story of atomic espionage were, moreover, brought up short by a series of dead ends. The ordinary uses of research do not suffice in telling this fascinating and shocking story. True, the voluminous transcripts of Congressional hearings, trials, the inquiries of government bodies, and the reports of special commissions offered a bewildering number of facts. But significant areas, never opened up for public scrutiny, remained unexplored.

Much of the information necessary for a rounded account was locked away in the secret files of Counter-Intelligence and counter-espionage—and these are seldom opened to writers. Security still outranks curiosity or the often proclaimed right-to-know.

There was one major source to be tapped—the experienced memories of Soviet espionage agents who defected to the West. For the most part, these men and women tell what they know to the Central Intelligence Agency, to the Federal Bureau of Investigation, to Britain's MI-5, and/or to the French Deuxième Bureau—and then pray that they will be allowed to disappear from sight. If their existence is known, they do not respond to the queries of reporters and writers they have never before met. In fact, they devote themselves to forgetting, not remembering. For every ex-agent who is caught in the focus of public attention, there are many whose existence never becomes known except to specialists in Soviet espionage. Even those who shared the glare of sensational events speak fully only to their governmental questioners—and in private —or to people whose background and knowledge they trust. Igor Gouzenko, who years ago gave me what I believe to be his first interview with a newsman, was willing to let down the barriers because he knew me by reputation. "You will understand," he said.

What he meant was that he could employ with me the special shorthand of a special world. I have seen two former Soviet agents, meeting for the first time, plunge into what seemed like an interrupted conversation. There was no need to find a point of reference. Each knew immediately what the other was talking about, without any explanations. Never having been a Communist, I am in a sense an outsider. But I still remember the surprise of Whittaker Chambers when, after he got to know me well, he discovered that I was never a member of the underground party. Knowledge of the espionage world's shop talk has been invaluable to me in putting together this account of the greatest plot in history. Even in the testimony of former *apparatchiks,* there is much that remains meaningless to the untrained ear.

My major task in writing this book was to sort out the great mass
of unrelated public information—including what was ignored or
misunderstood when it flashed across the screen of our contem-
poraneity—to fill in the gaps with material from my own files, to
consult my notes and my recollection, and to place it all in context.
Because every chapter could of itself have been a small book, a
second task was to boil away the fat of nonessential though interesting material.

Of necessity, I read many hundreds of news stories even though
they merely echoed one another. There were, however, rewards in
this—for buried away among the twice-told tales I found a fact or
an allusion which lit up a dark corner of spying's netherworld.
Much-plowed ground, like the Report of the Royal Commission
which studied the documents taken out of the Soviet Embassy in
Ottawa by Gouzenko, yielded important insights. Of considerable
value were the reports and hearings of the House Un-American
Activities Committee, the Senate Internal Security Subcommittee,
and the Joint Congressional Atomic Energy Committee—not available when the earlier books on this subject were written. The Report
of the Royal Commission in Australia which sifted the disclosures
of Vladimir Petrov was also of value. Wherever it would not be
improper or indiscreet, I have identified other sources in the course
of my narrative.

I am deeply indebted to two books which guided me in recount-
ing the history of nuclear research and in describing the complex
problems of technology solved by the Manhattan Engineer District:
Men and Decisions by Lewis L. Strauss and *Now It Can Be Told*
by Leslie R. Groves. Security reports and testimony, buried away
in the 992 pages of *In the Matter of J. Robert Oppenheimer: Transcript of Hearing Before Personnel Security Board*, corroborated
what had previously been subject to controversy.

A final word:

This book is a tale of many men and many cities—of mixed
motives, misplaced idealism, and ruined lives, of duplicity and inno-

cence. For communism is not the monopoly of traitors. It reaches out in its many disguises to honorable men who do not know why or how or even that it has touched them. Subversion in our time does not lurk in Jacobin cellars: it openly manipulates hopes and causes before betraying them. In narrating actions and effects, my intent is not accusatory. Knowledge of what is past can deflect the course of future events. Since communism, as a paramilitary philosophy and a plan of attack, gains its strength by compounding the weakness and ignorance of others, a delineation of its methodology may serve to increase the will to resist it.

Contents

"Espionage is a distinct and principal Soviet industry."
Vladimir Petrov, former NKVD chief in Australia

"Every member of the Communist Party is an agent to execute the Communist program."
Mr. Justice Jackson, in *American Communications Association* v. *Douds*

"When security is found to be excessive, it can always be cured by relaxing it. There is no cure for inadequate security. Information once compromised is information broadcast forever."
Lewis L. Strauss, in *Men and Decisions*

I

The Bridegroom Cometh

———————

The date: May 17, 1938.
The place: Buffalo, New York.
The mission: Espionage.

ON that day, Arthur Alexandrovitch Adams, whose alias combined the ludicrous juxtaposition of a blatantly Russian middle name and an honored American patronymic, crossed the Canadian border into the United States. Immigration officials took only routine notice of him, paying but casual attention to the Canadian birth certificate he carried with him. Customs officials had no reason to suspect that the sole contraband in his possession was a master plan, well-memorized, for penetrating the secrets of his host country. The United States was at peace, and to most people the potential enemy spoke with a German accent.

Arthur Alexandrovitch Adams was but one more traveler crossing the unguarded frontier which separates the United States and Canada. It would be years before American security agencies would know that the birth certificate he carried was fraudulent, obtained

3

from a secret member of a Toronto Communist cell who bore the portentous name of M. S. Milestone. It would be years, too, before these agencies learned that a group of Americans in New York, on instructions from the Fourth Section of Red Army Intelligence, had already prepared for Arthur Adams a safe cover for espionage. But at that moment neither Adams nor his superiors in Moscow could have known that he would play a key role in history's greatest plot: the theft of America's most closely guarded nuclear secrets and the formation of an effective apparatus which, in its Phase Two, would confuse public thinking on atomic energy, influence the deliberations of Congress, and muddy up the waters of international policy.

Only in the eyes of a handful of scientists, working in their laboratories, could the gleam of an atomic age a-borning be detected. Yet it was easily foreseeable that the American-British-Canadian project, once it was discovered, would be the target of Communist spying. The catalogue of military and diplomatic espionage by the Soviets was in the late 1930s grim and long.*

* In the June 19, 1951, issue of *Look* magazine, the Washington correspondent for the Cowles newspapers, Fletcher Knebel, compiled a partial list of "the secrets Russia got":

"*Military:* H-bomb theory, A-bomb theory and plans, Panama defense details, proximity fuse, data on Oak Ridge gaseous diffusion plant, cosmic ray research, facts about Chalk River atomic plant, details on Hanford atomic plant, Uranium-235, Los Alamos atomic layout, identity of atomic scientists, mathematics of atomic aircraft, date of A-bomb test, plans for earth satellite, RDX high-explosive, turbo-prop aircraft data, Jeep plans, Edgewood Arsenal research-equipment blueprints, radiation data, B-29 plans, aircraft production figures, date of Normandy invasion, our progress in breaking Russian codes, 'Dina' explosive, sonar anti-sub devices, Torpex explosives, anti-sub aircraft radar, guided missiles progress, battleship radar, airborne distance indicator, scanning radar, waterproof maps, production, distribution and storage of weapons.

"*Industrial:* Photographic processes, high-octane gas, synthetic rubber, industrial solvents, hundreds of chemical formulas, sugar-refining processes, layout of United States and Canadian research laboratories.

"*Diplomatic and political:* Secret Far Eastern dispatches, secret European dispatches, secret messages from embassies in Moscow, secret sessions of the Canadian Parliament, Justice Department espionage files."

The Communists had given it new dimension by including in this time-dishonored practice industrial, technological, and scientific espionage—preying on the private sector by stealing patented processes which they could as easily have bought in the open market. They enlisted in this activity on a mass basis the nationals of Western countries whose loyalties were subverted and whose idealism was corrupted. No longer was a spy a shameful creature stealthily lurking in the back alleys of society. The Soviet *apparat* could claim men of stature and intellectual attainment—men who spurned money and justified their acts as moral. But the master Soviet accomplishment—an operation which Vladimir Ilyich Lenin would have lustily applauded—was the manipulation by trained agents of world opinion and of the scientific community, at a time when the cold war had barely begun to form its icicles.

In 1938, no reader of spy thrillers would have looked twice at Arthur Alexandrovitch Adams or considered him a menace. He was a frail man, obviously racked by pain, who seemed incapable of the taxing pursuit of espionage. A doctor would have said he was arthritic. He himself attributed his ailments, in the privacy of the *apparat,* to the beatings he had received at the hands of the Tsarist police during the abortive Russian Revolution of 1905. This was his small boast. On a higher plane, he spoke of an intimate association with Lenin in the early days of Communist revolutionary activity—a claim which must have had some basis in fact, since it was accepted by his superiors at the Center in Moscow. The extent of his disability was later described by one of his accomplices:

He was a pretty sick man. . . . Many is the time I had to send my secretary down to get him out of bed. He was rheumatically crippled and had fallen out of bed and injured his eyes. So we were always under the impression that he would injure himself. . . . It would paralyze him completely. He would have great difficulty . . . in sitting in one position, and he would be all hunched up, and it would take at least one hour before he would come to himself.

Yet Adams was a man to watch. He was an Old Bolshevik, one of the elite of Soviet communism until Stalin began to slaughter them by the thousands in the grisly cellars of Moscow's Lubianka prison. More significant, he was a highly trained agent—a veteran and charter member of the secret police created by Felix Dzerzhinsky under orders from Lenin when the Bolsheviks overthrew the democratic government of Alexander Kerensky. Known originally as the GPU, the organization took many names over the years, but its function was always the same—to inspire terror in the Russian people and to prey on the non-Communist world.* In 1924, Dzerzhinsky would report confidently on the success of his efforts:

The OGPU not only works energetically by paralyzing the espionage of foreign citizens in the USSR, but it also has succeeded in creating a network of information Intelligence agencies in all other large centers of Europe and North America. Responsible workers of the OGPU are detailed to all the diplomatic and trade missions of the USSR abroad. The total strength of the Foreign Department of the OGPU is 1,300, including employees of the foreign section in Moscow. The OGPU has rendered service to the Commissariat of Foreign Affairs and the staff of the Red Army in supplying secret information both of a political and military nature.

At the time Arthur Adams entered the United States, however limpingly, that modest 1,300 had grown into an army of some nine thousand highly-trained "master spies," almost 200,000 sub-

---

* In 1923, the GPU (*Gosudarstvennoye Politicheskoye Upravelenye*) became the OGPU by the addition of the word *Obedyedinnoye* to its name. In 1934, the entire name was changed to NKVD (*Narodyny Komisariat Vnutrennikh Dyel*), by which it is still popularly known. By 1946, when the Kremlin dropped the term "commissariat" for the more respectable "ministry," the NKVD became the MVD (*Ministerstsvo Vnutrennikh Dyel*). At the same time, because of some division in function, the MGB (*Ministerstvo Gosudarstvennoy Bezopasnosti*) was created. After Stalin's death, Malenkov placed internal security in the hands of the KGB (*Komitet Gosudarstvennoy Bezopasnosti*). There is often some confusion as to whether a particular agent is NKVD or Red Army Intelligence. This is due to the overlapping of activities. Often the agent himself does not know who are his masters.

ordinates, and half a million *novators*—the dupes, innocents, and (as the NKVD calls them) the "in-the-dark" informants who consciously or otherwise supplied information to the Center in Moscow. Adams had been part of this operation as it grew and refined its techniques, his particular specialty the United States. As early as January 1919, he had been assigned to an espionage mission in this country. But the Soviets, full of revolutionary arrogance, were clumsier than they needed to be. Adams was caught redhanded, and was forced to leave New York "voluntarily" two years later. Only slightly deterred by this contretemps, he returned in 1927, ostensibly as the official representative of Amo, the Soviet Union's first and still inefficient automobile plant. A smattering of engineering and technical lingo helped him maintain this cover, as it did in all his other missions. The year 1932 saw him back again in New York, this time as a member of a group then negotiating with Curtiss-Wright for the purchase of airplanes—with side trips for the apparatus.

His next venture, in 1936, was an assignment from both Red Army Intelligence and the NKVD. In the glow of the Popular Front and as a reaction to Hitler's rise, Soviet espionage had taken a great leap forward. Young men in the federal government, researchers and technologists in American industry, and graduate students in the great universities had made the blinding discovery that Utopia and the Soviet Union were synonymous. In the darkness of their blazing noon, they were eager and ready to make a compound of moral treason and sophistry, excusing the betrayal of principle and common decency with the argument that they were "helping the working class" or "fighting fascism." The blow to American complacency delivered by the great depression still shook them and furnished additional rationalization. But though they contributed to the flow of information into the Soviet Union, they were for the most part rather poor agents. Only the innocence abounding in most Americans had prevented more than random discoveries of Soviet espionage, and these made such little impact on the public consciousness that until the Gouzenko disclosures there were still people who insisted that it existed only in the minds of "Red-baiters."

The slips which occurred troubled Moscow, however impervious to their significance this country might be. Though the Soviets have put espionage on a mass-production basis, precisely because they rely on quantity to make up for quality, security remains an important factor. It was "to inspect the posts" in New York, Washington, Pittsburgh, Detroit, and points west that Arthur Alexandrovitch Adams was sent on his penultimate trip to the United States, in the guise of visiting relatives. Discipline had to be imposed, procedures tightened, and the small seed of fear planted in the minds of those who held professional rank in the Soviet Union's proliferating underground cells. The possibility of defection had to be scotched—and it was very real. Though the West had yet to understand the meaning of the great purges, or even to be really aware of them, they were a topic of much talk among the *apparatchiks,* who learned every day of the disappearance of this or that official in the Soviet hierarchy. For them, the need for exegesis was not necessary.

Like every espionage service, both the NKVD and Red Army Intelligence knew the drill. Stalin, through the Center in Moscow, decided to crack the whip. It is an index of the importance of Arthur Adams that he was selected to do the cracking. His orders were specific. No matter how ingenuous Americans might be, the network was to operate with the same care, using the same methods that obtained in London, Paris, or Berlin. An espionage apparatus, if it is properly organized, is like a chain that can be tugged in only one direction. This means that if Counter-Intelligence discovers one agent or link, and if that agent talks, he can only give information about his subordinates. The higher, and critical, links in the chain cannot be pulled in or arrested.

The Center in Moscow has all the pertinent, and some impertinent, facts about the entire network—the table of organization, so to speak. But it communicates directly only with its representatives in Soviet embassies and consulates. It maintains contact via the diplomatic pouch and short-wave radio. Messages are sent in code (at the Soviet Embassy in Ottawa there were five cipher clerks, each one using a code not known to the other four) and a set of cover names is used for individuals, organizations, and places. An embassy is known as *metro*, the NKVD is *the Neighbor*, passports are *shoes* (and those who supply forged or fraudulent passports are *shoemakers*), a legal front for espionage such as the Amtorg Trading Corporation in New York is called *a roof*, local Communist parties are referred to as *the corporation* (members are *corporants*). A hide-out or hiding place, such as the house on Gay Street in New York's Greenwich Village, where couriers off the ships brought messages for processing in the early 1930s, is a *dubok*. Anyone working for the apparatus is *nash*—"ours."

The Center divides any apparatus into two parts, the "legal" and the "illegal." This has nothing to do with the nature of the work being done, but of those who are doing it. A Soviet national, protected by a diplomatic passport and the immunity it gives, is a "legal" agent. So, too, is any Russian on official business—the member of a purchasing mission, a dance troupe bringing ballet and enlightenment to the Americans, or anyone who can offer a "legitimate" reason for being in the host country. The "illegals" are agents traveling under false papers who have submerged their identities—the "faceless men"—or natives of the country in which the network has been set up. If caught, they have no protection and expect to be sacrificed.

There is a free two-way communication between the Director at the Center in Moscow and the resident directors, but it stops there. The resident director is known to his agents by a cover name —"Al" or "Carl" or "Fred"—though he knows exactly who they are. They in turn use these cover first names with their subagents unless they are dealing with people known to them professionally or socially. If an agent is apprehended or defects, he can merely give the cover name to the authorities and supply some sort of description. At the time that Arthur Adams was "inspecting the posts," Whittaker Chambers knew the identities and histories of those who supplied him with information. But security was so lax within the apparatus that he knew the name and much of the personal background of his superior, Colonel Boris Bykov. It is ironic that in time Adams, the inspector, should make the same mistake of talking too much to his sources. But even during its most secretive phases, Soviet Intelligence failed to observe all the rules. As Igor Gouzenko once remarked to this writer:

"What does it matter? They work on such a mass-production basis that the loss of one agent is sometimes beneficial. The Americans arrest him, and they are lulled into thinking that they've broken up the whole network. Meanwhile, nine or ten other networks remain untouched."

From the detailed confessions of Soviet agents to United States security agencies, it is known that in 1936 procedures were tightened, minimizing, though not eliminating, the continual threat of ideological defectors, double agents, and inadvertent discovery. As the *apparatchiks* grew into their new discipline, fewer and fewer of them were able to learn, as did Whittaker Chambers and Hede Massing, of the personnel and scope of parallel apparatuses in the United States and abroad. The veterans of the October Revolution who had been subverted into the dirty business of spying either accepted the new ways, or, if they persisted in their romantic notions, were eliminated—to be replaced by younger professionals "academically" trained, for whom 1918 was but a childhood memory. If there were still intramural leaks, they ceased to be the rule and became the exception.

When Arthur Adams returned to Moscow, the relatives he had been "visiting" knew only that he was involved in "important work." If they had any educated guesses as to the nature of that work, they did not confide them to the Federal Bureau of Investigation. His superiors at the Center were, however, given a full report on the strengths and weaknesses of the organization in America and an evaluation of the agents there. Possibly as a result of his findings, at least one Soviet agent was "eliminated" in New York because of his weakness for female companionship and the bottle. This much is certain: Moscow was convinced that Arthur Adams had done his job well, that he was capable and trustworthy enough to be given another American assignment. After a period of observation, mandatory after an agent has been exposed to the corrupting influences of capitalist society, he was tapped by the Red Army General Staff, Military Intelligence, Fourth Section, for what was to be his most important and most delicate mission: to head the "illegal network" in the United States.

This was not a snap decision. It was made at a very high level and for reasons the world would not guess until more than a year later. To get a false passport and to lay the groundwork for adequate cover both take time. The preparations began on December 19, 1937, when one Samuel Novick, a naturalized American citizen in the radio and electronics business, wrote to the Immigration and Naturalization Service that Arthur Adams ("a skilled radio engineer") had been working for him in Canada for ten years— a falsehood Novick would attempt to deny under oath many years later. Behind the plan to install Adams in the United States as a resident director was a long-range projection of Joseph Stalin himself. At that time, the Soviets and the Nazis had already put out the first feelers for what would burst on the world as the Hitler-Stalin Pact in the late summer of 1939.

Communist leaders were fully cognizant that this pact would be the signal for a Nazi attack on the West. And Stalin, who always assumed that others would act as he did, took it for granted that this would lead to a diplomatic rupture between the United States and the Soviet Union. Under those circumstances, the entire "legal" apparatus—the Embassy, the consulates, and Amtorg would be forced to shut up shop. The "illegal" apparatus would therefore become Stalin's only way to continue plundering the United States of its industrial techniques—an operation vital to the backward Soviet economy, which was struggling to drag itself back to the position Russia had held in 1913, before World War I and the 1917 Revolution had crippled it. Stalin knew that his overtures to Hitler, though more than reciprocated, would not be consummated in the pact for some time. He could afford to plan carefully.

The Center did not foresee that events beyond its control would compel it to act on a crash basis—to send Arthur Adams to his new assignment ahead of schedule. Those events concerned Whittaker Chambers, like Adams an "illegal," whose battle with his conscience had led him to break with the Soviet underground early in April of 1938. His defection had caught the Communists flatfooted and sent agents throughout the United States diving for cover. Colonel Boris Bykov, resident director of several groups and Chambers' superior, was immediately summoned to Moscow, disgrace, and a bullet in the back of the head. For a brief period, everyone even remotely connected with Chambers was put "on ice," * and even those who were relatively safe lived in a period of panic. They had no way of knowing that Chambers would remain silent—or that when he spoke up, goaded by the implications of the Hitler-Stalin pact, his disclosures would be brushed aside by President Roosevelt.

When Arthur Alexandrovitch Adams was given the order to salvage what he could of the demoralized American apparatus, he was already in Canada. The dates would so indicate, for there was little over a month between the time that NKVD "disciplinarians" began looking for Chambers and the day that Adams crossed the border. Air travel was rare in those days, and the Center would have been reluctant to catapult Adams from Moscow to Buffalo so rapidly. This would be particularly true in an operation where Stalin was concerned. (In a totalitarian state, there are no excuses for failure.) In any case, Adams had been thoroughly briefed as to the nature of his original assignment. The necessary cover had

* The underground phrase is to "go private."

already been provided and reliable contacts alerted. All of American industry, with its techniques, processes, and know-how—what Stalin lacked after twenty years of revolutionary mismanagement—awaited his plundering fingers.

In a city like New York, a man preserves his anonymity so long as he pays his rent, does not get too friendly with bartenders, and avoids trouble with cab drivers. But a spy, watching the reflections in store windows at all times to see if he is followed, feels that he must establish himself as a solid citizen, as if he were in Paris and had to account for himself to a prying *concièrge*. Adams checked in at the Peter Cooper Hotel and, almost before his bags were unpacked, had given the identification signal to Jacob Aronoff, a lawyer with offices at 165 Broadway. The two men, with Philip Levy, a small businessman who knew only that there was a profit in it somewhere, set up Technological Laboratories, Inc.—a business which was all name and no activity. Years later, Levy complained to a Senate committee that the deals with Adams, Aronoff, and his associates netted him no cash.

There were others on hand to make solid the Adams claim that he was an engineer and a machine designer. Eric Bernay, whose record shop just east of Times Square featured domestic Communist and Soviet music, went into "partnership" with Adams. Bernay was also the head of Keynote Records, whose musical social protest was financed by party funds and at least one Park Avenue angel. This was no surprise, for Bernay had at one time been business manager of the *New Masses*. His contribution was to put Adams on his payroll for seventy-five dollars weekly, a not ungenerous sum in 1938. Adams also used as a base Novick's Electronics, Inc., a company which received six million dollars in defense contracts for secret radar equipment—and a Navy accolade, the coveted "E" for excellence in production. To pad out Adams's income, a Hollywood businessman and secret party member was given $1,875 by Adams. This money was dutifully paid back, seventy-five dollars a week, as "salary." But none of these pre-

cautions were really needed. The idea that the Soviet Union in-
dulged in espionage, using the Communist Party as a base, was
then being received by most Americans with laughter or indignation. Even during the period of the Hitler-Stalin Pact, it was considered a sign of paranoia to think of the Communists as anything
other than overzealous idealists.

The Arthur Adams apparatus, which grew and grew until it
included well over one hundred agents, began modestly enough.
There was Julius Heiman, a millionaire businessman. Like a good
father, he inculcated his daughter with his ideas and put her to
work at the Soviet Embassy. Heiman's mink-lined beliefs included
a fierce hatred of the system which had given him his wealth and
a fatuous love of the "worker's fatherland." The underground
snapped the whip, and Heiman went into the steel business. This
gave him a legitimate excuse to run courier errands for the network, particularly to Stockholm, then a leading transfer point for
Soviet agents delivering information or taking out instructions.

A touch of glamour which Alfred Hitchcock would have appre-
ciated was furnished by Leon Josephson. His brother Barney
"owned" Café Society, a large and pleasantly decorated nightclub
on New York's Sheridan Square, which provided some of the best
jazz music of the period. While the greatest of hot musicians beat
it out on the bandstand to the applause of college boys and jazz
buffs, other business was transacted in the back rooms. There was,
however, nothing romantic about Leon Josephson. He had earned
his wound stripes and hash marks in Stalin's secret service. His
associate at one time had been George Mink, one of the NKVD's
peripatetic executioners. This sinister man's prime coup had been
the ambushing of Ignace Reiss, who had incurred Stalin's displeas-
ure by breaking with the espionage *apparat* and denouncing the
Great Dictator as a "murderer." In 1935, an espionage arrest for
Josephson ended happily when the Danish police released him.

One Rebecca Victoria Singer Stone was also involved, though
her day of glory did not come until Adams was on the run from

the FBI and needed willing confederates to help him evade arrest. Victoria Stone ran a jewelry shop on Madison Avenue—it is still in business—which she had set up with funds furnished by Julius Heiman. When the House Un-American Activities Committee questioned her in the late 1940's, her answers were vague and contradictory—and a report to the Congress in 1948 stated that she would be cited for perjury. She never was.

This was the nucleus. Before the apparatus could be worth its salt, Adams needed men and women with roots in the government and industry—the unsuspected *novators,* who were already in a position to deliver the facts, figures, and secrets demanded by the Center in Moscow and designated by the schoolboy term of "tasks." The documents which Igor Gouzenko, file clerk at the Soviet Embassy in Ottawa, turned over to the Royal Canadian Mounted Police, show how tidily the Center assigned these tasks and how conscientiously the agents did their homework.

It is popularly believed that a resident director, filling his manpower requirements, turns to the local Communist Party for recruiting suggestions. This is not so. The Center has only contempt for non-Soviet party members. The local parties have done their job when they have enticed idealistic or warped people into membership or the "front" periphery. The selection is done by the Center, which submits a list of candidates to the "Comintern rep" —Moscow's gauleiter—much as Classification in the United States Army will furnish the names of riflemen or typists to the units that need them.

The mission of the resident director is known, of course, in Moscow. And at the disposal of the Center is the largest file in history of possible talent. This is what the NKVD, Red Army Intelligence, the Comintern, and subsidiary espionage groups innocuously call the Central Index. Millions of dossiers—*zapiski*—are kept up to date for the use of enterprising recruiters. Every party member, past or present; every fellow traveler; every sympathizer who has put his name to petitions or contributed to party causes;

every person who has had dealings, business or social, with officials of Iron Curtain countries—each one has a personnel folder in the acres of filing cabinets kept by Central Index.

Also the subject of Moscow's solicitous interest are foreign politicians who are considered vulnerable, trade unionists active on labor's left bank, intellectuals infected by the more polite forms of the Marxist virus, businessmen who put profit above the national interest. The strenuous efforts of Communists in the United States, Canada, and Western Europe to organize "unions" of scientists had but the secondary purpose of mobilizing for agitation. The primary motivation was to search out men and women adept at the white magic of our time, to sound them out, to learn their weaknesses—all for the benefit of that *zapiska* which at the proper moment could provide the name of a strategically placed individual. The system worked when atomic espionage became the Kremlin's major area of interest.

Another myth, that the Soviet espionage apparatus shies away from party members in its recruitment of spies, is also untrue. The Center prefers them. Of course, once one of the faithful has been tapped, he breaks off all connection with the open party, cuts himself off from Communist friends, and may even pose as a critic of the Soviet Union. But even here there are major exceptions. Steve Nelson, a "hero" of the Abraham Lincoln Brigade and the Spanish Civil War, doubled in brass as commissar of California's Alameda County party and as an operative in the atomic spy ring.

The Center will reach out in any direction as it invades a given sector of "capitalist" society. But it prefers the indoctrinated Communist, whose background has been thoroughly investigated, who has been observed by his superiors, who has been tested in a thousand small ways, and whose loyalty to country, family and friends has been thoroughly compromised. Whittaker Chambers was selected for a highly sensitive assignment in 1933 even though he had been an editor of the *Daily Worker,* editor-in-fact of the *New Masses,* and author of a short story widely acclaimed by

MOSCOW as representative of the true Bolshevik spirit and dramatized for agitprop use. And the Center has been vindicated during the four decades of its depredations. Cash-on-the-barrelhead operatives, like our own Francis Gary Powers of U-2 fame, feel no compunction about bowing to the inevitable. But given the army of Communist spies, the number who have defected (or talked when arrested) has been miniscule.

This, as Stalin used to say, is no accident. Every party member has filled out an exhaustive questionnaire giving a host of biographical detail. He is told that this is for the exclusive use of his immediate superiors, but it ends up always at the Central Index, where it is thoroughly studied, then placed in the *zapiska*. The questionnaire is then supplemented by the judgments and evaluations of fellow Communists—and becomes a better guide for psychological analysis than any of the tests devised by our own Central Intelligence Agency. Further light is cast on the "subject" by the comments elicited from him on party associates. One questionnaire issued by the Communist Party USA to its members began with:

DEAR COMRADE:

Below you will find a questionnaire to be used as a guide in writing your biography. Please be advised that the Central Commission wants a detailed and frank statement from you, one that will enable it to know you as well as you know yourself. Please use as much paper as necessary (on one side only) and be assured that this document will be treated in strict confidence and properly safeguarded.

The suggested topics delved not only into the member's background but also into that of his family and friends. It demanded one kind of important information: "Name all your recruits into the party, giving their present whereabouts and functions, as well as their social and occupational background. State whether they are at present in the party and if they dropped out, why." If any of the member's recruits later defected, this would be a warning to the Center. Defection can sometimes have a chain reaction. The Center is also deeply interested in the sexual habits of the people it honors by inclusion in the Central Index. Sexual deviation in a party member, sympathizer, or a likely subject for espionage recruitment is of more than considerable interest to the Center. It is not so much a question of blackmail as of exposing a man's weaknesses. Repeatedly the Center's queries to resident directors, as it seeks to develop outside sources, are directed to information on sex, liquor, and love of money. Agents, in reporting on their "contacts," are asked to give:

Personal positive and negative characteristics:

(a) Inclination to drink, women friends—or good family man;

(b) Lover of good things—or inclination to solitude and quietness;

(c) Influence of wife on actions—or independence in making own decisions;

(d) Circle of acquaintances and brief character sketches of them.

When the Center ran through likely possibilities for the new Adams network, it was armed with its *zapiski*. The validity of its judgments was such that not a single one of the people chosen reported Adams' approach to American security agencies. What little is known about the ring was discovered by the Federal Bureau of Investigation in its ceaseless check on suspected agents. Because the original target was industrial espionage—not involving the federal government—almost nothing is known of who did what to whom by Arthur Alexandrovitch Adams and his agents. When their activity impinged on the military—the ring was successful in stealing American bombsight secrets—more became known.

But forces and events were on the move. In university laboratories, scientists had begun their long battle to penetrate the secret of the atom and to harness their discoveries. A scientific revolution which would eventually bring obsolescence to weapons systems and military strategy was in the making. Agents throughout the West picked up the signal and reported it to the Center. The Kremlin was informed, though in the early stages it showed but small interest. When it became clear that the atom contained within it physical and political forces which could reshape the world, Stalin pricked up his ears. The orders went out for the espionage vacuum cleaner to suck in every fact, every technique. Perhaps by accident, the assignment in the United States to organize the operation which would transmit this new theory and technology fell to Arthur Alexandrovitch Adams, friend of the Lenin who had midwifed an equally earth-shaking revolution.

I I

Target: Atomic Know-How

SIMPLICITY is the mother of confusion. In the debate over atomic energy which has raged since Hiroshima, some have claimed that the Soviets knew nothing until Klaus Fuchs and other espionage agents alerted them. Others have argued that the phalanx of atomic spies in the West contributed nothing to the Soviet state of the art. To this latter point, many scientists and intellectuals added a corollary, demonstrating that their logic was in this instance in inverse ratio to their Intelligence Quotient. They insisted that the secrecy demanded by the Manhattan Engineer District and the Atomic Energy Commission "aided" the Soviet advance and "hurt" the United States. And accepting Soviet claims of success, they simultaneously failed to observe that, if true, these achievements had occurred behind a hermetic wall of secrecy.*

* To this day, Western scientists do not really know if the Soviet Union has been exploding nuclear devices or bombs. Having little knowledge of their atomic weaponry, we assume for safety's sake that they are bombs. Those who chronically assert Soviet superiority also forget that in the "scale of violence" two twenty-megaton bombs are far more effective than one fifty-megaton *device* such as the U.S.S.R. recently set off in the atmosphere.

The extremes of opinion have oversimplified the facts. In general theory, the Soviets were in the mid-1930s not far behind the Western nations. Russian science, when not tied to a Marxist-Leninist *mystique,* has ranged from adequate to excellent in its theoretical aspects. In the experimental and the practical, however, they have been hindered by the weaknesses of the Soviet economy. This was particularly true in the nuclear field, where great amounts of capital, a highly sophisticated industrial plant, and the willingness to risk time and materials on what may be a dead end in research are required. Soviet science has always moved timidly and taken the safe course. Soviet technology has "made do" with what it had at hand, never striking out boldly but relying on the pioneering of the West.*

Until the very late thirties and early forties, Soviet scientists could read all the journals of Western scientists. These were imported by the Soviet Academy of Science and carefully studied. And from them, the Kremlin's scientists could, by theoretical induction, arrive at accurate conclusions. But it was never a question of knowing that atomic fission could release energy in quantities hitherto unknown. (Einstein's theoretical $e=mc^2$ was never classified information.) The question was how to release and harness that energy, how to produce in sufficient quantities the elements necessary to bring this about—and what those elements were—and how to squeeze from the lemon of the Soviet economy sufficient funds to experiment in a field where billions of dollars were merely a down payment.

Given these circumstances, the Kremlin took a calculated risk that it could allow the West to expend the intellectual and financial blood and sweat of harnessing the atom. What was being done in American, Italian, and French laboratories was open to the world

* The one Soviet leap forward in rocketry, the development of a powerful booster which gave it a temporary lead in space, was conditioned by an inability to keep pace with the West in miniaturization and transistorization. With far less rocket thrust, the United States has been able to cram many times the number of instruments in far smaller capsules.

until shortly before the outbreak of World War II. And the Soviets always had a friend in the scientific court—Frédéric Joliot-Curie, a French Communist and one of the elite corps of nuclear scientists who could describe and annotate what the West had wrought. When secrecy was demanded—first self-imposed by the scientists themselves and later systematized as atomic energy became a military matter—the Kremlin knew that through the Center in Moscow it could reach out to some of the men involved, thumbing through the *zapiski* of the Great Index for leads and approaches. Aiding the network were the garrulous propensities of the scientific fraternity which to the very end could not quite believe that Big Brother was watching—and sometimes manipulating—them.

The mistake that the men of science made was that they confused ideas with techniques and capabilities. Dr. J. Robert Oppenheimer verged on an understanding of this when he told the Joint Committee on Atomic Energy in 1949: "History time and again shows that we have no monopoly on ideas, but we do better with them than most other countries." The idea of nuclear fission, and ultimately of the bomb, was never a monopoly or a secret. But translating that concept into an actual device was a monopoly and would have remained so for many years were it not for the wholesale theft of atomic secrets by the Soviets—and the leg up given to their scientists by those of Oppenheimer's colleagues who insisted that the mechanics of the bomb should be fully disclosed to the whole world after Hiroshima and Nagasaki.

In 1933, two years after Dr. Harold Urey and his associates at Columbia had discovered heavy water, one of the first major breakthroughs on the road to nuclear fission and the bomb, the Soviets were still groping in theoretical areas which German, British, and American scientists had long passed. In July of that year, W. A. Sobolov and M. G. Gurevich were announcing a "sensation" in atomic research which our own scientists must have considered quaintly old-fashioned. The "sensation" was duly reported in the English-language *Moscow Daily News*:

"Our discovery is only a preliminary step," Sobolov modestly explained. "It will provide a basis for developing new theories and guiding future research. Science is still far from penetrating the secret of the atom. But once it is grasped, new and undreamed sources of energy will be placed at the command of man.

"One gram of radium, for example, in its disintegration, emits 2 billion calories of energy. So far, however, we have made little progress toward harnessing this reservoir of power. The case with other elements is similar."

At the time Moscow "modestly" boasted of its scientific achievement, Dr. Enrico Fermi was working in Italy with a group of brilliant assistants, including the spy-to-be Bruno Pontecorvo. This group was already well on its way to the discovery of a process for making elements radioactive by bombarding them with slow neutrons—a step of such importance to science (and in time to the Manhattan Engineer District which created the atomic bomb) that the United States government was later forced to pay $300,000 in royalties to the Italian scientists. The "idea" behind the process was in the public domain, but the incentive and know-how of Fermi and his assistants were needed to give it concrete form. The idea for the next great step in atomic exploration was also known to Soviet scientists, but it took two German scientists to make it, and a third German scientist to understand it.

Science had become a kind of detective story in 1938, when Dr. Otto Hahn and Dr. F. Strassmann, two chemists, determined that when uranium is exposed to neutrons under the right conditions, an isotope of barium is created. Not fully comprehending what they had discovered, Hahn wrote to the physicist, Dr. Lise Meitner, whom he had smuggled out of the Third Reich, where she had been persecuted for her Jewish antecedents. From Copenhagen, Dr. Meitner wrote back explaining the significance of the experiment. "She pointed out," Hahn later told Lewis Strauss, the inspiration and financial backer of much early nuclear study, "that what had happened was that we had fissioned the uranium atom. The use of the word 'fission' in that connection, I think, was made for the first time."

As a physicist Dr. Meitner was also able to do the computation necessary to a full comprehension of the experiment. She nailed home mathematically the fact that in splitting the uranium atom, a minute amount of matter had been transformed into tremendous energy. Applying and confirming Einstein's formula, Dr. Meitner reported to Hahn that the energy released (e) equaled the mass of matter (m) times the square of the speed of light (c^2). (Light travels at the rate of 186,000 miles per second.) This discovery, as Lewis Strauss has pointed out, was "more exciting than anything which had occurred in physical science since the discovery of radio-activity by Becquerel forty-two years earlier." The atomic scientist Leo Szilard reported that the Physics Department at Princeton was "like a stirred-up ant heap." Szilard, a Hungarian refugee, had none of the reservations of the "modest" Soviet scientists about the future of nuclear energy. He wrote immediately to Strauss that the new discovery "might lead to a large-scale production of energy and radioactive elements, unfortunately, also perhaps to atomic bombs." His letter is dated January 25, 1939.

From that day on, nuclear research was sicklied over by the morbid cast of this thought. Szilard was not the first man to con-sider the explosive possibilities of the atom. But he had seen imme-diately the import of Dr. Meitner's calculations. His ideas spread quickly to others in the scientific community, if only because Szilard sought them out to discuss ways and means to push the work. Among those who shared his confidence—and in time his enthusiasm—were Dr. Edward Teller and Dr. Enrico Fermi. They were top-rank men, respected by their colleagues. (It was only when Teller triumphed over Oppenheimer in 1950 and won Presi-dent Truman's assent to build the hydrogen bomb that Teller's reputation was assailed by politically minded scientists.)

Henry Adams wrote many years ago that, in scientific research, a "law of acceleration" applies. Knowledge is gained slowly at first, but the progression is geometric, not arithmetical. On February 13, 1939, Szilard was again writing to Strauss that "almost every day" new knowledge became available, forcing him to change his projected course of action. Yet in that same letter, he could prophetically outline what direction academic and government-sponsored nuclear research would take.*

Slow neutrons seem to split a uranium isotope which is present in an abundance of about 1% in uranium. If this isotope could be used for maintaining chain reactions, it would have to be separated from the bulk of uranium. This, no doubt, would be done if necessary, but it might take five or ten years [it took five] before it can be done on a technical scale . . . We would have the task immediately to attack the question of concentrating the rare isotope of uranium.

By February 22, 1939, Szilard and Fermi were at hard work, fairly certain that they could create a chain reaction with U-235, and Szilard was "beginning to give attention" to a process for concentrating this isotope. Early in March, the two scientists had advanced far enough in their experiments to believe that there was a fifty-fifty chance of success, and Strauss had agreed to finance the purchase of a quarter ton of uranium oxide for their use. And now the question of security arose. It is significant in view of the later controversy that the scientists thought of it first and tried to win agreement for some kind of voluntary secrecy. They had a healthy respect for German science. They were also aware, like most people at that time, that war with the Nazis could come at any moment. Being many of them refugees from Hitler or Mussolini, they were dedicated to the idea of keeping their work out of the hands of the Axis Powers. Their American and British colleagues, commendably anti-Nazi, though tending to be myopic in the left eye, concurred. The major leak was Joliot-Curie in France—conceited, selfish, a Communist, and ambitious. He, of all the Western

* Lewis L. Strauss, *Men and Decisions* (Doubleday, 1962).

scientists, insisted on publishing those results of nuclear research he knew—which were considerable.*

At this point, it was a matter of time, money, and adequate facilities before the bomb became a reality.

Had not war and the MED (Manhattan Engineer District) intervened, it is probable that the first use of nuclear energy would have been in the power plant of a submarine. On March 17, 1939, Enrico Fermi met with the Navy's Technical Division to brief its members on the new discoveries. Fired by his speech, the Naval Research Laboratory immediately began experiments to separate U-235. This laboratory, under Admiral Harold G. Bowen, leaped the decades and was working on the basis of a technical memorandum written by Ross Gunn days after Fermi's talk. It set forth plans for a nuclear reactor which, by providing power for submarine propulsion, would liberate underwater craft from the dangers of surfacing in order to recharge their batteries. It also made a submarine's range almost limitless and removed the need of a rendezvous for refueling with surface vessels. In that memorandum, the atomic submarine was, at least theoretically, born. Under President Roosevelt's directive, however, all nuclear research was assigned to the MED under the crash program that produced the bomb. It was not until the war's end that the United States Navy could resume its work.

The first alert for the Soviet Union that something might perhaps be added to the dimensions of war came in July 1939, when Leo Szilard and Edward Teller visited Albert Einstein, then vacationing at Peconic Bay, Long Island. The scientists engaged in nuclear research had arrived at several conclusions: (1) their own experimental chain reaction had reached a point where further studies

---

* Under pressure from Joliot-Curie and the British scientist P. M. S. Blackett (later to be quoted approvingly by the Kremlin for his support of its position on international "control" of atomic energy), an important paper by Szilard and Walter H. Zinn, *Instantaneous Emission of Fast Neutrons in the Interaction of Slow Neutrons With Uranium,* was published despite their protests.

could not be privately financed; (2) success in manufacturing an atomic bomb had moved from the realm of possibility to that of probability; and (3) government action was needed to corner the most important source of uranium, the mines in Katanga, then part of the Belgian Congo. Strauss had been urged to intercede with President Roosevelt, but he had wisely absented himself from that felicity by pointing out to the eager scientists that his close association with Herbert Hoover would make him *non grata* at the White House. The intermediary most likely to impress the President, it was decided, would be Einstein.

The Einstein letter to Mr. Roosevelt, dated August 2, 1939, was not delivered until two months later—the President was too occupied by the impending war to see Dr. Alexander Sachs, who had been chosen to present it. But the ideas and urgent requests it made appealed to the Rooseveltian temperament. Not only did he have confidence in Einstein, but the element of the bizarre and innovational made the proposed action precisely the kind of gamble to stimulate and intrigue a man of such far-ranging interests. In fairly short order, President Roosevelt had set up a high-level advisory group made up of himself, Vice President Henry Wallace, Secretary of War Henry Stimson, Chief of Staff George Catlett Marshall, Dr. Vannevar Bush, and Dr. James B. Conant. The Navy had already begun its researches, but since it was not represented on the policy committee, the assignment for building the plant and creating the bomb fell under the jurisdiction of the Army's Corps of Engineers.

From that point on, everything about the research project was presumably so hush-hush that even mention of atomic energy was kept out of the newspapers. The American public and the Nazis remained thoroughly in ignorance. The same cannot be said of the Communists. Starting in the early 1930s, the Center in Moscow, working through Red Army Intelligence, Fourth (Industrial) Section, had been systematically placing its operatives in orbit around the great men of science in the West. J. Robert Oppenheimer, not quite out of the top drawer scientifically but a man with great administrative and public relations talents, had by his own admission joined "just about every Communist front" in the country and gave his money and prestige to party causes. Dr. Einstein never quite realized that his incomparable mathematical genius made him no match for the casuistry of those who camped on his doorstep. In the middle echelons there were the naïve to offer cover and the committed to hide behind it.

In the early stages of the atomic project, the Center's interest was routine and precautionary. For many years the conscious agents and their unwitting *novators* had run a vacuum cleaner over the complex of American industry and government, sucking in whatever information came close to the nozzle and dumping it in Moscow. The atomic project became one more area of operations with a not very high priority. According to a former *apparatchik,* moreover, "if in 1942, the Soviets had been handed a complete blueprint of the nuclear process, they wouldn't have been able to do a thing with it. They were too busy preventing disaster on the military front, industry was being transferred helter-skelter to the Urals, and the main question for Stalin was survival. Nevertheless, the Communists knew, because that is their nature, that they would live to fight another day. And so every scrap of information on our atomic progress was important to them—to save them time, to give them a know-how they lacked, and to permit them to catch up quickly once the Nazis had been defeated."

From the start, the apparatus foresaw no great difficulties in plundering the atomic project. In the earlier phases, it was imbedded in an academic community too thoroughly conditioned by the Popular Front and the Spanish Civil War to doubt that the Soviet Union was idealistic, misunderstood, and more sinned against than sinning. The apolitical members of that community tended to judge their colleagues by themselves, and they failed to realize that in the ideological struggle the criteria of science do not apply. The problem of security was further complicated when the entire program was placed in the hands of the Corps of Engineers. For General Groves, who was tapped to head the MED, though justifiably suspicious of Soviet and home-grown Communists, was never really able to understand the language of the scientific club or comprehend its ingrained bias. In surmounting the tremendous physical obstacles of building the bomb, he did an excellent job. He was a first-class administrator, and he knew how to avoid the bureaucratic pitfalls of wartime Washington. But he was a military man dealing with civilian prima donnas unaccustomed to security restrictions. That he rubbed them the wrong way was probably inevitable. But that he gave in to their quirks—grudgingly, to be sure—as if the scientists on the atomic project were not bound by the same rules of conduct as others involved in the war effort, led to serious trouble.

In justifying his espionage activities, Klaus Fuchs told British security officers that "General Groves regarded scientists as long-haired eggheads whom it was necessary to humor because scientists had to produce something which the Army wanted." This was only part of the story, though it discloses more about the scientists than it does about General Groves. He considered them a breed apart, to be accepted on their own terms. He was, moreover, somewhat dismayed that many of them were "foreigners." Had he been handed an all-American team, his reaction to their shenanigans about security would have been different.* But precisely because the scientists were what they were, General Groves sat uncomfortably on the point of his ambivalence—and the Center in Moscow profited thereby.

Colonel John Lansdale Jr., security officer for the MED, had

---

* In describing his relations with the scientists on the project, Groves complained: "If I went to a laboratory or on to a plant and failed to speak to somebody who was there or didn't see him [there was trouble]... even at Oak Ridge I had to go back at the expense of about three hours one day to speak to a superintendent that I had failed to see when I went through the plant, and when he spoke to me, I had not answered him... I say that so you see why certain people were not removed."

been one of those who urged more stringent measures to protect
the techniques of atomic production, but he was overruled by General Groves. Years later, he gave his views of the problem. "I certainly can't overemphasize the extremely frustrating, almost mad-
dening, let me say, tendency of our more brilliant people to extend
in their own mind their competence and independence of decision
in fields in which they have no competence," he said. "The scientists," he noted, with some of the old bafflement still in his voice,
"believed that their judgment as to what people needed to know,
as to what was security and the like, was as good or probably
better than [that of] others."

The scientists acted on a series of principles. The first of these
was that the military had no sense and no brains—and therefore
could be justifiably ignored; the second that compartmentalization
of information, a prime rule of security, was ridiculous. The directive at Los Alamos, as well as the other MED installations, made
it clear that no man on the project was to know any more than
was absolutely necessary for him to carry out his work. Many of
the scientists were irritated by this violation of their sacred right
to hold bull sessions. As a result, even the technicians were privy
to facts which would be valuable to those whose interest might be
suspect. The scientists also had a tendency to put personal loyalties
above security and on a number of critical occasions withheld
derogatory information from the military. Finally, they refused to
believe that communism was anything more than political theory.
In this, they had support from the very military they deplored.
Colonel Lansdale, who considered the 1954 investigation of Dr.
Oppenheimer a "manifestation of hysteria" and McCarthyism,
described his wartime experiences with the Pentagon brass:

In the War Department I was being subjected to pressure from
military superiors, from the White House and from every other
place, because I dared to stop the commissioning of a group of
fifteen or twenty undoubted Communists. I was being vilified, being
reviewed and re-reviewed because of my efforts to get Communists

out of the Army and being frustrated by the blind, naive attitudes of Mrs. Roosevelt and those around her in the White House which resulted in serious and extreme damage to this country. . . . I stood up in front of General McNarney, then Deputy Chief of Staff of the Army, and had him tell me that I was ruining people's careers and doing damage to the Army because I stopped the commissioning of the political commissar of the Abraham Lincoln Brigade, and the guy was later commissioned on direct orders from the White House.

To a degree, the same thing was true on the Manhattan project. Though General Groves was personally anti-Communist, he arrived at the formula that once a man had been attached to the work it would be more dangerous to fire him than to keep him on. The first major security decision dumped in the lap of Groves involved Dr. Oppenheimer, director-in-fact of the preliminary experiments and deeply involved in the project. Few people have questioned Oppenheimer's loyalty. But as a "security risk," he presented a real problem. By his own admission, he had contributed regularly through the party to Communist causes, lent his name to Communist fronts, and attended Communist meetings. His wife numbered among her friends a high-ranking Communist activist and espionage agent. His former mistress, whom he still visited, was a member of the party. This is the bare skeleton of his record. The security people in the MED, moreover, were opposed to granting him clearance, as this colloquy between Colonel Lansdale and Roger Robb, counsel for the Gray Board, which investigated Oppenheimer years later, will attest.

Mr. Robb: Mr. Lansdale, it is true, is it not, that the security officers down the line below you in the Army hierarchy were unanimous in their opposition to the clearance of Dr. Oppenheimer?

Mr. Lansdale: Virtually so, yes. I say virtually so because I cannot precisely now recall that it was unanimous . . . I should think that the answer was yes. Let me add this: That had I been confined to the bare record, I might possibly have reached the same conclusion. In other words, if Dr. Oppenheimer had not been as important as he was, I would certainly have stopped with the record and used my every endeavor to persuade the General [Groves] that Dr. Oppenheimer ought to be dispensed with. However, in view of his importance to the project, we made a tremendous effort to reach a settled conclusion in our own minds. At least I did, and I am sure the General did.

MR. ROBB: You mean if he had not been an important figure you would just have discarded him as a nubbin and gone on to something else?

MR. LANSDALE: Oh, absolutely.

General Groves, however, overruled his own security officers and approved the appointment of Dr. Oppenheimer to the top position in the atom-bomb project. It is a decision he still defends—and the wisdom of it will never be known until the records of the Center in Moscow are opened to public scrutiny. Given the need of success at any cost (and the conviction among scientists that Hitler's much-touted "secret weapon" was the A-bomb), the Groves decision may have been justifiable. But the fact remains that Groves condoned breaches of security by Oppenheimer subsequent to his clearance and brushed aside later reports of his security officers which should have been sufficiently disturbing to cause a review of this decision. Groves stood firm on his original directive that clearance be granted "irrespective of the information you have concerning Dr. Oppenheimer."

The second serious mistake in those early days of the MED was the appointment of Dr. Edward U. Condon, a physicist then employed by Westinghouse, to handle administration and personnel. Groves wanted a man with an industrial background to relieve Oppenheimer of detail and to serve as liaison between the harassed military and the touchy scientists. But from every standpoint,

Condon was a dead loss. Colonel Lansdale testified secretly to the House Un-American Activities Committee years later that he considered Condon a security risk. His ambiguous role during and after the war led the Committee to brand him "the weakest link in our atomic security"—a charge which gave him a cachet in certain circles. Though Oppenheimer recommended Condon, Groves has since said that "the responsibility was primarily mine."

From the start, Condon was a troublemaker. He was dissatisfied with the primitive living conditions at Los Alamos and complained because he was not given a big enough house. He had a small coterie of young scientists—many of them members of the Communist cell at the University of California's Radiation Laboratory at Berkeley. And his cantankerous behavior antagonized the military without satisfying the scientists. At the Oppenheimer hearing in 1954, Chairman Gordon Gray asked this question of Groves:

MR. GRAY: You said that Dr. Condon had been unsatisfactory in every respect. Does that include security? Did you have anything in mind on security in that regard, or loyalty?

GENERAL GROVES: I would say not in giving any information, but in setting up. He set up the rules at Los Alamos—at least I always felt that he was the man responsible for the rules—that tended to break down compartmentalization. He was the man who was primarily responsible at Los Alamos for the friction which existed. There would have been friction anyway. But the intensity of the friction that existed between the military officers who were trying to do the administrative operations out there so as to enable the scientists to work at science—Condon was the one who built all that up.

Condon lasted six weeks, then submitted his resignation. It was gratefully accepted, though Groves warned Oppenheimer to get Condon to put his reasons down in writing. To this day, Groves is convinced that Condon wanted out because he did not believe that the bomb could be constructed. But this was not the end of it. Every time a friend of his was being nudged off the project for security reasons, Condon would write a blistering letter to Oppenheimer, or telephone him, protesting the outrage in highly intemperate language. (In the postwar years, when some of these scientists were called to testify, they took the Fifth Amendment, but Condon still considered any investigation of their backgrounds a violation of the Constitution.) Condon, however, was later brought back to the project and placed in charge of certain experiments at Berkeley. That these experiments led to a dead end may have been fortunate. Groves has testified that Condon "just didn't do an honest day's work in our opinion"—running off to Pittsburgh for "his own family convenience."

Just before the first bomb was exploded at Alamogordo in 1945, Groves learned that a group of scientists had been invited to the Soviet Union. His firm rule was that no one connected with the MED should go for fear of an inadvertent leak. Just before the plane was to leave, Groves discovered that Condon had wangled an invitation. Groves objected strenuously and had Condon's passport withdrawn. "He made a terrific battle to go," Groves told the Gray Board. "That battle was so unrealistic and so completely lacking in appreciation of what was the best interest of the United States that you couldn't help but feel that either he was such an utter fool that he could not be trusted, or else that he put his personal desires above those of the welfare of the country." It should be noted that Dr. Oppenheimer shared Groves's distaste for Condon after the Los Alamos fiasco.

Whoever may have been responsible for it, one fact was obvious from the start: the MED leaked like a sieve. There was an unwarranted exchange of information, men were repeatedly kept on despite the protests of the security officers, and compartmentalization was disregarded. The breakdown of security was not restricted to intramural activities. When the atomic pile at Hanford, in Washington, suddenly quit (because of bad experimental techniques at the University of Chicago Metallurgical Laboratory) it became known to people in New York within forty-eight hours—people who were not on the project. Given this situation, it is no wonder that "information was pouring out"—to use Colonel Lansdale's phrase—to the Soviets from the very start. The MED was tailor-made for the Center in Moscow, and it took full advantage of this state of affairs.

III

The Slow Beginning

FROM the moment that Dr. Einstein wrote to President Roosevelt, the Center in Moscow knew that the United States had embarked on the greatest scientific adventure since the beginning of time. The Kremlin, however, gave the matter little more than passing attention. Stalin, who considered himself a military expert, did not believe that wars were won by physicists. Like the old-line British military men, he thought of combat in terms of massed troops, bayonets, and artillery. Even the German concept of fast-moving *Panzer* units—an application of old cavalry tactics to a mechanized age—did not impress him. Not long before World War II broke out, he "liquidated" Marshal Tukhashevky, the greatest strategic mind ever developed by the Soviet Union, and scrapped the in-depth defense, which would have been able to cope with a Nazi onslaught—in favor of heavy troop concentrations at his borders. He also rejected Western concepts of strategic bombing.

If the Americans and the British wanted to play with test tubes, abstruse equations, and "atomic piles"—whatever those may have been—it was all right with Comrade Stalin. He was at peace with

Nazi Germany, and a plan for the division of the world, one part Hitlerite and the other part Communist, was safely locked away in the Kremlin vaults. Reports to the Center indicated that even if the Western scientists could effect a controlled chain reaction, the means of applying this knowledge in time to change the course of the war were remote. The possibility of packaging nuclear fission in a bomb was beyond the ken of his own scientists. His Intelligence confirmed this in the opinions it received from some physicists in the United States and Britain who were perfectly willing to conduct their experiments at government expense though convinced that the atomic age would be a long time in dawning. One such was Dr. Condon—and he was far from being a voice in the wilderness. Einstein, Szilard, Fermi, Teller, and Oppenheimer—to name but a few of the optimists—disagreed, but Stalin knew better.

This, of course, did not deter the Center from paying attention to the facts and figures it received. Good Intelligence services operate on the pack-rat theory. And any information which the enemy tries to conceal is of interest and significance, and isolated facts which in themselves seem meaningless can often be pieced together to form an important pattern. As a matter of routine, the great Index in Moscow was combed for the names of Western scientists who might be involved in the atomic effort, and trained analysts began a study of the *zapiski* to determine which of them could be approached. How these scientists could be reached, and what their weaknesses might be, was the subject of a careful report to both Red Army Intelligence and the NKVD.

In October 1941, the Center began having some long second thoughts. Dr. Klaus Fuchs, a German scientist who had taken refuge from Hitler in England, was active in nuclear developments. In that month, he had reported to the Center that experiments in nuclear fission were moving ahead at a pace few would have previously considered possible—and with Stalin's approval, tentative mobilization of an atomic spy ring was begun. On December 2, 1942, Fermi and a group of his fellow scientists made the break-through. In a primitive uranium and graphite pile, built under the stands of the athletic field at the University of Chicago, they succeeded in achieving the first controlled—and sustained—chain reaction. It was now a question of refining the knowledge gained, of making the necessary calculations, and of designing a bomb which was small enough to be carried by the planes of that time. When this information reached Moscow, it could not be ignored. The implications were too clear. Stalin knew that his beleaguered country could not compete in any race for the bomb. But from that day on, the Center gave high priority to the theft of atomic information.

It is one of the major ironies of the great plot that had Stalin made a forthright demand for inclusion in the atomic project, he would probably have won President Roosevelt's assent. Harry Hopkins might have carried his battle to the White House and, as he usually did in such matters, convinced the President that to refuse would harm the American war effort. (There is no instance on record of a firm United States refusal of a Moscow request once it reached Hopkins.) But the Communist mind tends to be highly suspicious of goals too easily attained. (Walter G. Krivitsky, head of Soviet Intelligence in Western Europe, was promoted to the rank of general for stealing from a safe in the Nazi Foreign Office the text of the Berlin-Rome-Tokyo pact which created the Axis, even though Richard Sorge in Japan had already delivered it to the Center.)

Stalin never quite accepted the extent of American naïveté, good will, and/or submission to Moscow. Marx and Lenin had predicted the openhanded response of the "capitalists" to the Revolution, but Stalin was certain that any friendly gesture from the West was a trap. Having been a bank robber, he elevated theft to a national policy. Instructions were therefore forwarded to the resident director in New York, Arthur Alexandrovitch Adams, and to the "legals" at Amtorg, the Soviet consulate in New York, and its counterpart in San Francisco, to get cracking. The co-ordinator in the early stages was Adams, equipped with some technical knowledge and, as chief of industrial espionage in the United States, having a smattering of contacts in the scientific community.

Adams did not have to seek for recruits. The apparatus was in being, though semidormant. The great Index had already been combed for the dossiers of men considered likely prospects for invitation to the espionage and subversion waltz. At the University of California in Berkeley, the Radiation Laboratory which was to figure in the creation of the bomb had already been infiltrated. The Federation of Architects, Engineers, Chemists, and Technicians—whose local organizer was Marcel Scherer—served as invaluable cover both for Communist activity and for party recruitment. The FAECT had its members at the University of Chicago's Metallurgical Laboratory, which produced the first atomic pile, and at Columbia's SAM laboratory, which developed the gaseous diffusion process for Oak Ridge.* There was a small Communist cell at Berkeley, made up of scientists whose names would figure in later investigations of atomic espionage. Dr. Clarence Hiskey, one of the few caught red-handed (and a "protégé" of Adams) worked at both SAM and the Metallurgical Lab.

(In 1941, the FAECT was thoroughly "interlocked" with the special section of the Communist Party which worked among scientists. Secret minutes of an FAECT meeting early that year indicate how great was the interest in the Radiation Laboratory at Berkeley:

Ray Dunn stated that it would be necessary to obtain complete personnel list of employees with the Radiation Lab, and that this could best be obtained from the personnel office * * * raised an objection to this procedure stating that filching of such a list would probably come to the attention of the FBI and would cause trouble for the FAECT . . .

---

* SAM stood for the initials of the laboratory's code name "Substitute Alloy Metals."

A confidential report on the FAECT, moreover, quoted Scherer as having stated that many FAECT members had been accepted for jobs in the Radiation Laboratory. And, the report continued, "Incidentally, all personnel is directed through Scherer. He has an office on the campus and interviews people all the time . . . It is not farfetched to say that all applicants are either members of the FAECT or have to become members before or after they are accepted as employees of the Lab. Scherer told a girl that he would guarantee her a job if she would join the FAECT—a job at the Lab.")

Of considerable significance was the presence in California of Steve Nelson—"hero" of the Spanish Civil War, high-ranking party functionary, and an honor graduate of the Lenin Institute in Moscow, whose curriculum includes techniques of espionage, subversion, guerrilla warfare, and revolution. Nelson had other qualifications. He was a friend of the Oppenheimers, or more precisely of Mrs. Katherine Oppenheimer, whom he had intercepted in Paris as she prepared to go to Spain in 1937 to learn what she could about the death of her Communist husband, Joseph Dallet. It has been reported that Dallet was executed for showing signs of political deviation, a common practice in that sanguinary conflict. Nelson, however, convinced the widow of what may be the truth, that Dallet had died bravely in combat—then sent her back to the United States. From this episode had grown a friendship which persisted after the Mrs. Oppenheimer-to-be drifted out of the Communist Party. This friendship was a windfall for the apparatus. Dr. Oppenheimer's sympathies were well known to the Center, but his importance required that he be handled with the utmost care.

In addition to the scientists already imbedded in the nascent atomic project, there were trained consular officials who could act as the recipients of all information gathered by the agents. In San Francisco, Gregory Kheifets and Peter Ivanov, both vice consuls, handled this chore. In New York, Pavel Mikhailov, also a vice consul, was of sufficient rank and stature in Soviet Intelligence to be sent to Canada to inspect the operations of the spy ring later exposed by Igor Gouzenko's defection to the West. Adding the Mata Hari touch was Louise Bransten, the blonde and green-eyed heiress to a two-million-dollar fortune, who was on intimate terms with Kheifets. Mrs. Bransten's home was used to entertain important party functionaries and to impress party members or fellow-travelers vital to the party's undertakings. On trips to New York, she would visit Mikhailov, leading security officials to believe that she may have doubled as a courier. When the Los Alamos project was begun, the apparatus reached out to less exalted "contacts" such as David Greenglass, who succumbed to the pressure of his sister and brother-in-law, Ethel and Julius Rosenberg. In time, Harry Gold, perhaps the hardest-working agent in the Soviet espionage corps, was taken off industrial spying and assigned to work with Klaus Fuchs.

The over-all boss of the Center's Operation Atom was Vassili Zubilin, Third (later Second) Secretary of the Soviet Embassy in Washington. Zubilin, like Adams, was an old pro, carrying the credentials of both Red Army Intelligence and the NKVD. Particularly beloved because of his part in the assassination of Ignace Reiss in Switzerland, Zubilin held the rank of major general in the secret police. In Europe, he had frequently used the cover name "Peter." In the United States, his *nom d'espionage* was "Cooper." * Zubilin (real name: Zarubin) was familiar with the American scene, having traveled to this country on several occasions between 1934 and 1937, carrying a false passport made out to the name of Edward Joseph Herbert.

Zubilin could not have had much of a life. His wife, Elizabeta, was also an Intelligence agent of some importance, and her job was to keep an eye on him. This may explain his major weakness. In 1953, Lieutenant Colonel Yuri Rastvorov, who broke with the

---

* The Center in Moscow is not given to irony, but it is interesting that "Peter" and "Cooper" Zubilin's chief agent, Arthur Adams, lived at the Peter Cooper Hotel in New York.

apparatus, told the Senate Internal Security Subcommittee that Zubilin "was fired from the service in 1947 because of alcoholism, and now he is retired, drinking peacefully." Only Zubilin himself or the Pavlovian specialists of the NKVD know whether he drank because he enjoyed it—or to forget the events of his full and jolly life. But alcohol had not dimmed his perceptions or slowed his hand during the four and one-half years that he ruled the apparatus in the United States. The now famous 1945 FBI report to President Truman detailing the ramifications of Soviet espionage in the United States, from Alger Hiss and Harry Dexter White to the atomic ring, recounts one meeting between Zubilin and Steve Nelson in San Francisco. The "source" of the information was a microphone planted in Zubilin's room.

Nelson advised Zubilin that his work on behalf of the apparatus had been predicated upon a note from Moscow which had been brought to him by a courier from New York and that Earl Browder was fully cognizant of the fact that he, Nelson was engaged in secret work for the Soviets . . .

Nelson also discussed thoroughly with Zubilin what were vaguely described by him as "Russian activities" to distinguish them from the political and propaganda work of the Comintern. In connection with these "Russian activities" he pointed out that a number of the officials of the Communist Party were alarmed by the fact that Soviet representatives would approach party members in California and give them specific assignments, presumably of an espionage nature, and would instruct them to say nothing to their superiors in the party regarding the assignments given them by the Soviets. Nelson suggested to Zubilin that in each important city or state, the Soviets have but one contact who was trustworthy, and to let that man handle the contact with party members who were to be given special assignments by the Soviets.

At the time of this meeting, Nelson complained to Zubilin about the inefficiency of two persons working for the apparatus. (These persons who later were identified through investigation . . . as Getzel Hochberg and Mordecai Rappaport, were relieved of their duties and actually transferred to other cities from those in which they had been working—Hochberg from New York to Detroit, and Rappaport from San Francisco Bay area to Los Angeles, Calif.)

Another entry in the report indicates how Arthur Adams transmitted information to Mikhailov in job lots:

Adams is known to be a contact of Pavel Mikhailov, acting Soviet consul general in New York City, who has been identified heretofore to an agent of this Bureau by Igor Gouzenko as the head of an important group of Red Army Intelligence espionage agents. For example, on the night of 25 October 1944, Adams was seen by Bureau agents to leave the residence of Jacob Broaches Aronoff carrying an extremely large and heavy case. Mikhailov drove an automobile up to the curb. Adams carefully put the case in the trunk compartment and drove off with Mikhailov.

But these instances of Soviet activity, and others to be described in later chapters, are hardly necessary to demonstrate the extent and success of Soviet espionage. There is far more concrete proof. When the Soviet Union began to build its atomic installation, its plutonium plant (PRS) was almost identical in size and specifications to "secret" Reactor 305 at Hanford, Washington. (As Admiral Strauss has pointed out, "The odds are astronomical against such a neat series of coincidences.") Comparing the figures, the conclusion is inescapable that Soviet engineers could have walked blindfold through the Hanford plant, so fully informed were they.

	Reactor 305	*Russian PRS*
Power	10 watts	10 watts
Diameter	19 feet	19 feet
Lattice spacing	8½ inches	8 inches
Loading	27 tons uranium	25 tons uranium
Rod diameter	1.4+ inches	1.6 inches

The Soviets were not only able to get the specifications of reactors. One of the messages transmitted by Gouzenko when he was the cipher clerk at the Soviet Embassy in Ottawa gave the exact amount of U-235 being used daily at the Metallurgical Laboratory. Another reported when the first test at Alamogordo was held. Greenglass supplied the design of the implosion lens used in the bomb. Fuchs turned over every scrap of information he could lay his hands on—which was a great deal. Donald MacLean, when he was stationed at the British Embassy in Washington, had a permanent pass to the Atomic Energy Commission Headquarters, which allowed him to move in and out alone. Bruno Pontecorvo carried in his head much experimental and theoretical knowledge. The Communist cell at Berkeley was a constant source of information. Dr. Hiskey not only passed on top-secret data about the work at Columbia and the University of Chicago, but helped Arthur Adams in recruitment work.

So up to the minute were Soviet scientists that they even picked up the slang and jargon of the MED and adopted it as their own. A few indiscretions during the postwar period, when Bernard Baruch was attempting to work out United Nations control of nuclear energy with the Soviets, indicated to him—more than all the security reports—that the Communists had stolen the secret and the techniques. In his book *Men and Decisions* Lewis Strauss recounts one anecdote demonstrating this point:

Dr. Charles Allen Thomas, chairman of the board of the Monsanto Chemical Company, who was a key figure in the early years of the Manhattan Project, recalls another of these interesting coincidences. Scientists at that time were intrigued by the ease with which some atoms could stop certain neutrons. "One of them," said Dr. Thomas, "compared the process with the ease of hitting a barn when it presented a broadside target. As a result of this chance remark, the unit of measure for nuclear capture cross-sections became known as the 'barn' and this function of atoms is still measured in 'barns,' just as distance is measured in miles. When we first learned of Soviet nuclear technology some years later, we were surprised to hear *they* were measuring these same cross-sections in terms of 'barns,' even though the closest word to 'barn' in the Russian language is 'bahrahn,' which means mutton . . . I leave it to you to say who has been whose lamb chop," concludes Dr. Thomas. This incident only suggests that there was a fairly free flow of scientific information—in one direction.

Adding to this scientific free flow was Joliot-Curie, later to become head of France's atom project. (He was fired in 1950 because of his membership in the Communist Party and his participation in a Communist "civil disobedience" campaign among French scientists.) Shortly after the liberation of Paris, MED agents were flown to France to meet with Joliot. Their job was to determine just how far along the Germans were in their own nuclear experiments. He was the man who would know. All during the occupation, he had allowed Nazi scientists to make use of his cyclotron in Paris— working along with them. The fact that the United States and the British were so pressingly curious about what the Germans had achieved in atomic energy was enough of a clue for Joliot-Curie.

Joliot and several German refugee scientists had developed some patents in the nuclear field just before the Nazis captured Paris. The refugee scientists, who had fled to England, freely assigned their rights to the British—but Joliot held out for payment. In November 1944, he began to clamor for his money and insisted that one of these refugee scientists visit him in Paris to discuss the matter. The British agreed, instructing the scientist, Hans von Halban, to give Joliot only the "barest outline" of what was being done in the United States, Canada, and Great Britain. But Joliot was able to pry loose considerably more than that. General Groves, who had not been informed of the Halban trip, assesses the significance of the visit in these terms: "Vital information relating to our research had been disclosed—information that had been developed by Americans with American money and that had been given to the British only in accordance with an agreement [under which they had committed themselves not to divulge anything to a third country]. It confirmed facts that Joliot might have suspected but which he otherwise could not have known. The information had always been scrupulously regarded as top secret." From this point on, Joliot began throwing his weight about. He demanded full partnership with the United States and Britain in the atomic project—something which war-torn France could not have afforded at the time—and threatened to go to the Soviets if he were turned down. It is a fair certainty that he had already confided what he had learned from Halban to one of the Soviet Union's many agents in France.

With Allied security so lax, Communist curiosity so great, and the stakes so high, the wonder is that it took the Soviet Union as long as it did to make and explode its first nuclear device. The exigencies of war and the country's industrial backwardness are in part responsible. So too was the operative Red axiom: There is an American way and a Soviet way in technology—and the Soviet way is to copy the American way. Stalin wanted American money and American know-how to cross every "t" and dot every "i" before he joined the atomic age. The decision was made for him.

On July 16, 1945, the test bomb was exploded at Alamogordo. President Truman and Secretary of State Byrnes were at Potsdam for the Big Three Meeting, and it took several days for the news of this success to reach them.

On July 24, Mr. Truman decided to inform Stalin. Byrnes described the scene in his memoirs:

At the close of the meeting of the Big Three [that afternoon], the President walked around the large circular table to talk to Stalin. After a brief conversation the President rejoined me ... He said he had told Stalin that, after long experimentation, we had developed a new bomb far more destructive than any other bomb and that we planned to use it very soon unless Japan surrendered. Stalin's only reply was to say that he was glad to hear of the bomb and he hoped we would use it.

Byrnes was surprised at Stalin's "lack of interest" and expected to be questioned at length the following day. Stalin never brought up the subject again. It is indicative of American innocence that Byrnes concluded that "because the Russians kept secret their developments in military weapons, they thought it improper to ask us about ours."

But on July 22—two days before President Truman "broke the news" to Stalin and not many hours after he himself had learned of the success at Alamogordo—the Center in Moscow cabled to its chief spy in Canada, Colonel Zabotin (cover name, "Grant"):

Take measures to organize acquisition of documentary materials on the atomic bomb!

The technical process, drawings, calculations.

On August 9, 1945, three days after the bomb had been dropped on Hiroshima and even before President Truman had returned from Potsdam, the Center in Moscow received this message from Colonel Zabotin in Ottawa:

Facts given by Alek [Allan Nunn May]: (1) ... The bomb dropped on Japan was made of uranium 235. It is known that the output of uranium 235 amounts to 400 grams daily at the magnetic separation plant at Clinton [Oak Ridge].

The Center had zeroed in the project.

I V

The Assault on Berkeley

ON March 29, 1943, at 11:15 P.M., the telephone rang at 3720 Grove Street, Oakland, California. Steve Nelson was not at home, but his wife took the call. Dr. Joseph W. Weinberg, a scientist working at the Radiation Laboratory in Berkeley, told her he was very anxious to see Nelson and that it had to be that night.

"He won't be home until late," Mrs. Nelson said, "but if it's important, you can come here and wait for him."

It was not until 1:30 A.M. that Steve Nelson arrived at his house. After a brief greeting, the two men got down to cases. "I have some information for you that may be very useful," Weinberg said. "I can't leave it here because it must be back at the Radiation Laboratory the first thing in the morning. It belongs to someone else, and it's in his handwriting." Then Weinberg proceeded to read aloud, while Nelson took it down—what security agents described as a "complicated formula dealing with the Radiation Laboratory's research into the military use of atomic energy."

Several days later, Nelson made his regular "contact" with Peter Ivanov, nominally the Soviet vice consul in San Francisco but actually one of the agents assigned to the atomic project by the Center in Moscow. The two agents agreed to meet at the "usual place." Late that night, the two men met briefly in the middle of an open field on the grounds of the St. Francis Hospital in San Francisco. Nelson handed Ivanov an envelope. On April 10, 1943, Vassili Zubilin, of the Soviet Embassy and the NKVD, visited Nelson's home. He gave Nelson ten bills of an unknown denomination—payment for an assignment well done. As he counted out the money, Nelson exclaimed: "Jesus, man, you count out money like a banker."

This series of events came at a midpoint in the successful drive by Soviet espionage agents to gather every possible fact, figure, and blueprint of the technical and theoretical process for building the atom bomb. The FBI (and subsequently the Counter-Intelligence Branch of the Ninth Corps area) was either physically present or electronically apprised of the meetings. One FBI agent had crouched behind a bush at the St. Francis Hospital grounds when Nelson handed the envelope to Ivanov. Surveillance of various Communist groups and individuals at Berkeley and in the Bay area had been carried out for some time. San Francisco was an important wartime port, and the Bureau knew that two very active underground groups—one at the University of California and the other in the Bay area—presented a danger. Rich patrons of the party served as hosts to high-ranking functionaries and to likely recruits. The Soviet Consulate in San Francisco served as a point of embarkation for espionage.

The catalogue of those who plunged into underground work—as well as of those who hung their clothes on a hickory limb but did little more than dip their toes in the water—is long, and the significant names will be listed in this account. The very numbers are significant—there was more activity in the Bay area than anywhere else in the United States with the exception of New York and Washington—for the apparatus could count on the temporary Communists and their fellow-traveling friends to supply the leads for professional agents. For the FBI, trying to cover all bases simultaneously, the numbers made counter-measures that much more difficult. When Steve Nelson met with a group of people, was he wearing his espionage or his party-organizer hat? Was it necessary to watch all those who attended? Perhaps more important: If espionage was on the agenda, was it directed to the atomic energy project?

When the MED began setting up its security defense, the FBI had long been on the scene. But the Bureau was under strict instruction not to impinge on the prerogatives of the MED. What MED leads it discovered through its watch on other spies, it was simply to pass on to the proper Army authorities. Before Weinberg paid his visit to Nelson, the FBI had been told by Major General G. V. Strong, head of G-2, to "keep out of our business." Only because of the Bureau's surveillance on the Bay area Communist Party in general—and Steve Nelson in particular—had it been able to "overhear" the conversations which took place at Steve Nelson's house.

For Ninth Corps Counter-Intelligence, the first "hard" indication that the Soviets were interested in the atomic project had come late in 1942. It was discovered then that one George Charles Eltenton, a chemical engineer doing secret research at the Shell Oil Laboratory in California, had been recruited by Vice Consul Peter Ivanov. Eltenton, Soviet-trained and dedicated to the ideology of his teachers, was a close friend of the rich Louise Bransten. Through her, he had been able to meet on a social basis (and to become friendly with) Communist and pro-Communist students and professors at the University of California, and to tap those designated by the Center for espionage work. It was Eltenton's assignment to evaluate them and then to put the question direct: Will you transmit data to us?

Early in 1943, Lieutenant James Sterling Murray, assigned to the MED by Ninth Corps G-2, learned from a confidential informant that an unidentified scientist had turned over secret information on the project to a member of the Communist party in San Francisco. This material was in turn given to Ivanov, taken to the Soviet Embassy in Washington, and sent out of the country by diplomatic pouch. The only name the investigators had as a start in running down the scientist was "Joe." But there were other clues.

"We had certain key things to go by in information from the confidential informant," Murray said. "The informant advised us that this particular scientist had a wife from Wisconsin, that he was very young and just shortly out of college, and that he was working solely in a certain physics field. We were able to go through the personnel records and, by examination, narrow the field down to two or three, one of which was Weinberg. Subsequently we were able to identify him as the man." This identification of "Joe" did not come quickly. The March episode, however, quickened apprehension. G-2 knew that the wall had been breached—and badly. By May 1943, a decision had been made to put a top-drawer man on the job of breaking what was known to be a spy ring. "Joe" had given Steve Nelson more than technical data: the MED timetable and the scope of its experiments.

The man called in was Lieutenant Colonel Boris T. Pash, chief of Counter-Intelligence for the Western Defense Command and the Fourth Army. Pash had been intensively trained in espionage and subversion procedures. The American-born son of the Metropolitan of the Greek Orthodox Catholic Church in this country, he spoke Russian and was not bound by any sentimental preconceptions of communism or the Soviet Union. By pulling together all the information gathered by his own and other security agencies, he discovered the existence at the Berkeley Radiation Laboratory of a tight Communist cell, strategically placed, and operating behind the front of the party-line Federation of Architects, Engineers, Chemists, and Technicians—a CIO "union" with members at all the atomic project installations from coast to coast.

At first it was believed that "Joe" might be a cover name, that behind this name was Giovanni Rossi Lomanitz. Why? Because of

Lomanitz's past history. "We were able to procure that," says Pash. "Lomanitz was affiliated with some Communist-front organizations and actually was reported to be a Communist Party member." By the painstaking and systematic process of elimination, which is the only basis for good Counter-Intelligence, Colonel Pash and his men began nailing down the facts. "In our operational work," Pash reported, "we were able to procure a photograph of four men, and I had one of our men working on that photograph to determine the background of the personnel on that photograph." Three of the four men in the picture were Lomanitz, David Bohm, and Max Friedman, all scientists at Berkeley. The fourth was Joseph Weinberg. In the early part of June 1943, Pash was able to report to his superiors that he had succeeded in the first part of his assignment. But this was just the beginning.

"We found out," Pash has said, "that Lomanitz was a member of the Communist Party. From the conversations"—presumably taps had been placed on their telephones—"we had sufficient information to determine that both Weinberg and Bohm were members of the party." Though the evidence against Weinberg seemed the most damning, the consensus of those evaluating it was that Lomanitz was the most dangerous of the agents working with Steve Nelson, the ex-officio chief of the cell at the Radiation Laboratory. The question then was how to get rid of these men without creating a stir among the rest of the scientists. At both the laboratory and Los Alamos, security was anathema—and everything the military did was subject to deep suspicion. The simplest way out was to order cancellation of draft deferments. With General Groves's sanction, steps were taken to put Lomanitz in uniform. He had frequently proclaimed a passionate desire for combat duty, and it was thought that there would be very little kickback if his wish were granted.

As it happened, Groves and Pash miscalculated. Lomanitz had no taste, in the old British Army phrase, for cold steel. Instead of going off to war, Lomanitz set up a tremendous outcry that he was being "framed" for "union activities." He appealed to his draft board to continue his deferment, sought other jobs when the Radiation Laboratory would not intercede in his behalf, and delayed his induction by one month. More important, he wrote to Dr. Edward U. Condon, complaining that he was being railroaded into the Army. He also called on Dr. Oppenheimer at Los Alamos to come to his rescue. Condon wrote to Oppenheimer an "insulting" demand (Oppenheimer's word) that the atomic project fight to keep Lomanitz out of the Army. But Oppenheimer did not feel too insulted to fire off a telegram to an MED official stating that Lomanitz's work was "pre-eminently satisfactory." Though he knew why the induction had been ordered, he added: "Urge you support deferment of Lomanitz or insure by other means his continued availability to the project." (After Lomanitz had been drafted, Oppenheimer continued to seek his assignment to the atomic project.)

Between Lomanitz's notice of induction and his final entry into the Army, however, he found time to participate at least once more in the work of the Communist cell at the Radiation Laboratory. On August 12, 1943, Murray, now a captain and still continuing the physical surveillance of Joseph Weinberg, learned through that most reliable of "confidential informants"—the tapped telephone —that a meeting was to be held at Weinberg's house on Blake Street in Berkeley. Along with two MED investigators, he posted himself in the vicinity of the Weinberg house. His account, told under oath:

At approximately 9 o'clock I observed a man known to me to be Steve Nelson, and a woman known to me to be Bernadette Doyle [one of Nelson's most trusted assistants] approach the Weinberg home and enter therein. After their entry into the Weinberg home I, in the company of agents Harold Zindle and George Rathman, went to the roof of the apartment house which was immediately next door to the Weinberg home, and from an observation post on the roof I was able to look into the second-story apartment of Weinberg.

I noted Weinberg, Steve Nelson, and Bernadette Doyle, in company with at least five other members, some of whom were employed by the Radiation Laboratory, seated around a table in the dining room of the Weinberg apartment . . .

Q: Do you recall the other persons around the table in Weinberg's apartment at this meeting you are describing?

MURRAY: I don't recall all. I know Giovanni Rossi Lomanitz, David Bohm, Irving David Fox, Max Friedman . . . I believe the meeting broke up about 10:15 P.M. . . . I ran down to the street floor again and observed Nelson and Doyle leaving together. They turned east on Blake Street, and I turned east on Blake Street and was immediately in front of them. We proceeded up the street approximately 100 feet in that fashion, at which time I thought, for the purposes of the record, that I should make some face-to-face contact with Mr. Nelson, and so I swung on my heel and started west on Blake Street, and in so doing I touched the shoulder of Nelson. We both immediately pardoned each other, and I continued west on Blake Street.

Q: . . . Were there any FBI agents present, to your knowledge?

MURRAY: To my knowledge, the FBI was surveilling Steve Nelson and Bernadette Doyle until such time as they entered the Weinberg residence.

What the purpose of this meeting may have been is not a matter of public record. The assumption, from the investigative records, is that it was a council of war to determine why Lomanitz had suddenly lost his immunity, what might be done to restore him to the good graces of the MED authorities, and a review of security to protect the cell from further incursions by the FBI and the Army. Certainly no order was given to call a temporary halt to the activities of the cell. According to MED security officials, the flow of information to Steve Nelson and Peter Ivanov continued unabated.

One theory holds that the members of the cell convinced Nelson, who, as a trained agent, would have folded the tents for a while, that a frontal attack would be the best strategy. It was no secret that General Groves was anxious to keep the scientists happy. He might agree to drastic action in individual cases, but he could not afford to slow down the work of the project. Though in this case Dr. Ernest Lawrence, head of the Radiation Laboratory, protested vigorously, Lomanitz's blatant Communist record and his zeal for proselytizing could explain the MED's concern. An organized protest was something else again.

On August 26, when Oppenheimer was on a visit to Berkeley from Los Alamos, Weinberg and Bohm decided to make another attempt to "save" Lomanitz. From the nature of their conversation, it is clear that they were attempting to find out just how much Oppenheimer knew of their work with the apparatus. He brushed aside their accusations that Lomanitz had been "framed" and reassured them that their jobs were safe as long as they lived up to security regulations and desisted from political activity. But he was troubled by the meeting. For one thing, he was responsible for bringing Lomanitz into secret work. Beyond this, he had been in general charge of recruiting scientists, and he had for some time been aware of the ideological commitments of certain individuals at the Radiation Laboratory and at Los Alamos.

That day he dropped in to see Lieutenant Lyall Johnson, security officer at Berkeley, and told him he had some information to give, hinting at espionage. Johnson immediately reported to Colonel Pash, then busily at work trying to plug the information leaks at West Coast atomic installations. Pash knew that Eltenton had, through an intermediary, suggested to one or more people in the MED that they furnish data to the Soviet Union. He suspected that Oppenheimer had been one of those to whom feelers had been put out. Pash also had a surveillance report showing that Oppenheimer had spent the night with his mistress, Jean Tatlock, an on-again-off-again Communist who still maintained her associations with party functionaries. Pash, therefore, assumed that Oppenheimer had come to make a clean breast, and an appointment was arranged for the following day.

At the time, Pash was convinced that Oppenheimer was actively involved in espionage for the Soviets. In fact, on June 29, 1943, he had sent a memorandum to Colonel Lansdale, security officer for the Manhattan Engineer District, stationed at the Pentagon. The information he transmitted came in part from the FBI, in part from his own investigations. Subject of the memorandum was Julius Robert Oppenheimer. It read:

1. Information available to this office indicates that subject may still be connected with the Communist Party . . .

(a) Bernadette Doyle, organizer of the Communist Party in Alameda County, Calif., has referred to subject and his brother, Frank, as being regularly registered within the party.

(b) It is known that the Alameda County branch of the party was concerned over the Communist affiliation of subject and his brother, as it was not considered prudent for this connection to be known in view of the highly secret work on which both are engaged.

2. Results of surveillance on subject, upon arrival in San Francisco on 12 June 1943, indicate further possible Communist Party connections.

(a) Subject met and is alleged to have spent considerable time with one Jean Tatlock, the record of whom is attached.

(b) He attempted to contact by phone and was later thought to have visited a David Hawkins . . . a party member who has contacts with both Bernadette Doyle and Steve Nelson. [Hawkins, whose field was philosophy, was subsequently hired as historian of the Los Alamos project.]

. . . In view of the above there exists [the] possibility that while subject may not be furnishing information to the Communist Party direct, he may be making that information available to his other contacts, who, in turn, may be furnishing or will furnish such information, as it is made available to them by subject, to the Communist Party for transmission to the U.S.S.R.

The memorandum concluded with the recommendation that (1) Oppenheimer be separated from the atomic project or that (2) the Espionage—and riot—Act be read to him in order to let him know that the government would not tolerate any further leaks. It also suggested that Oppenheimer be told that there was a possibility of violence against his person at the hands of Axis agents— an excuse to assign him two bodyguards for the purpose of continuous surveillance.

This was the background of the Pash-Oppenheimer meeting on August 27, 1943. Pash had the office wired for sound, with an officer in the next room recording the conversation—something Oppenheimer was not aware of at the time nor years later, when he first challenged the suspension of his security clearance. To Pash's surprise, Oppenheimer launched into a discussion of Lomanitz. The colonel cut him short. "Well, that is not the particular interest I have. It is something a little more—in my opinion, more serious." There was a pause, and Oppenheimer shifted without transition to the Eltenton affair.

(Later Colonel Pash recalled: "It was my definite feeling at the time that the interview Dr. Oppenheimer had with me was the result of Lomanitz's situation. I felt definitely at the time that Dr. Oppenheimer knew or had reason to know that we were investigating or making an investigation which was more thorough than a normal background investigation. It was my opinion that Dr. Oppenheimer wanted to present this information to us for the purpose of relieving any pressure that might be brought on him for further investigation of his personal situation.")

The story Oppenheimer told seemed straightforward. All it lacked was four important names. Three scientists on the atomic project, he said, had been approached by a Professor "X" with the suggestion that they transmit data to him. "X" in turn would

pass it on to George Eltenton. It would then be microfilmed by a
Soviet official at the consulate in San Francisco and sent to the
U.S.S.R. "He told me," Pash testified in 1954, and this was borne
out by the recordings, "that two of the men [approached] were
down at 'Y,' as we called it, that was Los Alamos, and that one
man had either gone or was to go to site 'X,' which, I believe, was
Oak Ridge." But Oppenheimer refused flatly to identify the professor or the three scientists.*

Several months later, and only after he had received a flat order
from General Groves, Oppenheimer disclosed that Professor
Haakon Chevalier, known then only as a vociferous fellow traveler,
had been the intermediary who carried Eltenton's message. But
before he did, Counter-Intelligence had been feverishly attempting
to identify the three scientists and the unidentified professor. A
search through personnel records showed that a scientist was, in
fact, about to be transferred from Los Alamos to Oak Ridge. On
Pash's recommendation to General Groves, the transfer was canceled. This was based on the security principle that though the
espionage attempt had failed, the fact that it had been made was
in itself suspicious. Obviously, there had been something in his
past that made the Center believe he might be susceptible. Again
on a security principle, it was important that his field of knowledge
not be widened by allowing him to move to another atomic
installation.

Identifying Professor "X" was another, and more difficult, matter. On November 22, Counter-Intelligence headquarters in San
Francisco reported to Colonel Lansdale the result of their search:

... A record check of all professors and associates at the University of California was made with the Federal Bureau of Investigation and the results thereof contained in a progress report
from the office dated 20 October 1943. A continued survey has

---

* For a fuller account of Oppenheimer's disclosures and the extent of
Communist infiltration of the atomic project, see Chapter V.

been made and it is believed that it is entirely possible that the professor might be one of the following. . . .

Nine names were listed, with descriptive material. They included Lomanitz, Friedman, Bohm, and Weinberg. After Weinberg's name there was the notation, "has been known to commit at least one espionage act." But Haakon Chevalier's name was not among them. By the time Oppenheimer had broken his vow of silence, the trail was cold. The only tangible result was a recommendation by Counter-Intelligence that "it is not believed that (Oppenheimer) should be taken into the confidence of the Army in matters pertaining to subversive investigations." Eltenton was outside the jurisdiction of the Army, since he worked for the Shell Oil laboratory and was a civilian. Chevalier remained untouched. Weinberg, who had been slated to go to Los Alamos at the recommendation of Oppenheimer, had his orders canceled and remained at the Radiation Laboratory.* When the war ended, Lomanitz returned to his old job at Berkeley. Bohm continued to work for the MED at the University of California until 1946. Only Robert R. Davis, who had joined the Communist Party out of curiosity and on the urging of Lomanitz, was asked to resign—even though his membership had been of very brief duration and probably meaningless.

If any sinister conclusions seem to be implied by this lack of action on the part of the government, they can be quickly dispelled. It was one of the overriding fears of General Groves that anything done to call attention to the atomic project would serve to alert the Nazis. The most public act would be a trial for violation of the Espionage Act—a trial which would have to be conducted under the rules of Anglo-Saxon jurisprudence. This would have broadcast far and wide the fact that the United States was working on the bomb. General Groves had trouble enough keeping the words

---

* On April 26, 1949, Weinberg testified in secret session before the House Un-American Activities Committee and denied all the charges against him. He was indicted for perjury, tried, and acquitted—in part because the committee refused to turn over to the prosecution the transcript of his testimony.

"atomic energy" and "uranium" out of the papers. And to this extent, he was right: Though the Nazis knew of American-British-Canadian interest in atomic research, seized German records show that they never suspected the magnitude of this effort or gave it serious consideration.

V

Oppenheimer: Room at the Top

AN accident of history made Dr. J. Robert Oppenheimer ("Oppy" and "Opje" to his friends) the "father" of the A-bomb. As director at Los Alamos, he guided the translation of scientific theory into an overwhelmingly devastating weapon. In another, quieter era, he would have been a kind of intellectual *flâneur*—charming, gently arrogant, quick at ideas, brilliant in conversation, whimsical in the exact sense of the word.* At Los Alamos, he demonstrated that though his scientific genius was definitely second to that of an Enrico Fermi or an Edward Teller, he had a great and extraordinary organizational capacity and the ability to ride herd on the prima donnas of research in nuclear energy.

It was his personal tragedy that this great achievement was compromised by an ideological conflict which went beyond his comprehension. He was charged with the responsibility of safeguarding the awesome contrivance that he created. That others were more lax or more bemused than he may condition the verdict of

* *Time* described him as the "thin, angular man with the chill blue eyes."

history. Oppenheimer, however, was the man on the scene. If he stumbled, as the record would seem to indicate, it may be because he allowed his heart to rule his mind and his past to determine his future. Certainly he remains an enigma in any account of the great plot to steal the atomic secret and its complex techniques.

It is not the purpose of this narrative to sit in judgment on his actions or to determine whether or not he was a part of the conspiracy. In a sense, this is an academic question for the keepers of dossiers to answer. By his own admission, he was contributing $150 a month to the party, handing his money to a notorious activist, Isaac Folkoff (Whittaker Chambers knew him as "Volkov"), until he was tapped for the atom-bomb project. That the party and the espionage apparatus in the United States considered him to be *"nash"* (one of ours) may or may not be significant. On the other hand, that the Atomic Energy Commission's Security Board cast doubt on his probity does not prove its members to be the Devil's kin.

The Center in Moscow could not have cared one way or another. A study of Oppenheimer's *zapiska* indicated that he was a target. Despite his distress over the Finnish war and the Hitler-Stalin Pact, he had remained on good terms with Communist friends and associates. His wife, Katherine, had drifted out of the party. But she still retained considerable affection for Steve Nelson, one of the party's most important functionaries.

Oppenheimer becomes important in any account of atomic espionage because of the men who surrounded him, because of the information he gave MED security officers, and because of the great interest which the apparatus showed in him. Beyond this, it is all conjecture. The facts speak for themselves, but they speak differently to different people.

This, then, is the record:

In any infiltration of the Los Alamos project, the Center knew Oppenheimer would be of prime importance. Counting on past experience in dealing with the scientific mind, it hoped to enlist

him. Failing this, it was ready to settle for his benevolent neutrality.
There were hands in plenty at the Radiation Laboratory and at
other installations connected with the MED to supply the pieces
which, when put together, form the jigsaw picture. But in espionage there is always room at the top—and only a laggard apparatus
would have ignored so likely a prospect. The first step was to make
the approach, direct or flank, which sounds out the prospect. In
most cases, this is a delicate operation. The guiding mind of the
Zubilin-Adams *apparat,* however, was certain that by using Steve
Nelson the risk would be held to a minimum.

In the spring of 1942, Steve Nelson called Katherine Oppenheimer. She already knew that he was in the San Francisco area,
this knowledge having come from a friend of hers who had worked
in Albacete, headquarters of the International Brigades during the
Spanish Civil War. According to Mrs. Oppenheimer, she invited
the Nelsons and their baby to a picnic lunch at the Oppenheimer
home. It is of some interest that Oppenheimer had not yet been
appointed director of Los Alamos. But obviously the apparatus
knew that he had from the very start been active in the preliminary
work—serving on a committee of scientists under Arthur Compton,
doing some of the necessary calculations, and consulting "more or
less regularly with the staff of the Radiation Laboratory on the
program for the electromagnetic separation of uranium isotopes."

In 1954, Oppenheimer described his meetings with Steve Nelson:

MR. ROBB: You knew he was a Communist Party functionary?
MR. OPPENHEIMER: I knew he was a Communist and an important
Communist . . .
Q. At the time Steve Nelson was at your house you had some
connection with this project, did you not?
A. Oh, yes.
Q. How many times did Steve Nelson come to your house?
A. I would say several, but I do not know precisely.
Q. Did you ever go to his house?

A. I am not clear. If so, it was only to call for him or something like that . . .

Q. Can you give us any idea how long these visits were?

A. A few hours . . .

Q. Was he a man of any education?

A. No.

Q. What did you talk about?

A. We didn't talk about much. Kitty and he reminisced . . .

Q. Did Nelson tell you what he was doing in California?

A. No. I knew he was connected with the Alameda County Organization (of the Communist Party).

Q. Did Nelson ever ask you what you were doing?

A. No . . . He knew I was a scientist.

The security files tell a different story. If accurate, they are evidence that Nelson carried out his apparatus assignment by asking Oppenheimer to turn over secret information to the Soviet Union. The approach was typical. There was talk about the heroic role of the Red Army and the fact that the Soviet Union was being shut out by the United States from receiving technical data which would help defeat the Nazis. Since the Soviets and the Americans were fighting the same enemies, Oppenheimer would be righting a wrong by giving help to those killing his country's enemies. What Oppenheimer is alleged to have answered is still classified information. But in the charges made against him by the Atomic Energy Commission there is the flat statement that "several years prior to 1945 you had told Steve Nelson that the Army was working on the atomic bomb."

Early in 1943, Oppenheimer was officially appointed director of the Los Alamos project—although it was not until July that, on categorical orders from General Groves, he was given clearance. But before he had taken up his duties, he was visited at his Eagle Hill house by Dr. Haakon Chevalier, a professor at the University of California. During the course of the evening, Chevalier followed Oppenheimer into the kitchen and discussed with him the possibility of turning over secret data to George Charles Eltenton. This information would, in turn, be transmitted to the Soviet Union. Oppenheimer, according to his account, rejected the idea violently. Since then he has given conflicting accounts of this conversation. But one fact he has never challenged—that months passed before he reported it to MED security officers, and this after it became obvious to him that they already knew something about the episode. When he finally talked, he also discussed a group of scientists at Los Alamos and at the Radiation Laboratory who were Communists. He attempted to explain why he had hired some of them and permitted others to be hired.

Oppenheimer had two long meetings with the MED's top security officers, Colonel Pash and Colonel Lansdale, in the course of which he discussed at great length not only the Chevalier-Eltenton incident but also his knowledge of the Communist affiliations of scientists working on the atom-bomb project. These conversations were recorded, and though Oppenheimer subsequently stated that he had been telling a "cock-and-bull story"—and that he had been an "idiot"—the transcripts are perhaps the most revealing documents on the lax security within MED. The *dramatis personae* of Oppenheimer's disclosures included Eltenton, Giovanni Rossi Lomanitz, Oppenheimer's brother Frank, and a number of others at Los Alamos and at the Radiation Laboratory who were Communists and, by Oppenheimer's own criterion, of "divided loyalty." *

Since those for and against Oppenheimer have taken a passionate view of the events described, the best source seems to be the transcript of the critical conversations, as taken down from the recordings. (Here and there in the recordings, voices overlap or a speaker's words fade, but at no significant points. These breaks

---

* It should be noted that in 1954, under oath, Oppenheimer denied any knowledge of the Communist affiliations of the people he had so freely discussed with Pash and Lansdale. It was these contradictions which led Thomas Murray, a liberal Democratic member of the Atomic Energy Commission, to file a minority report which held that Oppenheimer was "disloyal."

are denoted by asterisks in the transcript.) The first meeting, between Colonel Pash and Oppenheimer, took place in the New Classroom Building of the University of California at Berkeley on August 26, 1943. Present was Lieutenant Lyall Johnson, who had been informed the previous day by Oppenheimer of an espionage attempt on the atomic project made some six months earlier. After some preliminary remarks, the talk turned to Giovanni Rossi Lomanitz.

From the transcript:

MR. OPPENHEIMER: What I wanted to tell this fellow (Lomanitz) was that he had been indiscreet. *I know that that's right that he had revealed information.* I know that saying that much might in some cases embarrass him. It doesn't seem to have been capable of embarrassing him—to put it bluntly.

COLONEL PASH: Well, that's not the particular interest I have. It is something more, in my opinion, more serious. Mr. Johnson said there was a possibility that there may be some other groups interested.

O: I think that is true, but *I have no first-hand knowledge that may be, for that reason, useful,* but I think it is true that a man, whose name I never heard, who was attached to the Soviet consul, has indicated indirectly that he was in a position to transmit, without any danger of a leak, or scandal, or anything of that kind, information which they might supply . . . I have been particularly concerned about any indiscretions which took place in circles close enough to be in contact with it . . .

P: Could you give me a little more specific information as to exactly what information you have? You can realize that phase would be to me as interesting, pretty near, as the whole project is to you.

O: Well, I might say that the approaches were always to other people who were troubled by them, and sometimes came and discussed them with me; and that the approaches were always quite indirect so I feel that to give more, perhaps, than one name, would be to implicate people whose attitude was one of bewilderment rather than one of cooperation. I know of no case, and I am fairly sure that in all cases where I have heard of, these contacts would not have yielded a single thing.

That's as far as I can go on that. Now there is one man, whose name was mentioned to me a couple of times—I don't know of my own knowledge that he was involved as an intermediary. It seems, however, not impossible and if you wanted to watch him it might be the appropriate thing to do.

He spent quite a few years in the Soviet Union. He's an English * * * I think he's a chemical engineer. He was—he may not be here now—at the time I was with him here, employed by the Shell development. His name is Eltenton . . . He has probably been asked to do what he can to provide information. Whether he is successful or not, I do not know. But he talked to a friend of his who is also an acquaintance of one of the men on the project, and that was one of the channels by which this thing went . . .

P: Anything that we may get which would eliminate a lot of research work on our part would necessarily bring to a closer conclusion anything that we are doing . . .

O: I don't know the name of the man attached to the consulate— I think I may have been told or I may not have been told and I have, at least not purposely, but actually forgotten. These incidents occurred of the order of about 5, 6, 7 months ago . . . I have known of two or three cases, and I think two of the men were with me at Los Alamos—they were men who were very closely associated with me.

P: Have they told you that they . . . were contacted for that purpose [divulging information]?

O: For that purpose . . . the form in which it came was that an interview be arranged with this man Eltenton, who had very good contacts with a man from the embassy attached to the consulate who was a very reliable guy (that's his story) and who had a lot of experience in microfilm work, or whatever the hell . . . [Emphasis added.]

Oppenheimer would not budge from his position that it was his "duty not to implicate" those of his colleagues who had been approached or the name of the man who had made the contact. He suggested that Colonel Pash investigate those in the project "who have been generally sympathetic to the Soviets and [are] somehow connected peripherally with the Communist movements in this country"—a designation which applied to him and to a dozen other scientists in the atomic-bomb project. He also informed Pash that the scientists who had been approached "were considering the step, which they would have regarded as thoroughly in line with the policy of this government, just making up for the fact that there were a couple of guys in the State Department who might block such communications." After all, the United States was sharing some of its atomic data with the British. Why not with the Soviet Union? "There is a great deal of feeling about that," Oppenheimer said, "and I don't think that the issues involved here seem to the people (on the project) very different."

Almost in the same breath, Oppenheimer stated that Eltenton might be "dangerous" to the country, yet argued with Pash that the intermediary—Chevalier, though he still did not give the name —was not in his "honest opinion" really involved. To Pash's point that, if three contacts had been made, there might be others that Oppenheimer did not know about, there was an assent—but still no co-operation. Instead, Oppenheimer brought the conversation around to Lomanitz, whose "indiscretions" were already known, and suggested that they might "very well be serious." He suggested that MED plant a man in the Federation of Architects, Engineers, Chemists and Technicians (CIO), of which Lomanitz was a hard-working organizer. And then he offered the usual justification for not worrying about Soviet espionage:

My view about this whole damn thing, of course, is that the information that we are working on is probably known to all the governments that care to find out. The information about what we are doing is probably of no use because it is so damn complicated ... I do think that the intensity of our effort and our concern with the national investment involved—that is, information which might alter the course of the other governments and I don't think it would have any effect on Russia * * * it might very well have a very big effect on Germany ... I think they don't need to know the technical details because if they were going to do it, they would do it in a different way. They wouldn't take our methods—they couldn't because of certain geographical differences, so I think the kind of thing that would do the greatest damage would just be the magnitude of the thing.

As it developed, the Soviet Union copied every part of the nuclear project that it was able to. After the Soviet tests of nuclear devices, the same scientists who had claimed that different methods would be used argued that the very similarity "proved" the existence of independent research. Pash, however, was not interested in these theories. Though the FBI was not allowed to aid in maintaining MED security, it had informed General Groves that Peter Ivanov, Soviet vice consul in San Francisco and an important cog in the Zubilin-Adams apparatus, was working closely with Steve Nelson and Eltenton. It had picked up information on the atomic project from these agents and knew that in mid-December 1942, Eltenton had been assigned to find a way to get through to the atomic scientists. Just how much MED security had been able to learn, either independently or from the FBI, becomes apparent from the meeting between Oppenheimer and Colonel Lansdale on September 12, 1943. Again, it was Lansdale's aim to pry loose some names, although his hopes were not high.

COLONEL LANSDALE: I want to say this—and without intent of flattery or complimenting or anything—that you're probably the most intelligent man I ever met and I'm not sold on myself that I kid you sometimes, see? . . . Since your discussion with Colonel Pash I think that the only sensible thing is to be as frank with you as I can . . . We have not been, I might say, asleep at the switch, to a dangerous extent. We did miss some things, but we have known since February that several people were transmitting information about this project to the Soviet government.

DR. OPPENHEIMER: I might say that I have not known that. I knew of this one attempt to obtain information, which was earlier . . .

L: Now, we have taken no action yet except with respect to Lomanitz.

O: Are they people who would be in a position to transmit substantial information?

L: Yes, I'm so informed . . .

O: Well, Lomanitz by virtue of being a theoretical physicist would probably have a rather broad knowledge of the things he is working on . . .

L: All right. Now I'll tell you this: They know, we know they know, about Tennessee [Oak Ridge], about Los Alamos, and Chicago [the Metallurgical Laboratory at the University].

O: And the connection of all that?

L: And the connection. We know that they know that the method, I may state it wrong, that the spectographic method, is being used at Berkeley. They know, of course, the method involved. They know that you would be in a position to start practical production in about six months from, say, February, and that perhaps six months thereafter you would be in a position to go into mass production. Now, you and I know, of course, how accurate these figures are . . . We, of course, have acted. The people who are responsible for this thing have been willing to take some risks in the hope of some return. It is essential that we know the channels of communication. We never had any way of knowing whether we have— whether the ones we know about are—

O: Are the main ones . . .

L: All we know is that [secret data has] gone through several hands to the Soviet government, some through consular channels. And of course they have many means of transmitting information, perhaps you know. The fact that it goes to the consulate today doesn't mean that it's going to the consulate tomorrow. The fact that it goes through Joe Doakes today doesn't mean it's going through him tomorrow. Of course, that's our problem.

O: No, the only thing that it does mean is that an effort is being made to get it . . .

L: We know, for instance, that it is the policy of the Communist Party at this time that when a man goes into the Army his official connections with the party are thereupon *ipso facto* severed.

O: Well, I was told—I was told by a man who came from my * * * a very prominent man who was a member of the Communist Party in the Middle West, that it was the policy of the party there that when a man entered confidential war work he was not supposed to remain a member of the party . . .

L: That severance is not a severance in fact. It's merely to enable the person to state without lying, without perjuring himself, that he is not a member . . .

O: I'm quite clear about—not to pull any punches, my brother has made a severance in fact.

L: Well, we know that he has been a member.

O: Yes . . .

L: I'm quite confident that your brother Frank has no connection with Communists. I'm not so sure about his wife.

O: I'm not sure, either . . . The thing that worried me is that their friends were very left wing, and I think it is not always necessary to call a unit meeting for it to be a pretty good contact.

Then, apologizing for the direct and pertinent questions he was going to ask, Lansdale edged over to the case of the three scientists who had been asked to give information—and to the name of the intermediary for Eltenton.

L: I think we know now who the man that you referred to as approaching the other college project was. I wonder if you feel that you're in a position to tell me.

O: I think it would be wrong . . .

L: How do you know that he hasn't contacted others?

O: I don't. I can't know that. It would seem obvious that he would have . . .

L: When the trail is cold it's stopped, when you have no reason not to suppose . . . that another attempt was made which you didn't hear about because it was successful.

O: Possibly. I am very, very inclined to doubt that it would have gone through this channel.

L: Why?

O: Because I had the feeling that this was a cocktail-party channel . . .

L: Well, people don't usually do things like that at cocktail parties. I know. All the stuff that we've picked up has certainly not been at cocktail parties . . . Now, while I would like to have [the names of the three scientists who were contacted] very much, it's not as essential as that we know the contact. Because . . . we don't know that channel. Now we've got no way of knowing whether the ones that we've picked up or the names that I know of are identical with that man. Now, that's a simple reason why I want that name, and I want to ask you pointblank if you'll give it to me. If you won't, well, no hard feelings.

This request for the name of the intermediary was a recurring theme in the conversation. Lansdale had determined to play it gently with Oppenheimer. He was, after all, responsible to General Groves, who had placed the Los Alamos director in a special kind of category. Lansdale, moreover, was aware that an antagonized

Oppenheimer could do the project serious harm. He served as a buffer between the temperamental scientists and the military, yet continued to hold the loyalty of both. Lansdale's technique was to lead Oppenheimer by small steps to a reassessment of his obduracy, and he did so by pointing out that though he could understand a refusal based on "personal loyalty," the intermediary was not a close friend. Oppenheimer conceded this, and added, "I'm worried about it a lot," but he still balked. Lansdale pursued the point. Under what circumstances would Oppenheimer talk?

O: If I had any evidence or anything that came to my attention which was indicative that something was transmitted * * *

L: Well, I'm telling you it is. Right today, I can't tell you the last time anything was passed, but I think it was about a week ago.

O: I mean something that there is a reasonable chance is the man whose name I don't want to give you.

Lansdale changed tack:

L: Who do you know on the project in Berkeley who are now . . . or have been members of the Communist Party?

O: I will try to answer that question. The answer will, however, be incomplete. I know for a fact, I know, I learned on my last visit to Berkeley that both Lomanitz and Weinberg were members. I suspected that before, but was not sure. I never had any way of knowing. I will think a minute, there were other people. There was a—I don't know whether she is still employed or was at one time a secretary who was a member.

L: Do you recall her name?

O: Yes. Her name was Jane Muir. I am, of course, not sure she was a member, but I think she was. In the case of my brother it is obvious that I know. In the case of the others, it's just things that pile up, that I look at that way. I'm not saying that I couldn't think of other people. You can raise some names.

Lansdale did: Joseph Weinberg and David Bohm. The two scientists had, not long before, visited Oppenheimer to protest the induction of Rossi Lomanitz by the Army and to determine how deeply they themselves were in trouble. "Did they tell you at this recent meeting that they were members?" Lansdale asked.

O: No. What they told me was the following: That they were afraid that Lomanitz was forced out because he was a member of the union and that their history was also somewhat Red.

L: By "their" you mean the union or Weinberg and Lomanitz?

O: Weinberg and Lomanitz. That they felt that they, as they put it, would also be framed, and they asked my advice as to whether they should leave the project. That is what they came to discuss. I said in my opinion Lomanitz was not being framed, that if they were fulfilling three conditions I thought that they should stay on the project. The conditions were first, that they abided in all strictness to all the security regulations; second, that they had no political activity or contacts of any kind; and third, that they—

L: Now why isn't that—can you tell me the names of anyone at Los Alamos that have been or are now party members?

O: I can't tell you the numbers of any who are now, but I know that at least Mrs. Serber was a member.* She comes from the Leof family in—

* Mr. Robb questioning Dr. Oppenheimer before the Gray Board in 1954:
"Q: You mentioned Mr. and Mrs. Serber yesterday. Did you know them very well?
"A: I did . . .
"Q: Was Mrs. Serber's position one which would be described as highly sensitive?
"A: Yes.
"Q: She had access to a great deal of classified information?
"A: Yes.
"Q: What did you know of her background so far as Communist connections were concerned?
"A: I knew she came of a radical family, the Leof family. I was told and heard in the transcript of my interview with Lansdale that I said she had

L: The Leof family in Philadelphia.

O: And I know that my wife was a member.

L: That was a long time ago.* Now, do you know? Was Mr. Serber a member of the party?

O: I think it possible, but I don't know . . .

L: Now, have you yourself ever been a member of the Communist Party?

O: No.

L: You've probably belonged to every front organization on the (West) Coast.

O: Just about.

Then Lansdale gave Oppenheimer another of his gentle prods:

L: Now I have reason to believe that you yourself were felt out, I don't say asked, but felt out to ascertain how you felt about it, passing information, to the party.

This was the crux of the matter, and Oppenheimer must have wondered: first, if Haakon Chevalier had talked to any MED security officers; second, just how much Lansdale knew. He briefly stalled for time. "You have reason?" he asked, seeking an answer

---

been a member of the Communist Party. I have no current belief that this is true . . .

"Q: Was Mr. Serber at Los Alamos?

"A: Yes. He certainly was . . . He was head of a group in the theoretical physics division.

"Q: Likewise, I assume, in possession of a great deal of classified information?

"A: Indeed.

"Q: Did you have anything to do with bringing them there?

"A: Oh, yes. I was responsible."

* Oppenheimer, in his formal answer to the Atomic Energy Commission's statement of charges (1954): "In 1943, when I was alleged to have stated that 'I knew several persons then at Los Alamos who had been members of the Communist Party' I knew of only one; she was my wife . . . Later, in 1944 or 1945, my brother Frank, who had been cleared for work in Berkeley and at Oak Ridge, came to Los Alamos from Oak Ridge with official approval."

to both questions. "I say I have reason to believe," Lansdale answered. "That's as near as I can come to stating it. Am I right or wrong?" Oppenheimer gave the easy, and false, answer. "If it was," he said, "it was so gentle I did not know it." Lansdale pressed. "Do you have anyone who is close to you—no, that's the wrong word—who is an acquaintance of yours, who may have perhaps been a guest in your house, whom you perhaps knew through friends or relatives, who is a member of the Communist Party?" Certainly, Oppenheimer told Lansdale, then offered one name—not Chevalier. At this point, he made what can only be described as an incredible mistake; he began covering up associations which he should have been aware were known to Lansdale. Asked if he knew "a fellow named Rudy Lambert"—Lansdale did not add that he was an important agent of the NKVD—Oppenheimer answered, "I don't know; what does he look like?"

Again, asked if he knew Hannah Peters, he admitted a close friendship and volunteered that her husband was on the project. "How about a fellow named Isaac Folkoff?" Again, Oppenheimer ducked: "I don't know. I knew a Richard Folkoff who was a member of considerable importance." * The prod once more: "How about Haakon Chevalier?" This must have come as a shock, and Oppenheimer said he knew him quite well. "I wouldn't be surprised if he were a member of the party. He is quite a Red," Oppenheimer said.

At the very end of the interview with Lansdale, Oppenheimer suddenly returned to the subject of Hannah and Bernard Peters:

L: Well, is there anything else that you believe you can tell me that could give us any assistance?

---

* Oppenheimer's answer to the AEC statement of charges: "It was probably through Spanish relief efforts that I met Dr. Thomas Addis and Rudy Lambert. As to the latter, our association never became close ... Addis introduced me to Isaac Folkoff, who was, as Addis indicated, in some way connected with the Communist Party, and told me that Folkoff would from then on get in touch with me when there was need for money. This he did ..."

O: Let me walk around the room and think.

L: Sure, it's getting warm, isn't it?

O: I have been thinking about this . . . I should have told you before, but I have told you since—no, I haven't—but I will tell you now. You said Mrs. Peters was a member of the Party. I do not know whether her husband is or not, but I know that he was, in Germany, and that he was actually in prison there, and I know that he always expressed a very great interest in the Communists, and I think whether he is a member or not would perhaps partly depend on whether he was a citizen or whether he was working on a war job.

Prior to this, however, Oppenheimer had made a statement which—had it been known in later years—would have served to answer those who minimized Soviet espionage efforts and argued that they merely resulted in the collection of valueless gossip. Oppenheimer's views came in answer to this question: "Let me ask you this. How in your opinion would the Communists engaged in espionage on this project transmit their information . . . Would it be necessary for them to pass it in writing?" And Oppenheimer's answer:

"To be effective; it depends," he said. "I mean gossip could be effective, but it could only be effective on the first sort of thing we talked about, namely, the extent and purpose and dates of the project and how many people were involved, where they were involved, and if it were hopeful or not and stuff something like that. But if it were going to be anything of a technical nature, well, I won't say it would be impossible but it would be very difficult to find a method of transmission which would preserve the technical details without having some of it written down."

Lansdale knew that the Communists employed both methods. The Lansdale-Oppenheimer interview, running to more than fourteen thousand words, merely scratched the surface. It did not deal with the *modus operandi* of the espionage onslaught. In September

1943, the MED had discovered but a small outcropping of the Soviet iceberg. The perfidy of Klaus Fuchs was not known. Neither was the extent of the *apparat's* flank attack from Canada. Lansdale and Pash were aware of the activities of Giovanni Rossi Lomanitz and Joseph Weinberg. They had the first worrying intimations of the Arthur Adams apparatus—and of Dr. Clarence Hiskey's complicity at the Metallurgical Laboratory in Chicago. Despite the protestations of those entrusted with security, however, very little was done. In 1954, Oppenheimer would sketch for the record, with one telling example, the interlocking nature of the infiltration at Los Alamos. Under questioning by Gray Board counsel Robb, he also demonstrated that the error was not solely his own:

Q: Doctor, you knew a man named David Hawkins, did you not?
A: Yes . . . I believe we met him and his wife at my brother's at Stanford . . .
Q: You say that you understood that Hawkins had left-wing associations?
A: Yes . . . I understood it in part from the conversations we had and in part from my brother . . .
Q: When did you have the understanding first?
A: Prior to his coming to Los Alamos.
Q: What were the left-wing associations that you understood he had?
A: Well, my brother was a good enough example.
Q: What others?
A: He and the Morrisons were closely acquainted.
Q: Who are the Morrisons?
A: Phillip Morrison was a student of mine and very far left . . .
Q: Was he a Communist?
A: I think it probable.*

---

* Subsequent to his employment on the atomic project, Morrison admitted under oath that he had been a member of the party. So, too, did David Hawkins.

Q: Did you ever make known to anyone that you thought that Phillip Morrison was probably a Communist?

A: No.... When he came to Los Alamos, General Groves let me understand that he knew Morrison had what he called a background and I was satisfied that the truth was known about him.... He came late and he worked in what was called the bomb physics division.... Then after the war he built quite an ingenious new kind of reactor....

Q: What else did you know about Hawkins's left-wing associations?...

A: I think he had a brother-in-law of whom I have heard it said that he was a Communist...

Q: Did you know that Hawkins was a friend of Louise Bransten?

A: No...

Q: Hawkins wrote the manual of security for Los Alamos?

A: I don't remember that, but it would have been likely. I discussed security with him many times. His views and mine were in agreement....

Q: Wasn't Hawkins, in fact, whether he had the title or not, pretty much your administrative assistant?

A: On the matters I have discussed, yes.

Q: Did Hawkins have access to all the secret information on the project at Los Alamos?

A: Most of it, I should think, yes.

Oppenheimer was not certain whether or not he had ever informed General Groves of the Hawkins "background." But when he was asked if he had continued to see Dr. Morrison after the war, he had a direct answer. He and several other scientists had dined with Morrison at the Hotel Brevoort in New York. "This," said Oppenheimer—and there must have been a small glint in his eye—"was during the time when [Morrison] was on a committee appointed by General Groves ... to consider the international control of atomic energy, and I was on a committee appointed by [Secretary of State] Byrnes to consider the international control of atomic energy. We were, with encouragement as well as approval, doing a little cross-talking to see what ideas there were in the technical group."

VI

Arthur Adams at Work

WHILE the Berkeley-Los Alamos apparatus was busily probing, recruiting, and stealing, the East Coast network was as assiduously seining the scientific world for the facts and figures of atomic energy. The two spy groups, however, were working in tandem— not independently, as the rule book dictates. Arthur Adams not only had direct contact with operatives such as Steve Nelson, but his own sources were being thoroughly developed. As the MED co-ordinated the work of the SAM laboratory at Columbia University with that of the Metallurgical Laboratory at the University of Chicago, Adams widened his scope. SAM had done the theoretical and preliminary research on the gaseous diffusion process for what became the K-25 plant at Oak Ridge. The Metallurgical Laboratory, later to be known as the Atomic Energy Commission Argonne installation, was the site of the first controlled chain reaction—the birthplace of the knowledge that led to the bomb.

Arthur Alexandrovitch Adams had a willing scientific helper at SAM and in Chicago. He was a brilliant young chemist named Clarence Francis Hiskey (Americanized from "Sczcechowski"), whose blatant Communist activities in his earlier years somehow failed to disturb MED security. Hiskey himself had the devoted assistance of his wife, Marcia Sands Hiskey, who served in an important, though less exalted, capacity. It was not until Hiskey had been off the atomic project for over a year that Army Military Intelligence reported fully on his background. A G-2 report, dated June 5, 1945, stated:

Hiskey was active in Communist movements while attending graduate school at the University [of Wisconsin] ... Allegedly Marcia, subject's wife, was a Communist. It was reported Hiskey had stated that the present form of government is no good, the Russian government is a model, and that Russia can do no wrong ... Also remarked that the United States government should look to Russia for leadership. Hiskey reportedly urged radical-minded young men to take ROTC training to provide for possible "penetration of the Communist Party in the armed forces of the United States." In various lectures he discussed communism ... Investigations conducted in 1942 revealed Hiskey read the Communist publications Daily Worker and In Fact, and he had definite Communist leaning ... Hiskey and his wife lived for approximately 2 years with —— whose brother was later president of the Young Communist League [cited as subversive by the Attorney General] at the University of Wisconsin.*

This bald and awkwardly stated resumé (written in the stilted jargon of Intelligence reports) was but a small part of Hiskey's background. Following his graduate studies at Wisconsin, he had gone to the University of Tennessee in Knoxville, where he was employed as an instructor of chemistry from September 1939 to June of 1941. During this period he was a member-at-large of the Communist Party—occasionally attending meetings of the sizable cell which had infiltrated the TVA. He was of sufficient importance

---

* This is, of course, merely an excerpt from the June 5, 1945, G-2 report. It is enough to indicate what MED security should have known when Hiskey was investigated at the time he was brought into the project.

to be invited to the convocations of the all-powerful Central Committee of the Communist Party held two or three times a year to receive political reports and the "line" from Earl Browder and other leaders. Following these meetings, there were a series of "seminars" headed by important party functionaries, in which specific areas of party work were discussed. Hiskey was assigned to the seminar headed by Marcel Scherer, national head of the party's activities among chemists, engineers, and scientists. (He was also the power-behind-throne of the FAECT, the CIO Communist-dominated union of which Lomanitz, Bohm, Hiskey, and others mentioned in this narrative were members.)

In July or August of 1941, Hiskey was a guest at the housewarming of Kenneth May, a party functionary in Berkeley, whose break over communism with his father, Dean Samuel May of the University of California, had brought notoriety to one and considerable embarrassment to the other. The "housewarming" was, in effect, a gathering of the clan, attended by many members of the party cell at Berkeley, officials of the FAECT, and congenial fellow travelers.

During the academic year 1941–42, Hiskey was teaching chemistry at Columbia University. There he became acquainted with Dr. Harold Urey, discoverer of heavy water and one of the nation's most prominent nuclear physicists, who asked him to take part in the highly important, highly secret research being done at the SAM laboratory. Urey would have had no interest, one way or another, in Hiskey's possible connection with the Communist Party. (A decade later, he would be among those defending the atom spies, Ethel and Julius Rosenberg.) But even a superficial check of Hiskey's past should have alerted security officials. It was not until much later that MED security became suspicious. Meanwhile, Hiskey was cleared for access to laboratory files and other secret information.

As a good Communist, Hiskey informed the party of his new assignment. This is standard operating procedure. No matter what the job, party members must let their superiors know of every move, every change in employment, every vacation trip. That he was now doing secret work at SAM was, of course, immediately relayed to Moscow. There is reason to believe that Hiskey had already begun supplying data to the Soviets when, at Knoxville, he had done research in the properties of rhenium. But with the switch to the atomic energy field, he came directly within the province of Arthur Adams. How many meetings between Adams and Hiskey took place is not known. However, in September 1943, when the personnel of SAM were transferred to the Metallurgical Laboratory in Chicago, Hiskey was already under suspicion.

As a result of some of the disclosures made by Dr. Oppenheimer in his various talks with security officials, it was discovered that Kenneth May's "housewarming" at Berkeley in 1941 had been more than social for some of the guests. On the agenda had been a small caucus, at which was held, according to an MED officer, a council of war "in connection with the party's organization of scientists on the campus, at Shell Oil (laboratories), and in other fields at Berkeley." A preliminary investigation by G-2 stated, in a report submitted to the MED on March 10, 1943, that Hiskey was "communistic," and it questioned his discretion and integrity. It was recommended at the time that Hiskey's reserve commission, which he held as a result of college ROTC, be revoked. He was retained at the Metallurgical Laboratory but put under surveillance.

That, in effect, was the end of the ball game for Hiskey. When Adams met him in Chicago's Lincoln Park, two Military Intelligence agents were tailing the scientist. They saw Hiskey give Adams an envelope, and the two men parted, each with a security agent behind him. Adams returned to his hotel room, where it was possible to identify him. Since the Army had no jurisdiction over civilians, the FBI was immediately notified and went into action. From that point on, Adams was the focus of intensive attention from the Bureau. He was "surveilled" to the Chicago–New York train, where one of the FBI men employed an old but effective trick—the briefcase switch. When Adams got off the train, he was carrying a briefcase stuffed with papers; the FBI had his briefcase in custody. The envelope from Hiskey was turned over to Manhattan Project scientists for examination of the contents.

"My God," said one of them, "this is part of the formula for the atom bomb."

"The question," in the words of an MED security officer, "was what to do with Hiskey. We had trouble with scientists when we tried to move one. Someone—I think it was Colonel Lansdale—found in Hiskey's record that he had a second lieutenancy in college in the ROTC. Providentially, he had not given [it] up, and we called the Adjutant General, and we had him call Hiskey to active duty amidst a great furor that we were doing it deliberately, and so on; and we transferred Hiskey, I think to the Canol project, I think, in Canada, where, in the Quartermaster Corps, he counted underwear until that went out of business. He was then transferred to an outfit in the South Pacific"—actually, to Scofield Barracks in Hawaii, where he ran an Army chemical plant and won several commendations for his work. "He was promoted under ordinary steps from lieutenant to captain with no interference from us, and he finally came out of the Army as a captain."

This, however, was only a small part of the story. For as soon as Hiskey learned that he was being called up for active service, he phoned Adams in New York. Adams rushed out to Chicago to get the facts firsthand. He advised Hiskey not to make an issue of his call to Army duty but ordered him to find a replacement who would continue to furnish information to the Zubilin-Adams apparatus. Hiskey agreed, and the following day found him in Cleveland, at the hotel of John Hitchcock Chapin, a chemical engineer and, like Hiskey, a group leader at the Metallurgical Laboratory. (His assignment in Cleveland was "secret even within the project.") Chapin had worked with Hiskey for about a year and a half, both at SAM and Chicago. They were friends, but not very close. According to Chapin, they hobnobbed on the project; that was all. The one interest in common, besides science, was "sympathy" for the Soviet Union. The meeting between Hiskey and Chapin can best be recounted in Chapin's words:

CHAPIN: I was told that Arthur Adams was a Russian agent, and told by Hiskey, that is—

Q: When did he tell you that?

A: . . . It must have been the spring of 1944. Yes.

Q: April 29 or 30, do you know?

A: It could have been . . .

Q: All right, what else did he tell you?

A: I have to think now. He asked me whether I would be willing to meet Arthur Adams at some future date.

Q: What was your reply?

A: After thinking about it awhile, I said, yes, I would be willing to meet him . . .

Q: Why did Hiskey want you to meet Arthur Adams? . . .

A: Well, to the best of my recollection, it would be to discuss whether or not I should hand out any information to Adams on my work.

Q: Was any arrangement made at that time between you and Hiskey for you to meet Adams?

A: No definite arrangement, that is—well, it was arranged that I would meet Adams sometime probably, no date or anything like that.

Q: Did you give Hiskey a key?

A: Yes. I did.

Q: Explain the circumstances. . . .

A: The key would be a means of my knowing if Adams ever did get in touch with me—would be a means for my knowing that that was Arthur Adams, or the man that Hiskey had spoken about. . . . It was an ordinary key. I think it was the key to the basement of our apartment or something else. It was an extra key I had.

Q: But the key was to serve as a so-called instrument of identity, is that right?

A: Yes.

Q: Did you ever see Arthur Adams?

A: ... Yes. He phoned (in the fall of 1944), and then he came around to our apartment sometime after that, and he did not come into our apartment actually, he came downstairs, and I went out and answered the doorbell, and went down to meet him, and he gave me the key, and I believe I asked him whether he would come up or not, and he did not, and suggested that we meet in a hotel room or something like that ...

Q: Did you go to the Stevens Hotel?

A: ... Well, I went when Adams was there in the room that he told me he would be in, and he suggested that he would like to—this again, I am trying to give you the essence of it—I honestly do not remember the details—the essence of it was that he would like to have me give him information on my work.

Q: What did you tell him?

A: I did not agree ...

Q: How long were you in his room?

A: Oh, I would guess about an hour or so ...

Q: In declining to furnish him any information, what reason did you give? What was your attitude to him?

A: I do not know ...

Q: Well, when you left the room of Arthur Adams ... did you say you would meet him again?

A: I do not think I agreed to meet him again, although he gave me his address ...

Q: Did you report your conversation with Arthur Adams to any of your superiors or anyone in the project?

A: No. I did not ...

Q: What happened to the key?

A: The FBI has it, so far as I know ...

Q: Did you know that Clarence Hiskey was coming to see you in Cleveland?

A: No. I did not.

On one point, Chapin could give no logical answer: Why had he agreed to meet a Soviet agent who was seeking classified information on the atomic bomb? The closest he came to any kind of explanation was in stating that he "must have considered the possibility of co-operating with Adams—at least thought about it." The thought stayed with him for some time. He had agreed with Hiskey that when he went to Chicago, he would write a letter to him, addressed to Marcia Sands Hiskey in New York (Clarence had divorced her and remarried) for forwarding. This letter was to be the signal that he was ready to talk to Arthur Adams. There was one more mystery. Chapin was not a member of the Communist Party, although he had always been outspoken in his praise of the Soviet Union. Yet Hiskey had made a blunt proposal that he meet a Soviet agent and supply him with information. Chapin was sure that Hiskey was simply taking "a terrifically long chance."

Q: Did you meet with Adams in the belief that Russia was our ally at the time?

A: Oh, certainly.

Q: And that you had in the back of your mind that it was not too great a breach of the confidence that was placed in you to divulge information to an ally?

A: That must have been in the back of my mind . . .

Q: Have you had the feeling that the secret of the atom bomb should be internationally shared?

A: Oh, I have made no secret of that. Yes, I have always felt that probably it should.*

---

* Chapin's explanation that he had pulled away from Adams because he got "cold feet" sounds eminently sensible. But his error in agreeing to see Adams lived to plague him. In 1946, he was asked to give a statement to the FBI, and he did so. (The Bureau knew the story, but wanted it from his lips.) In 1948, he was discharged from a post with a private company doing classified government work when he was denied security clearance.

Between the time that Hiskey asked Chapin to join the espionage apparatus and the first approach from Adams, G-2 had been busy on its own. On his way to Mineral Wells, Alaska, Hiskey stayed overnight at a United States post in Edmonton, Canada. While he was away from his room, a CIC agent, Charles Clark, searched his gear. Among Hiskey's clothes, Clark found a notebook full of data which General Groves later described as "top secret." From the FBI, G-2 learned that Hiskey was to have met a Soviet courier in Alaska who would pick up the notebook and deliver it to Arthur Adams.

The FBI had also begun to move in on Adams. He was put under a twenty-four-hour surveillance. An agent with technical equipment was stationed in a room next to Adams's at the Peter Cooper Hotel. About a half block away, at another hotel, the FBI set up a headquarters for a sixty-watt broadcasting station to direct the radio cars which maintained surveillance on Adams and his contacts. These contacts were in turn put under surveillance. From this, a diagram of interlocking relationships and activities began to emerge.

Steve Nelson arrived in New York. He was picked up by a Soviet consulate limousine which proceeded to Forty-fifth Street and Eighth Avenue. Adams was waiting at the corner. The two drove around for some thirty minutes, winding along the Central Park driveway and turning and twisting at random through New York City traffic. Then the limousine dropped Nelson and picked up Soviet Vice Consul Pavel Mikhailov. Some time later, after more aimless driving, Adams got out of the car. When Mikhailov stepped out, in front of the Soviet Consulate, he was carrying the briefcase Nelson had brought with him from the West Coast.

As a result of the FBI surveillance, it was noted that Adams frequently visited the jewelry store of Victoria Stone at 510 Madison Avenue and that he spent "about half his time" at her apartment. Microphones were planted in her telephone and in the fireplace of her apartment. Across the street in still another hotel, an agent monitored all conversations. By October 1944, Adams and his associates realized that they were being followed, but it never occurred to them that their phones were tapped—or if it did, they were unable to discover it and therefore felt safe. The surveillance became a kind of private war between the FBI and Adams & Co. Once a man with training knows that he is under surveillance, it is virtually impossible to tail him unnoticed. The briefcase switch, right after the Adams-Hiskey meeting in a Chicago park, could have been interpreted as misadventure by Adams, but he had been too long in the business to accept it as such.

The chase, as one former FBI man on the Adams case has said, became "a personal issue." Within ten to twenty minutes, the tail was spotted. Adams and/or his confederates always took precautions to backtrack. They would step into high-speed elevators and get off on different floors, go down into the subway and back up again, dash from one subway to another—in order to identify anyone who was trailing them. The FBI had strict instructions not to lose Adams or his confederates. Since it was impossible to take chances, the FBI men had to remain right at the heels of the subject they were following. Adams made the most of this, treating those who tailed him with contempt. Often in backtracking he would come face to face with an FBI agent, would say where he was going, at what time he meant to leave, and where he would go from there.

This heckling once caused Adams some embarrassment. He was on his way, in 1945, to an appointment with Steve Nelson. In order to shake his tail, he walked into the lobby of the Waldorf Astoria, turned a corner, and then doubled back—walking right into the man following him. His mouth open to make a sneering remark, he collided sharply with the FBI agent, lost his balance, and fell, his thick glasses skidding across the lobby. Peering and groping, Adams searched on his hands and knees for the glasses, while people glared at the FBI agent. From that time on, Adams stopped heckling his trailers. Very little was achieved by this surveillance in tracing new contacts. But it served to harass the espionage apparatus, to hamper its movements, and to make its work more difficult. The real leads came from the telephone taps and the hidden microphones in the rooms of Adams, Victoria Stone, and Eric Bernay.

One of the Adams contacts was Dr. Louis Miller, who practiced medicine during the winter on Manhattan's West End Avenue and in the summer from a bungalow in the Rockaways. Probably Miller was Adams's physician. But a check was made of his personal effects, and a number of cablegrams in code from Mrs. Adams in the Soviet Union were found. A search of the papers of another contact turned up the original Immigration and Naturalization file on Barney Josephson, brother of a onetime associate of spy and terrorist George Mink. Victoria Stone's jewelry shop, at which the FBI maintained a stake-out, was particularly rewarding to Bureau agents.

After the shop was closed for business, it would be visited by Julius Heiman—his daughter, Beatrice, worked at the Soviet Embassy in Washington and seemed to commute to New York—and others connected with Adams. Marcia Hiskey had a Post Office box in Brooklyn, at which she received mail addressed to her or simply to her number. At least once a week, and sometimes more frequently, Marcia Hiskey fulfilled her appointed task by delivering the mail to the jewelry shop. The contents of the letters she brought to Adams, it would not be unseemly to suggest, were known to the FBI.

In February of 1945, the special detail on twenty-four-hour surveillance duty realized that it was now a case of the hunter hunted. An FBI agent noticed that he himself was being followed. He stepped into a drugstore and phoned the Bureau's radio center which directed operations from the room near Adams's hotel. Except for the seriousness of the situation, there was something more than a little comic about what ensued. When agents were sent out to tail the newcomer, there was in effect a small procession—with subject under surveillance tailed by an FBI man, he in turn tailed by the mysterious third man who was himself being tailed by still another FBI agent. When the third man peeled off, he was followed to a building on Eighty-second Street off Fifth Avenue—the school for the children of Soviet diplomatic personnel, from whose upper story Oksana Kasenkina, the little Russian teacher, would leap for freedom after days of imprisonment.

The events of the following early morning offered the explanation for the countersurveillance. At 1 A.M., Adams stepped out of the apartment house where Victoria Stone lived. He was not wearing a hat, and to all appearances was merely taking her dog for a post-midnight stroll. Two FBI agents, standing by their radio car, observed him and followed on foot. Fifth Avenue was deserted, the shops were closed, and there seemed little likelihood that Adams could elude them. Then Adams did what any trained operative would have done. He waited until a late-cruising taxicab had almost drawn up to him, stepped into the middle of the street to flag it down, dropped the dog's leash, and hopped in—a clean escape. Against a move such as this, there is no checkmate. By the time the two FBI agents had dashed to their car, the cab had turned a corner and was gone.

Had Adams slipped away to rendezvous with another *apparatchik*? On the face of it, this did not seem likely. It became clear then that the apparatus had set up the countersurveillance the day before to draw attention from Adams, that he had been ordered to submerge—probably to surface elsewhere in the country where he was not known. This was bad news for the FBI, and it sprang into immediate action. Four hundred agents were routed out of bed or pulled from other assignments in an hour's time. They were posted at his hotel, Victoria Stone's apartment and jewelry shop, every place he had visited in his espionage peregrinations. But he could not be found. At FBI offices throughout the country, the teletypes began to clatter with descriptions of Adams. Railroad stations and bus terminals in the major cities were watched.

The system worked. When Adams and his associate, Eric Bernay, got off the train in Chicago, they knew that once more their trail had been picked up. Two FBI agents were waiting at the gates, and the surveillance was re-established. Perhaps resignedly, Adams continued his westward trek, while Bernay returned to New York. His first act was to call Victoria Stone to tell her that the strategic retreat had failed. Bernay reported that Adams had phoned him a few minutes after eluding the FBI. In his own apartment, Bernay had a suitcase packed with Adams's belongings and had met him at Grand Central Station. In thirty minutes, they were on board a train.*

Anger in his voice, Bernay said to Victoria Stone, "The goddam FBI picked him up at the station."

Adams tried to break free in Denver, failed, and moved on to Portland, Oregon. It was apparent then that Adams would attempt to leave the country. Normal procedure would have been to arrest him for espionage. But the Bureau in Washington could not get approval from either the Attorney General or the State Department. The FBI was given strict orders not to let him get away, but arrest was forbidden unless he boarded a ship. (The FBI men working on the case secretly hoped that he would cross over into Canada. There, the Royal Canadian Mounted Police would, they knew, act swiftly.) Even then, the charge was not to be espionage but violation of the immigration statutes or the Selective Service Act.

When Adams arrived in Portland, his welcoming committee consisted of practically the entire FBI contingent. He went directly from the station to the docks, where a Soviet freighter was tied up. Agents from the Portland office were there ahead of him, forming a cordon around the gangplank. Adams stepped out of the cab and approached to within ten feet of dockside. Then he spun on his heel, walking quickly away. Another cab took him uptown to a

---

* Bernay has admitted his part in the night's adventure but maintained that he had no idea what Adams was up to or that he was an espionage agent.

small movie house. He watched the film for about two hours and returned to the station. Back in New York, the cat-and-mouse game began all over again. Thousands of man hours and dollars were being spent, the Adams apparatus was fully alerted, and the Bureau knew that it was a matter of time before he eluded surveillance again. Urgent representations were made to the State Department for permission to make an arrest. But this was never forthcoming.

Eventually, Arthur Alexandrovitch Adams slipped away—this time with intent to flee the country. It required only a few minutes of headway for him to hide aboard a Soviet freighter in New York. He was never seen again in the free world—and it is rumored that for his successful theft of American military and scientific secrets, he was awarded a bullet in the back of the head. By Soviet standards, he had bungled. Like Hollywood, the Center judges its stars by their last picture.

VII

To Joe, With Love

IN the spring of 1949, a former Air Corps major heard a radio broadcast about a few grams of uranium which had disappeared from the Argonne Laboratory, an Atomic Energy Commission installation in Chicago. The United States Senate, in all its majesty, was embroiled in an investigation of what was either theft or carelessness. George Racey Jordan, the ex-major, contemplated the irony of this excitement. "If they're looking for uranium," he told a friend, "I can tell them about a thousand pounds that got away." As liaison officer, working closely with the Soviet Purchasing Commission at the air depot in Great Falls, Montana, he had seen far more than the passage to Russia of uranium during the years that Stalin was our "ally" and his every request tantamount to law. Major Jordan was not a professional soldier, though he had served as a flier in World War I with Captain Eddie Rickenbacker, but he followed orders.

His casual remark, however, set off a small war which filled newspaper columns and involved the House Un-American Activities Committee before he was vindicated. For it was repeated, along with his brief explanatory statements, to Senator Styles Bridges, a power in the Republican Party. Jordan was invited to visit Senator Bridges. He told his story in greater detail. "Are you certain you saw uranium?" Bridges asked. "Yes, sir," Jordan answered. "Could you be certain enough to testify?" Bridges pressed. Jordan was. "I will think it over for a few days and you will hear from me," Bridges told him.

Jordan heard instead from the radio commentator, Fulton Lewis, Jr. He repeated his story to Lewis who immediately reported it to the FBI. Special agents appeared at Jordan's house and at his office. They questioned him at length and photostated his diary and all other corroborative evidence. When, after many weeks, their investigation was concluded, Jordan appeared on the Lewis nightly broadcast and once more, interrupted only by questions, told of the wholesale movement of classified documents and war-precious materials to the Soviet Union via the Army's United Nations Depot at Great Falls.

The reaction was immediate: Public clamor for a thorough investigation and angry protests from Democrats still smarting from the Hiss case disclosures. Since at least one important New Deal figure had been mentioned, it was charged that Jordan was "in the pay of the Republican Party," that he was a publicity-seeker attempting to capitalize on the national concern over Communist espionage and subversion, and that he had invented his story out of whole cloth. So, as it must to men who speak up on the Communist issue, Major Jordan was subpoenaed by the House Un-American Activities Committee. When he took the witness stand on December 5, 1949, the mixture was not as before. The Democratic members arranged to be the only ones present, and their attitudes ranged from dubiety to the outright hostility of Representative Francis E. Walter.

The thrust of the investigation went to two points in Jordan's account: (1) Had shipments of uranium compounds been shipped to the Soviet Union at a time when the Manhattan Engineer District was seeking desperately to corner all supplies, and (2) had Harry Hopkins, the man closest to President Roosevelt, helped to expedite these shipments? The committee's irritation at Major Jordan should have been tempered by the witness who preceded him in the hearings—senior investigator Louis J. Russell. Reading from a long statement prepared by the State Department, Russell verified the fact that several shipments of uranium salts had indeed been shipped to the U.S.S.R., consigned to Colonel A. N. Kotikov, the Red Army officer who worked with Jordan at Great Falls. Also consigned to Colonel Kotikov were one thousand grams of heavy water, a rare and precious factor in early nuclear-fission experiments. Not immediately apparent was that at least two of these shipments had been obtained by subterfuge. Had the committee rested there, the interest in Jordan would have languished. It was only due to the earnest efforts of committee counsel Frank S. Tavenner to elicit the full story and the political determination of the majority members to blow Jordan out of the water that a full disclosure followed.

From the start, it was clear that during his period of service as a World War II "retread," Jordan had harbored no ill will toward the Russians but had in fact enjoyed very friendly relations with them. What had disturbed him were the irregularities at Great Falls, the manner in which standard operating procedure was ignored, and the general lack of ordinary security measures.

Jordan told of his early assignment to an East Coast port of embarkation, expediting the movement of planes by ship to the Soviet Union. The attrition of submarine warfare, in which two-thirds of a Murmansk-bound convoy would often be sunk, forced the Lend-Lease Administration to seek other means of getting American planes to the Russian fighting fronts. A route was worked out by the Air Force to keep the planes moving. They were flown by USAAF pilots to Great Falls, winterized for operational use in sub-zero weather, and flown to Alaska where Soviet pilots took over for the long flight over Siberia to European Russia. Somewhere

along the line, a decision was made to carry freight in the bombers
—and this was where the trouble began.

It was Jordan's job to inspect the planes when they were ready
to take off for Alaska and to give them clearance. At first, he kept
notes of his observations on backs of old envelopes. From time
to time, he copied these notes on sheets of paper. By 1944, his
concern was such that he began to keep a detailed diary, including
the names of all Soviet personnel who passed through Great Falls—
incoming or outbound. His account of these experiences, as told
to the committee, was the foundation from which Tavenner pains-
takingly drew a picture of Soviet deceit: *

"The air-freight movement was getting heavier, and in 1943
important Russian people used to go through with five or six suitcases," Jordan said. "I didn't stop them at that time because I
thought maybe it was legitimate. But when they started sending
the suitcases without people, I got interested, and sending fifty suitcases with armed couriers didn't seem proper and didn't have
diplomatic immunity so far as I could see. I let the first two or
three batches go through, and inquired of the State Department
and the War Department whether the bags had diplomatic immunity. I couldn't get an answer from the State Department, but
I did out of the War Department, and they said I was to be helpful to the Russians in every way."

Jordan also complained to his superior officer about this steady
stream of suitcases—neither Lend-Lease nor diplomatic mail—
which was being funneled through Great Falls. According to the
notations in his diary, he also made a trip to Washington in order
to get some clarification of his duties. As a result, he said, Lieutenant Colonel Robert S. Dahm of the Inspector General's office flew
out to the Lend-Lease base on January 25, 1944 to determine what
was going on. Jordan testified that on March 3, a team of ten

---

* Jordan slipped on one point. Although most details of his story were
eventually corroborated, he got his time sequence wrong and placed certain
acts in 1944 when, in fact, they had occurred in 1943.

inspectors arrived at Great Falls, spending two weeks gathering information. On April 7, Major Fred A. Farrar, an air inspector, also came to see for himself. Major Jordan repeated his story, then took the inspector to see the hangars and to meet Colonel Kotikov, who was beginning to show signs of annoyance at this sudden interest. The military expressed concern, but, according to Jordan, the State Department showed open hostility to his "interference."

> I went to Washington on that trip and walked up and down the corridors of the State Department trying to find someone who would tell me they [the Soviet couriers] had diplomatic immunity. I was passed from one room to another. The impression I got from the State Department was that I was being too officious, and I would be better off if I helped expedite the movement . . . I saw a John Hazard and he told me everything was known in Washington and that they understood thoroughly what was going on, and there wasn't anything for me to worry about, that I should help the Russians all I could.

Q: Tell us your experience with the suitcases? . . .

A: A notation in my diary says Colonel Pavel Berizine and Colonel Yakiv came through with a large number (early in 1944) . . . I could always tell when suitcases were going to arrive because one of the cargo planes would be put on the line and left unloaded, and the mechanics would tell me the Russians had told them to leave a plane empty for a very special assignment.

Jordan was also alerted by a sudden burst of generosity on the part of the Soviet officers:

> The Russians are always very close with their money. They don't spend anything they don't have to. I used to have to pick up their checks at the Officers' Club where I ate with them.
> This night the Russians, much to my surprise, invited me to Great Falls for a chicken dinner. There was a lot of vodka . . .

It happened I didn't drink. They suggested a toast to Stalin, Molotov, Roosevelt, and everybody else. I was suspicious, but I had left word at the control tower if a plane came in to call me at the restaurant, and a call came there. And I went to the field, and two armed Russian guards were standing over the suitcases. One of them tried to keep me out of the plane.

The suitcases were black, cheap patent leather, with white rope sash cord tied around them and gobs of red sealing wax over the knots. They screamed diplomatic immunity, and I said, "That doesn't look diplomatic to me." I ripped the cords off and opened about one-third of them. I had one of our own guards stand with a rifle on his shoulder so they would know I had a little protection.

It was twenty degrees below zero—"cold enough for the fillings to drop out of your teeth"—as Jordan began to examine the contents of the suitcases by the plane's overhead lighting and with the aid of a flashlight. His inspection was fairly sketchy. Frequently he opened a suitcase, got a general idea of its contents, and made a brief notation on the back of an envelope. (When he later transcribed these to a sheet of paper, he included some additional observations that were still fresh in his memory.) Jordan worked as rapidly as he could, knowing that the Russian officers might arrive from the town and interrupt him.*

Jordan's documentary evidence was subjected to chemical analysis and, by age tests of the ink and paper, proved to have been written at the time he claimed. In the notation of what he saw and

---

* Among the contents of the suitcases were a good many catalogues. He examined some of them fairly closely. Years later, he was shown Soviet catalogues. They were, as well as he could remember, identical except that the American descriptions had been translated into Russian. Since then, expert comparisons have been made of United States and Soviet industrial catalogues. They simply reproduced drawings and photos of the equipment in the earlier American version, passing them off as Russian. This observation has since been fully documented by Lloyd Mallan and others who made an intensive study of this practice.

read when searching the Soviet suitcases were technical terms used by atomic scientists and then still secret to all but a few Americans. These were convincing points, for those who sought to discount the Jordan story had hinted that his lists and diaries were forgeries. It is also doubtful that he would have been familiar with the names of unpublicized State Department officials like Alger Hiss and Assistant Secretary of State Francis Sayre. Here is what he set down:

Always just 50 black suitcases each load with 2 or 3 couriers—usually 3 weeks apart. Papers always cut close . . . Tass folders—Amtorg—Panama Canal Commission maps—Oak Ridge—memos from Sayre & Hiss & others—State Dep't. letters—films—reports—"secret" cut off—large folders on machine tools, electric tools & concrete data—furnaces—White House memo from H.H. about "hell of a time getting these away from Groves"—bomb powder [the Soviet term for uranium salts]—Donets—Duban—Siberian development—oil machinery maps—blast furnaces—memos from State, Agriculture, Commerce—thousands of catalogues and dry-looking scientific data . . . tremendous folders of shipping data.

Another load of suitcases—Aberdeen Proving Grounds—folders from Mexico City, Buenos Aires, Cuba—Sealed envelopes from Lomakin [a Soviet consul in New York who was later declared *persona non grata*]—Maps of U.S. auto companies marked strangely . . .

Look up words on memos & maps labeled Oak Ridge—Manhattan Engineering Dep't or District I think it was—Uranium 92—neutron—proton and deuteron—isotope—energy produced by fission or splitting—look up cyclotron—Map of walls 5 feet thick of lead and water to control flying neutrons. Heavy water hydrogen or deuterons.

Q: Did you know who Groves was?

A: No sir. I do now . . .

Q: To whom was this note addressed?

A: I have been asked that question before, and it is very difficult for me to remember because I didn't really attach much importance to it; but I would like to tell you that something else happened that makes me think I know. I remember two or three days later asking Colonel Kotikov who a Mr. Mikoyan was . . . Colonel Kotikov told me he was one of the three most important men in Russia. I am sure I asked Colonel Kotikov who Mikoyan was because I had seen the name and was trying to be cagey with him. I had never heard the name before.

Jordan recalled that in the suitcase with State Department papers, the folder marked "From Hiss" contained what seemed to be reports from the chief of the United States military mission in Moscow. "They had been sent through channels to Washington to the State Department, and somebody in the State Department had evidently photostated them and was sending them back," he said. "At the time, you must remember, I thought this material must be going through under authority, and I had no idea there was anything improper." But he also remembered that the thought ran through his mind: "This is something of a dirty trick to play on the chief of the military mission."

While Jordan was opening and examining suitcases, taking a hurried look at United States road maps on which the names of major industrial plants were written and puzzling over a very large blueprint marked "Oak Ridge," Colonel Kotikov stormed into the cabin of the plane demanding to know by what authority Jordan was perpetrating this outrage. "I will have you removed," he shouted. Jordan opened two or three more suitcases, explaining that he was doing his duty, that it was his job to inspect all cargo that went through the Lend-Lease base. Dismissing his rifle-at-the-ready guard, he walked to the barracks with Kotikov, who was now showing some nervousness, at his side asking whether the shipment would be held up and what Jordan intended to do. Where Kotikov had been threatening before, he was now placating. The shipment did go through, and if Kotikov reported the incident to the Embassy in Washington, no word was said either to the State Department, the War Department, or the Lend-Lease Administration.

The black suitcases, crammed with printed matter and documents, continued to go through. If planes were available, the shipment would go out immediately. From time to time, however, the suitcases were stored in a warehouse near the airfield. One courier would spread a blanket over them and sleep on it while another would stand guard. No such care was ever taken with ordinary shipments—in fact, the Soviet attitude was more cavalier than not about material shipped under Lend-Lease.

The majority members of the committee, particularly Representative Walter, seemed to have other fish to fry. Despite the testimony of their own investigator, they were out to prove that no uranium had been sent to the Soviet Union. They were further determined to show that the "H.H." who signed the White House note was not, and could not have been, Harry Hopkins. The two points were interlinked. For it was Jordan's testimony that whenever Colonel Kotikov wanted something done, he always threatened to take it to Hopkins, the Lend-Lease administrator in the early days of the war. At the Great Falls base, with many tons of equipment piling up for transshipment, there were always questions of priority. If there were any delays, Colonel Kotikov would call the Embassy in Washington and then put Jordan on the phone. Jordan would then get instructions from someone like General Piskounov or First Secretary Gromov, later discovered to be a high-ranking member of the NKVD. At one point, when there was a shortage of American fliers to pilot the planes to Alaska, Kotikov appealed to Hopkins, and almost immediately they began to pour in from air bases all around the United States.

"In one of the telephone calls," Jordan said, "Colonel Kotikov said that the Embassy had something very important to do with bomb powder, and would I expedite this particular shipment."

Kotikov, whose desk was next to Jordan's, kept a zealously watched folder marked "Experimental Chemicals," and from it he had extracted a sheet of paper to which he referred in this conversation with the Embassy.

JORDAN: I saw the word "uranium," and what he called "bomb powder" was actually uranium. He had it marked "uranium." I did not know what uranium meant and had no inkling at the time it would ever be important. I just knew that that particular shipment I had to expedite. The first shipment of uranium that was expected came from Denver.

Q: What was the approximate date?

A: I can't tell you that. I remember 420 pounds came from a firm in Denver.

Q: Do you remember the name of the firm?

A: I would like to keep my memory and what I now know separate. I know now the name of the firm and everything else, but I didn't know it at the time.

At this point, Representative Walter began boring in:

Q: Did you make a note in your diary of the shipment of uranium?

A: No, because it was not important to me.

Q: Was the shipment made about the time you were making entries in your diary, that is sometime in 1944?

A. Undoubtedly. We made thirteen copies of everything. I am sure the War Department can find one of them.

Q: I am talking about this shipment of uranium. Was that made in 1944?

A: Sir, I don't know.

Q: The reason I say 1944 is because that was when you were making the entries in your diary.

A: I didn't put in my diary the reports to the War Department. We covered many, many details in our reports to the War Department . . .

Q: I am directing your attention to the shipment of uranium. Did you make a note of that in your diary?

A: No, I never made any such note.

It was the second shipment—one of one thousand pounds of uranium, seemingly involving Harry Hopkins—that upset the majority members.

JORDAN: We had a 1,200-pound shipment that went through from Canada. That is the one Mr. Hopkins mentioned to me and said to expedite it and not mention it to my superiors . . .

Q: You say you talked to Mr. Hopkins on the telephone about this particular shipment?

A: The Russian told me there was a special shipment being handled in a very special way . . . and I got on the phone. When I got on the phone, he said, "Mr. Hopkins speaking" and asked if I had gotten the pilots I had asked for. I said I had. He said, "There is a certain shipment Colonel Kotikov will point out to you, and keep this very quiet."

Q: Mr. Hopkins said that?

A: Yes.

Q: When was that?

A: Two or three weeks before the shipment came through . . .

Q: How often did Mr. Hopkins call you?

A: That was the only time . . .

Q: How did you know it was Mr. Hopkins?

A: The Russian, Colonel Kotikov, told me it was Mr. Hopkins.

Q: But you personally did not know if it was Mr. Hopkins or not, did you?

A: Yes, I am pretty certain it was . . .

Q: What did he say?

A: I don't remember exactly what he said, but I knew from the conversation I had with him that I was to expedite this particular shipment, and this particular shipment came through and it was uranium. I don't think anybody but Mr. Hopkins would talk to me about uranium . . .

Q: And you also made the statement, which is a very serious one, that Mr. Hopkins told you "to keep quiet and say nothing about them, even to your superior officers, and not to leave any records of them."

A: That is correct.

Q: So far in answering our questions you haven't specifically testified you ever had a telephone conversation with Hopkins himself.

A: I said a moment ago I had a telephone conversation with Mr. Hopkins.

The Congressional Perry Masons went around and around, getting Jordan to repeat his story, putting words in his mouth which he had never uttered. With one breath they attempted to question the possibility of uranium shipments, but the next minute they cited the fact that export licenses for the uranium had been dated in 1943. Finally, Jordan snapped: "It is difficult for me to sit here and answer questions about minute details when I was working from five forty-five in the morning until eleven at night almost daily. We started in January 1943 and worked until September 1944, and much of this is telescoped in my mind together. It is difficult for me to tell you exactly when, but I know it was done, and I know it went through."

The hearing ended with a promise from Jordan to supply the committee with the names of people who might corroborate his story and to furnish the staff with all the records he had kept. By the time the full story was in, there would be, in his phrase, "clouds of witnesses" to back him up on hundreds of details. He had barely stepped off the stand, however, before Representative Walter announced to the press that Jordan's account was "inherently incredible." *Life* magazine stated in its story on the Jordan testimony that both the FBI and G-2 had investigated and found that there was no truth to his testimony—a charge cut from the whole cloth. *Newsweek* also expressed doubt in its reportage:

According to Sidney Hyman, who organized Hopkins' papers for Robert Sherwood, author of "Roosevelt and Hopkins" [*Newsweek* stated], F.D.R.'s confidant didn't have the faintest understanding of the Manhattan project until he read about the A-bomb being dropped on Hiroshima. Hyman said: "He didn't know the difference between uranium and geranium." It wasn't until weeks later that Hopkins talked with several of the atomic scientists and learned about the 'engineering feat of production.' "

Sherwood, on the contrary, dealt in detail with Hopkins's very early involvement in atomic energy matters. Vannevar Bush wanted to enlist Hopkins's influence with President Roosevelt to get the atomic project moving. Bush's proposal, according to the Hopkins account, was embodied in a letter to be signed by Roosevelt, and Hopkins was the man who took it to the White House. In another passage, Sherwood stated: "It will be noted that Churchill was conducting this correspondence on the atomic project with Hopkins rather than with the President, and he continued to do so for many months thereafter." Few bothered to check, and a researcher's faulty memory was allowed to discredit Major Jordan.*

Two days later, on December 7, 1949, the majority members— still meeting without their Republican colleagues—were jolted by the testimony of General Groves. For though the matter of Harry Hopkins was never settled—nor can it ever be—the first glimmer of the truth behind Jordan's account became apparent. So, too, did the shenanigans of the Soviet Purchasing Commission in obtaining the uranium and the failures of civilian agencies of gov-

---

* This phase of the Jordan case is cited not to argue the complicity or gullibility of Hopkins but to show how easily those who deplore the discussion of past actions will leap to conclusions without abiding by their own strictures against "character assassination." Without comparing Jordan's testimony to the available records, his detractors had already sat in judgment.

ernment to abide by the prohibitions against allowing uranium to be sold without the approval of the Manhattan Project. So well and carefully did the staff investigate that it was able to present documentary proof of facts which were not known to General Groves until the time they were developed by the committee.

The testimony of General Groves, corroborated in minute detail by former officials of the Lend-Lease Administration and the War Production Board—and backed up by intragovernmental correspondence, bills of lading, and other written records—is much too complex for a detailed recital. What it came to was this:

The Lend-Lease Administration received a request from the Soviet Purchasing Agency for two hundred pounds of uranium oxide and two hundred and twenty pounds of nitro-urano, a complex uranium salt. "There was a great deal of pressure being brought to bear on Lend-Lease, apparently, to give the Russians everything they could think of," Groves said. "There was a great deal of pressure brought to give them this uranium material." Before General Groves had learned of the request, it was granted and arrangements made for this shipment in 1943 to Kotikov at Great Falls. Groves was quite upset, but he felt that to revoke the permission would alert the Soviets to the significance of uranium to the United States. This might have been a somewhat naïve view, particularly since Groves knew at the time of Soviet espionage activities which had broken through to the secret knowledge that this country was working on the A-bomb. Nevertheless, he gave his approval.

The Soviet Purchasing Commission followed this by a request for eight tons of uranium oxide and eight tons of uranium chloride. This was turned down. The next request was for twenty-five pounds of pure uranium metal. The MED had not yet been able to purify uranium to the specifications sought by its own scientists, and the Soviets were given permission to purchase this uranium in the hope that they might find some metal refinery which had developed an adequate process. Finally, the Soviet Purchasing Agency was allowed to buy 2.2 pounds of impure uranium metal. (Groves believed that they would assume this to be what the United States was using in its experiments, thereby leading Soviet scientists astray.) Next, the Soviets asked for five hundred pounds of uranium nitrate and another five hundred pounds of urano-uranic oxide. This was turned down, but the Purchasing Commission set up a tremendous clamor that these salts were needed for medical purposes and for the hardening of gun barrels.

To quiet those within the federal government who insisted that the Soviet Union should have what it wanted, General Groves reversed himself, and a license for export was granted to an American supplier. Groves was certain that he had cut off all sources of supply and that the Russians would think that United States approval was based on a genuine desire to allow them this rare metal. The Soviets, however, instructed a dealer in metals to find it elsewhere. Without the knowledge or approval of General Groves, the export license was amended to allow the dealer to purchase the uranium in Canada—and it was shipped via Great Falls, as Jordan had testified. In June of 1944, another forty-five pounds of uranium nitrate was delivered to the Soviet Union—a fact that came as a considerable shock to some of the government witnesses testifying in 1949. It had been purchased for the Soviets by the Treasury Department. Among other gifts sent to Joseph Stalin were one thousand grams of heavy water—which, like graphite, was necessary in an atomic pile to slow down the fission process.

The sudden interest of the Soviets in uranium was the clearest indication that they were aware of American progress in nuclear physics. Prior to the request for 420 pounds of uranium salts, the Russians had never imported these compounds from the United States. Groves, of course, was aware of the significance of the continued Soviet demands for uranium. "From one month of the time I took over we never trusted [the Russians] one iota," he said. "Our whole security was based on not letting the Russians find out anything. We were not worried about Germany or Japan. We were worried about Russia." How then was the Soviet Purchasing Commission able to override his orders that no critical materials be shipped to the U.S.S.R.? Groves never met Harry Hopkins. He was certain that there had been no direct approach by Hopkins to MED officials. But the wartime mood was pro-Soviet, and this was reflected in the actions and attitudes of most in the Administration.

After all, President Roosevelt had said of Stalin, "If I give him everything that I can and ask nothing of him in return, *noblesse oblige,* he won't try to annex anything and will work with me for a world of peace and democracy." And Hopkins, at a giant Madison Square Garden Rally for Russian War Relief had said, in an apostrophe to Stalin, "We are determined that nothing shall stop us from sharing with you all that we have." (Cheers.) It is no wonder, then, that there was pressure on Lend-Lease and from Lend-Lease to release to the Soviets strategic materials necessary for the atomic program. "Can you tell us who exerted the pressure?" General Groves was asked.

GROVES: No, I can't tell you who exerted the pressure on Lend-Lease. Of course, it could have been internal pressure. At any rate we saw every evidence of that pressure, and I believe your files of Lend-Lease will show how they repeatedly came back. It was evident from reading the [official records] that we didn't want this material shipped, yet they kept coming back and coming back.*

This anxiety to please the Soviet Union was such that no consideration was given to the possible effects on America's war effort. General Groves recalls one incident:

---

* GROVES: There are two kinds of pressure in Washington. One is the kind that comes from above, that you realize what it is. The other kind is constant hammering, repeating and repeating in the hope that you wear down or that something slips. Nobody has a thousand batting average. I believe that it was the hope of the people who kept pushing and pushing that they might catch me out of town, or that some day I would say to give it to them to shut them up.

We were very anxious, in connection with the gaseous diffusion plant [then being built at Oak Ridge] to get certain equipment. If it had not been obtained, that plant would have been delayed in its completion. The Russians had a plant on the way. Of course, when I say they had it, you know who paid for it. That plant, some of it was boxed and on the dock when we got it, and I can still remember the difficulties we had getting it. One of the agreements we had to make was that we would replace that equipment and use all our priorities necessary to get it replaced quickly.

The Soviets, however, could not complain. They paid cash for the products strategic to nuclear research so far mentioned, hoping thereby to avoid the attention of the Manhattan Project. But other materials, in short supply and necessary for that research, to the sum of more than sixteen million dollars, they received as part of Lend-Lease. The catalogue:

9,681 lbs. of beryllium metal
72,535 lbs. of cadmium alloys
834,989 lbs. of cadmium metals
33,600 lbs. of cobalt ore and concentrate
13,766,472 lbs. of aluminum tubing (vital in the construction of an atomic pile)
7,384,282 pounds of graphite
25,352 lbs. of thorium salts and compounds
228 lbs. of beryllium salts and compounds
2,100 lbs. of cadmium oxide
18,995 lbs. of cadmium compounds
29,326 lbs. of cobalt compounds
806,941 lbs. of cobalt metal and scrap

It has been said that the uranium shipments would have been of little value to Soviet scientists, that the quantity was too small to matter. When asked about this, Groves stated: "Any amount would be of value in certain experimental work. That is, in anything to do with chemistry. After all, we designed and practically built the Hanford plant for separating plutonium and uranium when we had *one-millionth of a pound of plutonium.* The chemistry part could be very well handled." To activate an atomic pile, at least one ton of uranium would have been necessary. But at the time, the Soviets were not prepared to go into large-scale production. They wanted to know what the United States was doing and duplicate it in the laboratory. And this, with the help of enthusiastic Americans, they accomplished. When W. L. White was in Leningrad in 1944, he visited the bombed-out Kirov electrical plant and was shown what remained of Professor Joffe's famous laboratory. (Joffe was a nuclear physicist.) In the wreckage was a "curious contraption" described to him as a cyclotron, used by Joffe to split the atom. "Behind Urals, Professor Joffe has much newer, much better," White was told. "We have, like you call in America, Manhattan project." Like most Americans at the time, White had never heard of the MED. He thought the reference was to some industrial plant in New York.

If the Groves testimony was an eye-opener, there was more to come. When the House Un-American Activities Committee resumed hearings on January 24, 1950, the minority members, including Representative Richard Nixon, were present for the first time. In the interim, moreover, the committee staff had been delving into official papers and had come up with more evidence to corroborate the Jordan account of the happenings at Great Falls. Other military personnel were ready to come forward with statements of their own experiences, duplicating in kind what Major Jordan said in testimony.

Correspondence was put into the record from Lieutenant General L. G. Rudenko, chief of the Soviet Purchasing Commission, to Secretary of War Henry Stimson, insisting on the shipment of sixteen tons of uranium compounds. This had been followed by a memorandum to Groves from Colonel J. W. Boone, "acting for the Commanding General," for "information as to the supply of various forms of uranium" and asking for his recommendations "in order that materials can be made available." It was discovered that the earlier request for uranium compounds had been buried in long lists of desired chemicals, so as not to call attention to Soviet interest. Formal notification to the Lend-Lease Administration that the MED be "kept advised as to the progress" of negotiations for shipments of uranium was read into the record.*

On March 3, committee investigator Donald T. Appell took the stand. After Jordan's original testimony, the charge had been made and reiterated that (1) his account of the thousands of pounds of papers and other documents passing through Great Falls was a myth and (2) that had he really broken into the black suitcases and seen what he later stated on the stand, he would certainly have reported it to higher authorities or at least commented on it in his diary at some length. Obviously, it was argued, no reports were made, otherwise some action would have been taken. *Ergo,* Jordan was a sensation-seeker. These attacks had done much to discredit Major Jordan in the public eye—to the point that documented corroboration was ignored by the press and public. As usual, by focusing attention on extraneous matters, the thrust of the major facts was blunted.

Appell's testimony was direct and reflected the excellence of his investigative procedures. He had obviously combed such files as the State Department and other federal agencies permitted him to enter—and he had come up with far more than a prima-facie case that Major Jordan had been telling the truth and that United States authorities had been incredibly naïve.

According to the documents presented by Appell, the Soviet Pur-

* A curious exchange took place during the testimony:

"COLONEL CRENSHAW: General Groves' underlying philosophy was that the last thing in the world he wanted to do was to help the Russians in any way.

"MR. WALTER: Was he of that opinion, and did he take that attitude, *during the period when they were doing most of the fighting?* [Emphasis added.]"

chasing Commission had on January 19, 1944 attempted to formalize its practice of including large shipments of "diplomatic" cargo on Lend-Lease planes, and to increase the volume. In a letter to the International Section, War Department, the commission had requested that two C-47s a month be assigned to the transportation of "diplomatic mail." After a check with General Deane, head of the U.S. Military Mission in Moscow, the request was turned down on the ground that there was a shortage of cargo space. This refusal was subsequently reversed by General Bennett E. Meyers. The Soviets, however, had withdrawn their request before they had formal notice of General Meyers's action.

Nevertheless, the Soviets had shipped planeloads of so-called diplomatic mail—in violation of regulations—on January 28 (3,563 pounds), February 15 (4,180 pounds), February 17 (4,000 pounds), and February 28 (3,757 pounds). The G-2 report containing this information also noted that none of this had previously been known and added:

Major Jordan, who represents Air Staff at the ATC station at Great Falls, is reported to have examined one of the packages and found it contained blueprints of the A-20 plane, railroad guides showing long- and short-haul routes, and other technical data.

While the original request for special facilities was pending, however, the Soviet Purchasing Commission had made an end run—going to the Commanding General, Air Transport Command, asking for similar privileges. These had been granted. Subsequently, General Deane was once more notified. As he had in the first instance, Deane denied the Soviet request but was overruled by Averell Harriman, then ambassador to Moscow. But Jordan's complaints of Soviet irregularities were still echoing in Washington. On March 13, 1944 a special agent of Counter-Intelligence was sent to Ladd Field to interview Jordan. Here are significant excerpts of the CIC report:

... Major Jordan stated that he was desirous of conveying certain information to "Intelligence Authorities."

The following interesting information was supplied by Major Jordan:

The Soviet Union has made a practice of shipping freight to Moscow through the Alaskan Wing. This has been done for about two years. For the year 1943, the total freight shipped through Great Falls to the Russians was 768,254.2 pounds. This is to be compared with 433,112 pounds ... from 1 January 1944 to 5 March 1944.

This material has been sent by members of the Consular Service, Russian Army Officers, Russian Engineers, and families of Russians who pass through here and others. The freight is diversified in nature ... He added that, due to the shortage of personnel, the use of Russian-owned and operated aircraft, and the fact that a great deal of the freight is blanketed by diplomatic immunity, there is insufficient control over the material shipped to Russia. ...

There is an incredible amount of diplomatic mail sent to Russia through Great Falls ... All of this was protected from censorship by diplomatic immunity. It may be significant that it is not at all uncommon for the Russian mail or freight shipment to be accompanied by two men ... One man sleeps while the other watches the parcels and vice versa ...

This Agent observed that Major Jordan appeared to maintain accurate, detailed files and was very anxious to convey his information via Intelligence channels ...

It is recommended that a prolonged interview be conducted with Major Jordan; that his records be scrutinized for information of an Intelligence nature; and that he be contacted regularly.

It is further recommended that the facts contained herein be given due consideration, with a view to contacting the State Department in order that they be made cognizant of the situation and that corrective measures be taken.

There is no record that the first recommendation was heeded. *Three months later,* however, the State Department "took cognizance." On June 16, Charles E. (Chip) Bohlen requested a copy of the CIC report. A State Department memorandum noted the irregularity of permitting large quantities of nondiplomatic mail to pass through Great Falls without proper censorship or customs inspection and suggested that the matter be adjusted in Washington, or by the American ambassador in Moscow. On July 6, the State Department conferred with representatives of the FBI, the Office of Censorship, Military Intelligence, the Air Transport Command, the Immigration and Naturalization Service, the Bureau of Customs, and the Foreign Economic Administration. All present expressed concern, and a decision was made that regulations be "explained" to the Soviet Embassy.

Twenty-two days later, the State Department forwarded to the Second Secretary of the Soviet Embassy detailed instructions on the procedure for handling nondiplomatic mail and non-Lend-Lease freight. The Second Secretary gracefully accepted the gentle admonition and promised that henceforth there would be no more violations. His name: Vassili Zubilin, chief of the atomic espionage ring in the United States. How seriously he took his instructions may be determined by this: In the files, there is a report stating that on September 20, 1944, another irregular shipment went through Great Falls.

Representative Nixon summed up for the committee:

NIXON: As I see it at present, the issues are five . . . and I want to see which of the charges are still at issue.

First of all, the charge was made that if the shipments were going through, Major Jordan should have made a report. In this regard, he did make a report of the charges at least on two occasions. Is that correct?

APPELL: Yes . . . that is correct . . .

NIXON: Another point that was made was whether or not he tore radar equipment out of C-47 planes. As I understand, this particular phase of his story was questioned in an article in *Life* magazine, in which they said that the report that Mr. Jordan (did so) was preposterous . . . and it was further said that as a matter of fact no C-47s were equipped with radar at the time mentioned by Major Jordan.

The investigation of the committee, in addition to your own, has shown (1) that C-47s equipped with radar and going to Russia did go through Great Falls, and (2) that Mr. Jordan specifically asked permission of Colonel Gitzinger in Dayton to tear the radar out of a specific plane on one occasion. [It was against regulations to divulge information on radar or to ship radar equipment to the U.S.S.R.]

APPELL: That is correct, and he received that permission from Colonel Gitzinger . . .

NIXON: Another point that Major Jordan made was that certain documents were going through Great Falls under diplomatic immunity; that he broke into the cases, examined the documents, and that some of the material in there which he examined consisted of plans, secret material, and so on . . . I think it is clear from your testimony that that phase of Major Jordan's testimony stands up. Is that correct?

At this point, Appell said that the committee had another witness who would offer corroboration. In fact, there were many ready to take the stand.

NIXON: On the point of the so-called shipments of uranium, as I understand the case, first, there is no question about the shipments going through. Is that correct?

APPELL: As to the shipments of uranium and heavy water, [they] have been completely documented to include even the number of the planes that flew [them] out of Great Falls.

NIXON: Isn't it true that these shipments were made with the knowledge and approval of our officials?

APPELL: Export declarations on these shipments were approved by Lend-Lease and later by its successor organization, Foreign Economic Administration.

NIXON: And in the case of one shipment . . . General Groves and members of the Atomic Energy Commission learned about it [only] when this committee began its investigation. Is that correct?

APPELL: Yes, sir.

Only on the role played by Harry Hopkins in expediting the uranium shipments—and whether or not the note in one of the black suitcases had been initialed "H. H."—was there no corroboration. As Nixon pointed out, carefully underlining the point, Major Jordan's story had been substantially documented on four of five points—the critical ones. When Major Jordan took the stand once more, the atmosphere in the hearing room was considerably more cordial. There was little for him to add. But the committee counsel, Frank Tavenner, laid the groundwork for what was to come when he asked Jordan, "Were you acquainted with a Russian by the name of Semen Vassilenko?" Jordan replied that he was, that Vassilenko and three aides had passed through Great Falls on February 17, 1944—as he had written in his diary—with a cargo of the now-famous black suitcases.

When Jordan concluded his testimony, Tavenner called Victor Kravchenko, a former member of the Soviet Purchasing Commission and author of *I Chose Freedom*. Kravchenko told the committee that one of the commission's assignments was espionage, that its members collected secret technical and military information, that this information was referred to as "super Lend-Lease," packed in suitcases, and shipped to Moscow. In February 1944, Kravchenko himself had helped Semen Vassilenko pack a suitcase with secret metallurgical information.

At this point, Jordan might have rested his case. But there was one more refinement—an affidavit not read into the record. It was written by Royall E. Norton, a former Chief Petty Officer in the Navy, then a GI Bill student at Clemson College in South Carolina. Before writing the affidavit, he had consulted with the president of Clemson and with former Supreme Court Justice (and former Secretary of State) James F. Byrnes. The affidavit bears repetition:

A PBM—a Catalina type [plane]—was being loaded [in Kodiak] for the take-off to Russia. I had finished checking the cargo against my inventory when I noticed three extra parachute bags that obviously were not filled with parachutes.

I started to inspect them, and in the first one found a wooden box . . . I lifted the top to see what was inside.

The Soviet pilot, who was making a final check in the cockpit, saw what I was doing and put on a terrific scene. He tried to make me stop, yelling in English: "Personal gear—personal!" I went on long enough to see what was in the box. It contained a solid stack of blueprints, all of about the same size and general appearance, as if they belonged to a set.

I unfolded the top one and examined it fairly carefully. I had had some little experience in reading blueprints. This was very unusual and different from anything I had ever seen. But I had studied enough chemistry in school to recognize it as a highly complicated pattern of atomic structures. Protons and neutrons were shown.

In the lower right hand corner was a group of words, which were probably an identification of the blueprint. I cannot remember the terms, but I do recall the figure "92." It meant nothing to me at the time, as I had never heard of atomic energy or atomic bombs . . . This was undoubtedly a blueprint of the atomic structure of the 92nd element, uranium.

VIII

Gouzenko: The Shock of Recognition

THERE is a terrible sameness about the Soviet official face. The reporter in Moscow or Leningrad learns to recognize it almost immediately. It has nothing to do with features or racial type. It is an expression, not deadpan but withdrawn. It is the product of caution and training.

Eight years after Igor Gouzenko had walked out of the Soviet Embassy in Ottawa carrying the documents that would expose an espionage ring, he had not quite lost that official face. He stepped into the room at the Royal York in Toronto knowing the waiting reporter only by reputation and therefore warily, though the *bona fides* were reassuring. At that moment, he wore "the face." The reporter needed no introduction.

"I am Mr. Brown," said Gouzenko with the hint of a question in his inflection. The accent was Russian. The reporter wondered why members of the Soviet Intelligence *apparat* have such a fondness for the cover name of Brown. "Won't you sit down, Mr. Gouzenko," said the reporter. There was a smile of recognition at the name he no longer heard or could use—and the official face vanished. He was a pleasant-faced Russian, but the contours were firm and well-defined. A stocky man, he gave the impression of being short. More than anything he wanted to talk freely of his past, his present, his future. He wanted to discuss recent events in the Soviet Union, the position of the West, the failure of Americans and Canadians to understand the real nature of communism and the threat it posed. He wanted to tell of the novel he was finishing, *The Fall of the Titan*. (It was accepted by the Book-of-the-Month Club, and achieved both financial and critical success.)

It took no great intuition to realize that Igor Gouzenko was more than an entry in a secret police dossier, more than the flotsam of espionage. He was a man of character, stubborn as Russians can be, well read in politics and in literature, perceptive, and very talented. Fate, in catalysis with his needs and drives, had thrust on him his role as a protagonist in the never-ending drama of espionage and counterespionage. He took pride in the fact that his courage had projected him into the affairs of the world as the first to budge the rock of atomic perfidy and offer a brief glimpse at the underground world of spies and traitors. But he derived no pleasure from the notoriety and would have preferred to "surface" completely as Igor Gouzenko, the writer, the almost obsessive family man—as so many Russians are—the free citizen in a free society.

This, then, was the Gouzenko of 1953. What was the code clerk of 1945, recalled to Moscow for a more important assignment that might in turn lead to rank and power? He could be reconstructed only by extrapolation from known but two-dimensional facts. In effect, he had become the prisoner of his great exploit. And that exploit in turn was conditioned by the history of Soviet espionage, by the transcendent fascination of the atomic age, by his precise place in the unrolling story of Stalin's massive theft of the free world's nuclear secrets. In the unreality of the NKVD operation, he seemed slightly dwarfed, yet a pawn that acquired volition and direction. This diminution of the human species is common in the Soviet Union, where nothing is quite life-size except the State and its instruments of control. Yet the story of Gouzenko's exploit is an integral part of Gouzenko *qua* person and of his background.

Gouzenko was a student at the Moscow Institute of Architecture—one of the top five in his class and destined for a career of designing the wedding-cake palaces so dear to Stalin's heart—when he was tapped for training as a cipher clerk. He came from peasant stock, and his family shared the poverty that is normal to the vast majority in the Soviet Union. He had no *blat,* the Soviet equivalent of "pull." He was chosen to receive instruction in the Intelligence Administration of the Kuibishev Military Engineering Academy in Moscow—a coveted appointment. Having been a *Komsomol,* the Soviet equivalent of the Young Communist League, he was aware that from that moment on what little privacy he had been able to enjoy was ended. He was now part of the State, and a sensitive part at that.

It was no surprise to him that he was told to expect periodic investigations, special periods of unannounced twenty-four-hour surveillance, and continual scrutiny of his mind. Contact with foreigners was forbidden, and any new acquaintances were to be immediately reported. Association with girls was also forbidden without express permission from a superior. And it was made clear to him that the more trust was placed in him, the more suspect he would become.

"Each one who knows state secrets becomes an important and at the same time a dangerous person," Gouzenko was lectured. "The more an individual is trusted, the more closely he must be guarded. In your case, as a cipher clerk who will get to know the names and cover names of agents, and their secrets, there can be no relaxation ever—either on your part or on the part of the Special Section. Remember that at all times and watch your step."

When Gouzenko had completed his studies, he was assigned to Red Army Intelligence Headquarters. There he picked up the specialized vocabulary of Intelligence agents and became familiar with its table of organization. From a member of the *Otdel Spetsialnikh Zadanii*—the Special Tasks Branch—he learned the difference between "dry affairs" (regular espionage work) and "wet affairs" (the murder of an agent on whom suspicion had fallen). Telegrams from resident directors in other countries, calling for the "disposal" of once trusted men, passed through the cipher room and Gouzenko's hands. Intelligence Headquarters, housed in a large building at 19 Znamensky, processed the microfilm received from thousands of agents in the United States. Other thousands, according to Gouzenko, plied their trade in other countries of the world deemed important to the Kremlin. Agents spied on both the Yenan Communists and the Kuomintang in China. Microfilm was used whenever possible. Soviet scientists worked full time at adapting microphotographic techniques and equipment, stolen from Germany and the United States, to espionage purposes. A two-story white building, in the great courtyard of Intelligence Headquarters, was the processing laboratory, and it worked twenty-four hours a day.

After a time, Gouzenko carried a map of the world in his head as he followed the movements of agents through their reports to the Center. The same cover names would crop up repeatedly as he moved vicariously in faraway cities. The agent's reports on contacts, his fears of discovery, his request for instructions, his calls for money, the kind of codes he used—all of this built up a picture for the young lieutenant decoding the messages and encoding the Center's answers.

"It amazed me to note the psychological range employed in dealing with agents throughout the world," Gouzenko would write later. "Exhaustive files, compiled over a period of years at considerable cost, held histories on each agent, his motives, his habits, his weaknesses, his reason for being an agent. This knowledge was used to the best advantage when psychology was needed." These *zapiski*, making up the Great Index, were the source of leads on new agents when unexplored areas opened up to the Center.

People were bought, used and thrown over; many of them important personages in their own countries, being used wittingly and unwittingly by agents. Love, hate, resentment, anger, weakness of character and strength of character, courage and cowardice, were the tools used to get results by this monstrous, merciless and thoroughly efficient Soviet Intelligence machine.

If you . . . happen to be a person of some importance, or happen to be in a position whereby your knowledge might be useful, you are undoubtedly "intimately known" in the files in Moscow. This was clearly established by the varied approaches made on Soviet instruction when atomic bomb information was demanded. Astonishingly enough, it was shown there that when it comes to something really big, the money appeal isn't used. The appeal to "higher feelings" such as "the good of the world" proved most effective for Soviet Intelligence.

But the wide-eyed young Lieutenant Gouzenko quickly learned that these "higher feelings" were a carrot only for the dupes and outsiders. At the Center, the motivational force was fear. Good work was taken for granted. A small slip could lead to demotion and assignmer : to a penal battalion and front-line duty. A serious error usually meant death at the hands of a firing squad. At Intelligence Headquarters, there was a pervasive tension, a nervous strain which was never relaxed. Every man guarded his thoughts and watched his neighbor warily. For it was essential to carry out one's own assignments—and also to report the shortcomings of associates. Failure to do so made cipher clerks, lowly employees, and high-ranking officers subject to charges of laxness or ideological weakness. To turn in a friend was proof of loyalty, devotion to duty, and right thinking.

As the war progressed, the scope and importance of Soviet espionage increased. Stalin himself supervised its activities. Two tables of organization were set up—one for Tactical Intelligence, the other for Strategic Intelligence—each with thousands of technicians, scientists, and experts. Within Strategic Intelligence, a new branch of Special Communications was organized, to which Gouzenko and others with a knowledge of languages were assigned. It was organized like a foreign office, with "desks" for each country. Political and economic information was handled by an Information Branch. Scientific and technical information went to the General Branch. There it was first screened by a "security reader" who would make certain that the identity of the agent and his area of operations was deleted. According to Gouzenko:

Everything was broken up into small sections so that only a very few of the top people had the complete picture. What the spies sent in was turned over to these security experts for analysis. Every reference to the source of the material was washed out first. When a scientist or an engineer got a blueprint to study, it was only a blueprint to him. It was his job to study it and to determine how it fitted in with whatever else he knew or had on the subject— and to see whether or not it was useful.

Men from every scientific and technical institute in the Soviet Union were recruited for work with Intelligence Headquarters. Every new batch of data passed through their hands. They not only evaluated but drafted queries for the agents, demanding further types of information needed to complete the data. As Soviet interest in atomic energy began to build, the Soviet system of mass production espionage came in good stead. Detailed instructions would go to twenty or more agents, asking for the same information. When the first flow from the laboratories at Berkeley, the University of Chicago, and Columbia began, agents in Canada and the United Kingdom were ordered to duplicate it—and also to add pertinent new data.

In June of 1943, Igor Gouzenko was given his overseas assignment. His work had been highly rated by his superiors, and the "Five"—a screening group made up of representatives of the Communist Party's Central Committee, the NKVD, Red Army Intelligence, the Ministry of External Affairs, and the Ministry of Foreign

Trade—had attested to his efficiency and political reliability. He
had been briefed on the ways of the iniquitous West and instructed
to memorize a typewritten pamphlet marked "secret." The pamphlet was a guide to personal behavior. It warned:

Be careful . . . especially of women . . . There is something about
the environment of a train and the leisurely hours spent thereon
that provides opportunity for enemy agents to work their way into
your confidence. The best rule in this regard is simply: Do not
yield to cordial conversation with any foreigner . . .
Always wear a hat on the street . . .
Never overtip unless with a specific purpose in mind. That
might make you conspicuous . . .
Never permit yourself to be more drunk than your guest or your
host . . .
Keep your wives under reasonable control in shopping. Women
lean toward excesses in purchasing . . .
Americans are particularly adept at entangling you under the
mask of friendship. They like to employ a free and easy air in meeting you so that your natural caution is relaxed. They pretend to be
telling you secrets as a friend and, especially in drinking, you
might be inclined to fall in with the mood of the party . . . The
supposedly friendly American . . . is the most dangerous type of
foreigner.

The next step was to memorize his "legend." This was a false,
detailed background on which the biographical data supplied to
Canadian authorities was based. Gouzenko, for example, "learned"
that he had been born in Gorky and that he had studied at the
Economics Technical Institute there. No mention was made of his
Red Army rank. His official position was that of translator and
secretary employed by the Military Attaché. Even at the Embassy
in Ottawa, only those with whom he worked directly were to know
that he was the code clerk. The others, who would see him enter
and leave the guarded wing on the second floor, might guess but
never know. If "foreigners" questioned him about his duties, he

was to say that he read newspapers for important stories and translated them for his superiors.

Gouzenko's assignment to Ottawa was in the nature of a plum. For this once neglected post was being built up. Knowledge of Canadian scientific and military activity had become important to the Center. The exchange of information between the United States and Canada resulting from the wartime alliance presented a new opportunity. The St. Lawrence was an important staging area for convoys, and the Center wanted detailed information on the number of ships, the size and nature of their cargoes, the facts and figures on the effectiveness of Nazi submarine warfare. Of significance to this account, there was also the matter of Canadian participation in nuclear and weapons research. Therefore, the Center drew up a new table of organization for its espionage activities in Canada, with Colonel Nicolai Zabotin at its head and some of its best men under him.

At the Embassy, Gouzenko was placed directly under one Ouspensky, who later moved onward and upward to Washington. Ouspensky showed him the elaborate precautionary method of entering the secret wing. A bell was hidden under the bannister on the first floor. This alerted the guards and gave them time to take their positions. Having climbed to the second floor, those seeking entry found a steel-covered door, hidden by a velvet curtain. There was a slit in the door to permit a guard to determine who was seeking entry. A second door, bigger and more heavily reinforced by steel, was then opened. It led to a carpeted corridor and a series of other steel doors. The windows in the secret wing were painted white so that no one could see in. They were protected by steel bars and steel shutters. A radio blared endlessly so as to make eavesdropping by those within the secret wing impossible. Two incinerators occupied separate rooms. The first, an ordinary model, was used by those in the wing to burn every scrap of paper not deemed necessary. The second incinerator—a large and powerful one, specially designed for the Embassy—was used for the almost ritual burning of codes. This ceremony was carefully witnessed by the top echelon of the apparatus and supervised by the NKVD chief. Its primary purpose, however, was to provide for speedy incineration of all incriminating documents in case of emergency.* ("It's big enough and powerful enough to consume a human body," an NKVD official told Gouzenko.)

The Zabotin network included Fred Rose, a member of the Canadian Parliament; a rich Canadian professor, Raymond Boyer, who stole the formula of RDX, a secret and powerful high-explosive; strategically placed Army and civilian personnel; an atomic scientist, Dr. Allan Nunn May; two members of the key National Research Council; two employees of the Munitions and Supply Department, and others fortunate enough not to be implicated by the documents taken out of the Embassy by Gouzenko. In addition, there were several important members of the network whose cover names shielded them. Their activities and peregrinations would occupy the attention of the Royal Canadian Mounted Police's investigations. But the plaguing knowledge would remain that Zabotin, by his own admission to Gouzenko, was one of ten spymasters in the Center's "pioneer" invasion of Canada. The other nine remained untouched. If there were any outcroppings, only the RCMP was aware of them and could never discover enough to permit the government to mount a prosecution. Also to plague Canadian and United States authorities: the names of Americans found in the documents, but with insufficient information for legal action.

This was all in the future of an Igor Gouzenko still gawking at the easy freedom enjoyed by his "capitalist" hosts, the abundance of food, the outgoing friendship extended by the "enemy"—and the differences between what he was seeing or experiencing and

---

* It should be noted that prior to the arrival of Colonel Zabotin and his staff the secret wing and the other espionage arrangements in Ottawa had been inspected by an official using the cover name "Molier." He was, in fact, Pavel Mikhailov, Soviet vice consul in New York City and the confederate of Arthur Alexandrovitch Adams.

what he had been told about the "exploitation of workers" in Canada, the comparisons between life in Moscow and in Ottawa. These were reactions shared universally by those who are exposed to the West. The NKVD is, of course, cognizant of the erosion this works on the Communist will. As well as it can, it protects against the refusal of Soviet personnel abroad to return home by holding hostages—parents, children, brothers and sisters, a wife. In Gouzenko's case, however, there was a counterpull: his young son, born in Canada. Neither ideological or idealistic principles were uppermost in the minds of the Gouzenkos when, in September 1944, he was told that he had been summoned to Moscow. How would they feed the child properly in the Soviet Union? Where would they get the fresh milk and vegetables, the other foods, which in Ottawa were as close as the nearest shop? Lend-Lease shipments of food went first to the important bureaucrats and then to the troops. The rest of the population was on low subsistence rations or worse.

Gouzenko asked Zabotin to query the Center. Could he remain at some other job? In a few days, the Center replied that for the time being Gouzenko might remain, continuing his duties as a code clerk. This was a sign that he had not been recalled for punishment or because there was doubt as to his devotion to the Kremlin. Had there been the slightest suspicion of him, he would never have been allowed to remain in so sensitive a spot. But he knew, before his wife Svetlana said it, that this was only a reprieve. At that point, after searching his conscience, he decided that his duty lay with his young son rather than with an aging mother then close to death. His decision came at a moment when the work of the secret section at the Embassy was almost on a three-shift basis. Two agents in the National Research Council were systematically delivering everything in the files to Colonel Zabotin. Every night, there would be another package for microfilming, to be returned to its proper place in the morning. So great was the volume that a second photographic studio was pressed into service.

All members of the Embassy staff were furnished with still and motion-picture cameras to photograph anything of interest or importance. Zabotin himself, when asked to go fishing on the Chalk River with a member of the Canadian Army General Staff, scored a coup. He returned to the Embassy in great excitement.

"This does not mean anything to you," said Zabotin, "but there is a very important plant on the Chalk River. Moscow has been asking me for a description." Gouzenko did not know that this was Canada's atomic installation. "I asked my Canadian friend if I might take some pictures for my album. He said yes and even rowed the boat in close so I could get a good picture with good light. Moscow will be very happy."

But for Gouzenko, the work of the Zabotin network began to assume a completely different aspect. He had come to develop an attachment to Canada and the Canadians. His decision to defect had heightened his sense of identity with the people to whom he now gave his loyalty. In June 1945, when his replacement arrived, Gouzenko knew that he would have to take the terrifying step. To ensure a welcome and to repay the Canadians for the asylum he expected, Gouzenko began selecting documents to take out with him. The papers he thought important he dog-eared slightly, leaving them in the files.

As he said to this writer, "You get convictions only with documents—never just with talk." He selected those documents which would prove conclusively that wholesale espionage was the Soviet order of the day. And he chose those papers which would condemn three men he considered most reprehensible: Dr. Allan Nunn May, Canadian MP Fred Rose, and Communist organizer Sam Carr. (When the Canadian authorities studied the documents, many were called and more than a few were chosen—for a prison cell.)

The story of Gouzenko's last, heart-pounding visit to the secret wing, the rapid stuffing of documents under his shirt, the shaken walk down the stairs past the NKVD guards, and the fruitless attempts to deliver his precious cargo to Ottawa newspapers have been frequently repeated. Simply walking out of the Embassy, weighed down as he was by the incriminating documents, took incredible courage. Had he been discovered, he would have been shot on the spot—his body dumped into the big incinerator—and his family kidnaped and hurried off to the Soviet Union on a freighter.

He had taken only one precaution. Before making his raid on the network's files, he had pulled out two telegrams—one on the atomic bomb and the other concerning Fred Rose's activities— leaving copies. "If anything goes wrong, if they catch me," he told his wife, "you have these telegrams. Take them to the authorities, and they will give you protection." But this small bit of life insurance for his family made the exploit no less daring. He was one man against the NKVD. In his book, *The Iron Curtain,* Gouzenko summed up for himself:

I was born a very ordinary little man in Russia. I had never excelled in athletics. My triumphs seemed limited to the realm of studies. Dangerous living never appealed to me, and adventure always associated itself with unromantic danger in my mind. But that night of September 5, 1945, I came as close to becoming a hero as I ever will.

What saved Gouzenko's life was the fear and shock at the Embassy when his act was discovered. Had Colonel Zabotin bided his time, he might have trapped Gouzenko. But he could not know that the code clerk and his wife had spent a day being turned away from newspapers and government offices. Nor could he know that Gouzenko had returned to his apartment in despair. He was closer to the end of the road than he thought. At 7:05 P.M., there was a knock at the door, and Zabotin's chauffeur called out to him. Gouzenko climbed out to a rear balcony and made arrangements with an RCAF sergeant to take care of his wife and children and to call the police. Members of the Embassy staff were still in Gouzenko's apartment, searching—the entrance door forced open

—when the police arrived. From that point on, it was a matter for the highest levels of the Canadian government.

Gouzenko was spirited away to a safe hiding place. Meticulously, the Mounties questioned him, studied translations of the documents, and tracked down those implicated. Arrests were made, there were trials, and the guilty went to prison. The biggest catch, as Gouzenko had hoped, was Dr. Nunn May, the British physicist who was, he thought, safely out of it in London. A steadfast Communist to the bitter end, May confessed his own crimes but refused to implicate any of his confederates. Much of his story was either on the record or filed for reference in Gouzenko's mind. May and two others implicated by the Gouzenko papers were the first atomic spies in history to be apprehended.

Dr. Allan Nunn May had come to the attention of Colonel Zabotin not through any leads furnished by his agents or by the Canadian Communist Party. The order to contact the nuclear physicist came directly from the Director in Moscow. Early in 1943, Zabotin was told that May was a "very valuable source" and urged circumspection in the approach. "He is a *corporant,* and his cover name is Alek," the director informed Zabotin. "I consider it best to establish contact through Frank. Advise me immediately when you have established contact."

Gouzenko recalls that Zabotin was furious when he received the message. He had been working with secondary sources in gathering atomic bomb secrets, but the Center had failed until then to tell him that a member of the Communist Party (a *corporant*) was available through "Frank" (the high-ranking Communist functionary Sam Carr). So Zabotin went about it in his own way. It was quickly determined that Dr. Nunn May was one of a team of British scientists working at the atomic energy laboratory in Montreal—a part of the National Research Council. As such, he had the confidence of the director of Canada's nuclear work, Dr. Cockcroft, and access to most of the results of the work being done there and at Chalk River.

Lieutenant Angelov, one of the men working with Gouzenko in the secret wing at the Embassy, was assigned to make the contact. Angelov (cover name, "Baxter") used no subtlety. He knew that Dr. May had worked for an apparatus in England and needed no more than a shove. In Montreal, Angelov looked up May in the telephone directory and, with no warning, went directly to the house. Dr. May, who is described by Gouzenko as "a scholarly, meekish man," answered the doorbell.

"Dr. Allan Nunn May?" Angelov asked.

"Yes," May answered.

"Best regards from Michael," Angelov said softly, using the identity greeting May had used in London. Nunn May's manner changed, as if he had been struck a blow. Angelov later told Gouzenko that he gave the appearance of "a man who was trapped." He almost dragged Angelov into the living room, shutting the door behind them. Then, almost tearfully, he said:

"I have cut off my old connection with Moscow."

Angelov laughed. "We have an assignment for you," he said. "If you refuse, that will be trouble for you, not for us." There was a long silence. Finally, May asked wearily: "What do you want?"

"Everything you can tell us about the atomic bomb project in the United States and Canada. We want it in a hurry." May agreed to meet "Baxter" the following week. "We can meet here then, but after that there must be some other place," May told Angelov. "The security people keep a very close watch, you know." Angelov nodded curtly. From his briefcase he took out two bottles of whiskey and two hundred dollars in cash which he offered with a sardonic smile.

A week later, the report—ten single-spaced pages—was in Gouzenko's hands for encoding. He read it through and told Colonel Zabotin that it would be a bad idea to transmit it through telegraphic channels. Though the Center wanted speed, the process of encoding and decoding could lead to serious errors. The material was too technical. Zabotin agreed to send it by diplomatic pouch. But he ordered Gouzenko to put in code a second report from May. This, Gouzenko told the RCMPs, was a full description of the Canadian project and the Manhattan Engineer District. It described the work being done at Los Alamos, at Oak Ridge, at the Hanford plutonium plant, and at the Metallurgical Laboratory in Chicago. A list of men working on the project was appended. It included General Groves, Dr. Oppenheimer, and others who were "in immediate contact." The Center had some of this information already—but May, Zabotin, and Gouzenko had no way of knowing this. The Center, however, was double-checking on the data it had received from the Zubilin-Adams *apparat*—and testing Dr. May.

Allan Nunn May continued to supply information throughout the spring and early summer of 1945. Nunn May was not "just another scientist," as some have said. In fact, he may have contributed more to the Soviet effort than Klaus Fuchs—who entered the picture a little later—or Bruno Pontecorvo. General Groves's evaluation is contradictory. On the one hand, he told Senator Bourke B. Hickenlooper in 1946 that "it is very doubtful if May (had) anything but a general knowledge of the construction of the atomic bomb." But almost in the same breath, Groves said, "May had spent more time and acquired more knowledge at the Argonne (Laboratory) than any other British physicist." And the Argonne Laboratory was perhaps the most important MED installation, since it provided the experimental base for most of what was done at Los Alamos and Hanford. In 1954, Groves would say of some of the material May handed over to Lieutenant Angelov that it was "all-important." Certainly the Center gave Dr. May high marks. Though notoriously stingy with money, it presented him with another five hundred dollars.

The significance of May's espionage work is suggested by the role he played in the Canadian and United States research.* He was the senior member of the British team which was headquartered in Montreal, and he represented his colleagues on several inter-Allied committees. In January of 1944, he made his first visit to the Metallurgical Laboratory (Argonne) in Chicago. He returned to the Argonne in April of 1944 for a two-week stint at a time of critical experiments in the use of graphite as a retarding agent in the atomic pile. Again, in August of that year, he developed plans for the Montreal pile with Argonne scientists. A fourth trip involved intensive work "in a highly secret and important new field," today still wrapped in a top-secret classification. By 1945, a somewhat worried Groves vetoed a suggestion that May return to the United States because "I did not like him to have such a wide knowledge of later developments."

There were, of course, others in the Zabotin apparatus attempting to penetrate the atomic project in Canada. This was communicated to the Director in a series of messages.

Item:

Badeau [cover name for a member of the National Research Council] informs me that most secret work at present is on nuclear physics (bombardment of radioactive substances to produce energy). This is more hush-hush than radar and is being carried on at the University of Montreal and at McMaster University in Hamilton.

Item:

...Ask Badeau whether he could obtain Uran. No. 235, let him be cautious.

Item:

The Professor [Dr. Raymond Boyer] reported that the director of the National Chemical Research Committee, Stacey, told him about the new plant under construction: Pilot Plant... This plant

---

* Said the Royal Commission report: "May would have access to practically every document in the [Montreal] lab."

will produce "Uranium." The engineering personnel is being obtained from McGill University, and it is already moving into the district of the new plant. As a result of experiments carried out with Uranium, it has been found that Uranium may be used for filling bombs, which is already in fact being done.

The Americans have developed wide research work, having invested in this business 660 million dollars.

Item:

Badeau asks permission to change to work on uranium. There is a possibility either by being invited or by applying himself, but he warned that they are very careful in the selection of workers and that they are under strict observation.

Item:

Bacon [Professor Israel Halperin] is himself curious about the Chalk River Plant and the manufacture of uranium. He claims that there is a great deal of talk and speculation on the subject . . .

Item:

It has become very difficult to work with [Bacon], especially after my request for Ur 235 . . . Bacon explained to me the theory of nuclear energy, *which is probably known to you.* He refuses to put down in writing anything . . .

And this message from the Director in Moscow:

. . . Try to get from Alek [Dr. May] before departure detailed information on the progress of the work on uranium. Discuss with him: does he think it expedient for our undertaking to stay on the spot; will he be able to do that, or is it more useful for him and necessary to depart for London?

Colonel Zabotin answered the Director:

Facts given by Alek: (1) The test of the atomic bomb was conducted in New Mexico (with "49," "94-238"). The bomb dropped on Japan was made of uranium-235. It is known that the output of uranium-235 amounts to 400 grams daily at the magnetic separation plant at Clinton. The output of "49" is likely two times greater (some graphite units are planned for 250 mega watts, i.e., 250 grams each day). The scientific research work in this field is scheduled to be published, but without technical details. The Americans have already published a book on this subject.*

(2) Alek handed over to us a platinum with 162 micrograms of uranium 233 in the form of oxide in a thin lamina.

Item, Zabotin to the Director:

I beg you to inform me to what extent Alek's materials on the question of uranium satisfied you and our scientists . . . This is necessary for us to know in order that we may be able to set forth a number of tasks on this question to other clients [agents].

What the Director answered will probably never be known. If it was in the files of the Ottawa Embassy, Igor Gouzenko did not take it out with him. But Dr. Allan Nunn May had accomplished enough to merit a "well done" from his espionage superiors. Though the report of the Royal Commission in Canada did not so note, he also presented Stalin with a sample of enriched U-235. This was his most valuable contribution. An analysis by Soviet scientists opened to them that precious secret—the precise ingredients we were using in the bomb, extracted from nature at the cost of an untold number of scientific hours and hundreds of millions of dollars. This one gift was worth all the time, energy, money, and duplicated effort of the Soviet Intelligence service. The U-235 sample and a long scientific memorandum from May were considered so important that an NKVD colonel flew them to Moscow.

Nunn May left Canada two days before Gouzenko defected. But the manner of his going—and of his arrival in London—had been carefully planned by the Center, by Colonel Zabotin, and

---

* When this message was studied for the first time, it was assumed that this was a mistake. The message preceded publication of the Smyth Report on atomic energy by one day. However, the Smyth Report had already been written. At the very moment that Zabotin was reporting to the Center on this subject, President Truman, Secretary of State Byrnes, Secretary of War Stimson, and Fleet Admiral William D. Leahy—submitting to the strong pressure of the scientific community—decided to release the Smyth Report. The Zabotin apparatus in Canada knew before the American people what was going on at the White House.

by Soviet agents in Great Britain. When it became known that Dr. May was scheduled to be transferred to King's College in London, the Director queried Zabotin, asking him to work out all arrangements for a meeting between May and his London "contact." Zabotin radioed back that the meetings with the contact would be on "October 7.17.27"—that is, on any one of those three days—in front of the British Museum. This was standard procedure. If May could not keep the first appointment, or if he realized that he was being followed, he would attempt to complete the rendezvous on the 17th or the 27th. The time set was 11 P.M. "Identification sign: a newspaper under the left arm. Password: 'Best regards to Michael.' "

For reasons of his own, the resident Director in London insisted on modifying the arrangements, and the Center gave Zabotin new directions:

1. Place:

In front of the British Museum in London, on Great Russell Street, at the opposite side of the street, about Museum Street, from the side of Tottenham Court Road, Alek walks from Tottenham Court Road, the contact man from the opposite side, Southampton Row.

2. Time:

As indicated by you, however, it would be more expedient to carry out the meeting at 20 o'clock, if it should be convenient to Alek, as at 23 o'clock it is too dark. As for the time, agree about it with Alek and communicate the decision to me. In case the meeting should not take place in October, the time and day will be repeated in the following months.

3. Identification signs:

Alek will have under his left arm the newspaper "Times," the contact man will have in his left hand the magazine "Picture Post."

4. The Password:

The contact man: "What is the shortest way to the Strand?"

Alek: "Well, come along. I am going that way."

In the beginning of the business conversation Alek says: "Best regards from Michael."

Report on transmitting the conditions to Alek

Allan Nunn May never kept the appointment. Gouzenko's defection put the entire Zabotin apparatus on ice. Immediate instructions were sent to all Soviet personnel, however remotely they might have been connected with Zabotin's depredations, to stop all activity. Zabotin was summoned back to Moscow. Without informing the Canadian government of his departure, as protocol would dictate, he slipped across the border and departed the American continent on the Soviet ship S.S. "Suvarov." There are conflicting reports of his fate. According to some accounts, he died at sea. Press stories from Moscow reported that he suffered a heart attack on arrival. High-ranking Soviet agents who have since defected say that he was shot in the cellars of the NKVD's Lubianka Prison in the usual Communist manner—a bullet through the back of the head, a rubber ball in the mouth to absorb it, thereby preventing ricochet off the stone walls. Three other members of Zabotin's staff simply disappeared from Ottawa. The Soviet ambassador left for the Soviet Union "on a routine visit" but never returned.

Between October 1945 and February 1946, Scotland Yard's Special Branch kept a close surveillance on Dr. May. But having been told to desist, he was clearly grateful and made no attempt to make any contact with the British apparatus. On February 15, thirteen people were arrested in Canada. Simultaneously, the Special Branch picked up Nunn May for questioning. He showed no emotion—neither fear nor bravado. Asked if he knew of any leakage of atomic data in Canada, he professed complete ignorance. When he was confronted with the names of confederates, he blandly denied that they had any meaning to him. He was equally unmoved when it was suggested that he had given secret information to any unauthorized persons. Would he give the authorities any help? "Not," Nunn May answered quietly, "if it be counterespionage." What did he mean by that? "I would not want to give any information that might implicate my friends," he answered.

Five days later, on February 20, May was questioned again. This time the Special Branch let him know that it was armed with more than suspicion. What broke Dr. May was a quiet recital of the arrangements for his meeting with a London contact. His guilty mind convinced him that the Special Branch knew all. "I did not keep that appointment," he said composedly. "When I returned I decided to wash my hands of the whole business." But he showed no sign of anguish or repentance and refused to identify any of the people he had spied for—either before or during his work on the atomic project. His confession was as spare of details, and as self-serving, as he could possibly make it:

About a year ago, whilst in Canada, I was contacted by an individual whose identity I decline to divulge ... He apparently knew I was employed by the Montreal laboratory and he sought information from me concerning atomic research.

I gave and had given very careful consideration to the correctness of making sure that development of atomic energy was not confined to U.S.A. I took the very painful decision that it was necessary to convey general information on atomic energy and make sure it was taken seriously ...

After this preliminary meeting I met the individual on several subsequent occasions whilst in Canada. He made specific requests for information which were just nonsense to me ... But he did request samples of uranium from me and information generally on atomic energy.

May then described the two kinds of uranium he had delivered to Lieutenant Angelov—though not naming him—and stated that he had also written a report on atomic research. "This information," he said, "was mostly of a character which has since been published or is about to be published"—the "explanation" the Center had prescribed. May volunteered the fact that he had given "very little" information on the proximity fuse, noted that he had received two hundred dollars "against my will" and a bottle of whisky—but made no mention of the five hundred dollars he had subsequently accepted. And he insisted that he had not kept the appointment with his London contact because "this clandestine procedure was no longer appropriate in view of the official release of information."

The whole affair was extremely painful to me and I only embarked on it because I felt this was a contribution I could make to the safety of mankind. I certainly did not do it for gain.

Nowhere did he say that the information had gone to the Soviet Union.

Not that it would have mattered. He never said another blinking word, leaving it to his counsel at the trial. The Old Bailey, which had heard so much of Britain's routine evil, did not tremble when the defense told the court that, after all, Allan May's only crime had been to save foreign scientists some of the drudgery and some of the time required to develop their own atomic bombs. The Attorney General, Sir Hartley Shawcross, broke in eagerly to reassure the court. "My Lord, I think I ought to make it abundantly clear that there is no kind of suggestion that the Russians are enemies . . . The offense consists in the communication of information to unauthorized persons—it might be to your lordship, it might be to me or to anyone." On this warm note, the defense concluded: "He had nothing to gain, except what we all have to gain by doing what we believe to be right."

"Ten years of penal servitude," said My Lord.

But even before Dr. May stood in the dock of the Old Bailey, Solomon Lozovski, Deputy Commissar of Foreign Affairs, had reassured the Canadian government that no harm had been intended, that the Soviets had gotten nothing of value—and did not want it in the first place. His words are historic:

Soviet organizations have become aware that in the latter periods of the war certain members of the staff of the Soviet Military Attaché in Canada received, from Canadian nationals with whom they were acquainted, certain information of a secret character which did not, however, present great interest for the Soviet organizations. It has transpired that this information referred to technical data of which the Soviet organizations had no need in view of the advanced technical attainment in the U.S.S.R.: the information could be found in the well-known brochure of the American, H.D. Smyth, *Atomic Energy*.

It would therefore be ridiculous to affirm that delivery of insignificant secret data of this kind could create any threat to the security of Canada . . .

To take any other view, Lozovski warned, would be to succumb to the sensationalism of the corrupt Western press. In short, America's atomic secrets had been thrust upon a reluctant Soviet Union—bored, but unwilling to offend its faithful friends. This must have been cold comfort for Allan Nunn May or the thirteen arrested in Canada. That Lozovski's statement was in every particular a lie did not really matter.

I X

The Case of the Sad-Eyed Spy

HE looked incongruous in his old double-breasted, peak-lapelled, blue pin-stripe suit. The trousers were too long, and the fit was bad, as if he had taken it hastily from the hanger of a cheap ready-to-wear shop and put it on without bothering to wait for alterations. He would have looked far more appropriate in a druggist's smock, standing behind the counter of a lower East Side store—selling pacifiers to frantic mothers, making out prescriptions for cough syrup, and forgetting to charge the poorer neighborhood kids for their ice cream cones.

There was nothing distinctive about his round face and blurred Jewish features. Only his eyes spoke out with the kind of sadness that no single life could have accumulated—a sadness that is there at birth, the legacy of ghettos and constant flight, and the unfulfilled dreams that are older than Christianity. The eyes said, "How can you hurt me unless I let you?" They also said, "You caught me because arrest and conviction were the only honor left to me, the only bringers of rest."

Harry Gold stood in the doorway of a small room in the Old

143

Senate Office Building. He was flanked by two guards who towered
over him, but their presence was unnecessary. To Robert Morris
and William A. Rusher, counsel for the Senate Internal Security
Subcommittee, he said, "When we're through you can put a post-
age stamp on me and mail me back to Lewisburg prison. I wouldn't
want to run away." The penitentiary had become home, and its
laboratory, where he was pioneering in research on blood diseases,
was the refuge. The guards watched stolidly as Morris and Rusher
briefly discussed the manner in which he would be questioned. But
Harry Gold neither wanted nor objected to the hours ahead on the
stand. Once he began to speak, it was clear that he got a certain
enjoyment from it; the years in the underground, followed by the
years in prison, had never given him a chance to talk freely.

Gold's appearance before the Senate Internal Security Subcommittee, noted only by the slapdash immortalization in headlines
of its more sensational aspects, was in a sense the first revelation
of the man. Up to that time, he had been a series of notations
in the files of the Center and of the FBI, an object of curiosity,
and a witness constricted by the laws of evidence to disclose only
what was precisely germane to the trial of Ethel and Julius Rosenberg. The man in the rumpled suit was at best two-dimensional as
he faced an impassive jury and a hostile press. In the more relaxed
atmosphere of a Senate hearing room, Harry Gold could speak
in a soft monotone of the events and motives which led him to
his crucial association with Klaus Fuchs and David Greenglass—
both, like himself, confessed spies, though for far different reasons.

Harry Gold was never a member of the Communist Party and
"never had any desire to be one." He did not consider espionage
an exciting vocation and disliked most of the people he worked
for in the apparatus. What small sums of money he was given by
the Soviets came nowhere near compensating him for the time and
effort he gave in carrying out his assignments. In fact, they did not
even repay what he took out of his own pocket. Why, then, did
he spy? His tangential explanations are but a small part of the

story. Belief in the Soviet Union's noble experiment, a vague commitment to socialism, the bitter taste of anti-Semitism, gratitude to a friend who had helped him and then recruited him—were these enough to overcome the immigrant boy's devotion to science, his compunctions against betrayal, his love of family? Some deeper alienation must have been the compulsive factor, but certainly it is not easily apparent to the armchair analyst.

Certainly it has never been clear to Harry Gold.

When he was asked: "You never had much happiness in your life?" Gold answered emphatically, perhaps too emphatically, "I have been very happy." Then, with considerable irritation, he added: "There has been an incredible mountain, or a whole mountain range, of trash that has appeared—anywhere from saying that I got into this because I was disappointed in love ... through reasons that I felt inferior, and I wanted the adulation of people ... It is sheer balderdash ... I was cocksure. That was my only trouble. I was always sure I was doing the right thing. I did have qualms. I knew this much: I was committing a crime. I was fully aware that I was committing a crime. I knew that. And where we lived in South Philadelphia, it was, as I said, a poor neighborhood, but criminal deeds were looked down upon."

It was almost as if he were talking to himself.

"I couldn't kid myself. I was stealing. And to add to that I was stealing from Dr. Gustav T. Reich, who was research director for the Pennsylvania Sugar Company. And Doc Reich, well, so to speak, he sort of raised me from a pup. I started to work in the lab, cleaning spittoons, and when I finally left ... I think I was a capable chemist. Reich taught me a lot and made a lot available to me. I was violating that man's confidence ... I wasn't happy about it. But it seemed to me that the greater over-all good of the objective merited the means, or justified the means that I was using."

Perhaps the answer was in his life.

He was born in Bern, Switzerland, before the lights had gone out in Europe. The year was 1912, and his parents were in slow transit to the golden streets of the New World. At the age of two, he became part of the hopeful, grinding atmosphere of Jewish immigrant existence—which lives in poverty but does not admit of it. The Golds settled in Philadelphia, away from the protection of numbers shared by those who found their way to New York's Jewish slums, though with a ghetto of its own. The anti-Semitism he faced had nothing to do with not being admitted to the right clubs or fraternities. It was physical and violent—beatings at the hands of other children and the terror of what he later called the "brick-throwing, window-smashing forays" of raiders from the Neck, "a marshy section south of the city dump," whose inhabitants lived "under extremely primitive conditions and, amid the mosquitoes and filth, raised hogs and did a desultory sort of produce farming." This he could learn to take. But his father's experiences, described by Harry Gold in a long biographical sketch he prepared in 1950, cut much deeper:

When Pop first began to work for the Victor Talking Machine Company in 1915, the job was one which at that time had the designation of "lifetime." The company was run on a benevolently philanthropic basis, with a high wage rate, assistance if needed in buying a home, and gifts . . . at Thanksgiving and Christmas. The workmen were of a good, solid substantial type and their main criterion for judging the respect of a fellow employee was his ability at his job.

But, in 1920, things began to change. There was a mass influx of immigrant Italian workers, such as were needed in the changeover from the old craftsman technique to large-scale production. These newcomers were crudely anti-Semitic, and made Pop, one of the few Jewish workers, the object of their humor. They stole his chisels, put glue on his tools and good clothes, and in general made life intolerable for him. There was no point in protesting to the foreman, because that worthy was also full of hatred for the Jews . . .

Beginning about 1926, my father came under an Irish foreman at RCA, a man who was more bitterly intolerant than anyone Pop had yet encountered. He told Pop, "You Jew son-of-a-bitch I'm going to make you quit," and so put him on a specially speeded-up production line where my father was the only one handsanding cabinets. Then Sam Gold would come home at night, with his fingertips raw and bleeding . . . And Mom would bathe the wounded members and would put ointment on them, and Pop would go back to work the next morning. But he never quit, not my Pop. Nor did he ever utter a word of complaint to us boys, in fact he always tried to conceal his fingers from us.

Much has been made of Gold's sentimental attachment to socialism in his high school days and early manhood. Among his heroes was Eugene Victor Debs, Socialist Party candidate for President and a champion of labor rights, but there were many in the country who shared this kind of admiration for a man who put his cause above himself. In Gold's home, there was much talk of *Freiheit und Brüderlichkeit,* much reading of the *Jewish Daily Forward,* much admiration for Norman Thomas. But this was anti-Communist, or at least non-Communist, socialism. What Gold read in the crusading socialist press, moreover, affected him because it seemed much closer to life than "a dreary subject called civics" taught to him at school, which bore no relationship to "the actualities of Thirty-ninth-Ward politics as practiced in South Philadelphia in the days of the Vare regime." But as a thin, frail boy, Harry Gold had only revulsion when an older friend joined the Communist Party. "Bolshevism," Gold would write, "was just a name for a wild and vaguely defined phenomenon going on in an eighteenth-century land thousands of miles away."

Gold was graduated from a Philadelphia public high school in 1928, at the age of sixteen. It was not until two years later that he had saved enough money to go to college. But after two years at the University of Pennsylvania, majoring in chemistry and chemical engineering, he was forced to drop out. It was not until 1940 that he was able to complete his undergraduate education and earn a degree of bachelor of science. The need to help his family during the depression years—and the hours and days he devoted to doing the underground's bidding—slowed him up. Much of what he learned—knowledge which might have made him pre-eminent in the scientific world—he picked up at the various jobs he held. Dr. Reich, his mentor at the Pennsylvania Sugar Company laboratory, was as much responsible for this as any man. But the depression cut like a knife across this association, and in December 1932, "just ten days before Christmas," Gold was laid off.

Then it was that Ferdinand (Fred) Heller, a research chemist in the main lab, suggested that I should take my family to the Birobidjan area of Soviet Russia. He was serious, too. This was to me nonsense of course, because as bad as things were, I still considered this my home . . . But here was also the disgraceful specter and the deep ignominy of charity. And the first thing that followed my firing from work was the necessity for returning our new parlor suite (the first in sixteen years, and which was Mom's joy).

For five weeks, Gold searched for work. Then Fred Heller came bearing glad tidings. A friend of his, Tom Black, was leaving his job with a soap-manufacturing company in Jersey City for a better position. And Heller had arranged that Gold should get Black's old job. Gold's mother packed a worn cardboard suitcase for him, and with six dollars in borrowed money and a jacket lent to him by a friend, Gold boarded a Greyhound bus for Jersey City. He arrived at Black's apartment in the very early morning, at 1 A.M.

Tom was waiting for me in the hall downstairs; I can still see the huge, friendly grin in that freckled face crowned with those untamed reddish curls and the bearlike grip of his hand. We ate and then stayed up until 6 A.M. while Tom briefed me on soap chemistry and, in particular, on the "complicating circumstances" [that Gold was to say his mother was Christian and his father converted].

During those hours of anticipation, Black said to Gold: "You are a socialist. Fred Heller has told me that. And that's why I

brought you here for the job. I am a Communist, and I am going
to make a Communist out of you, too." Gold got the job the next
day, at thirty dollars a week, nineteen of which he sent home to
keep his family off relief. But with the job went the steady pressure
of Tom Black and his friends. Gold was taken to party meetings,
sent to the Workers' School in New York, where he picked up a
few pamphlets but did not enroll, and taken into a social group
in Greenwich Village which salted its Communist persuasiveness
with talk of the arts and of literature. Gold tried hard to find some
interest in the Communist Party, if only out of gratitude to Tom
Black and to Vera Kane, whose get-togethers at her Village apartment enriched his life. She was a "graceful" woman of thirty, warm
and gay, who gave Gold a feeling of belonging. His description of
the party, however, is caustic and true:

I met such assorted characters as Joe McKenzie, the seaman,
a young man with gaps in his teeth (due to his penchant, when
drunk, for slugging it out with Jersey City's outsize uniformed
police); an earnest old Pole who was an ex-anarchist; and a volatile
Greek barber who once, in petulance at a meeting which had
drearily degenerated into a discussion of Marxian dialectics, declared, "The hell with this stuff—give me five good men, and I'll
take Journal Square by storm."
These were at least sincere; but there were others, people who
frankly were in it only for the purpose of gratifying some ulterior
motives: a whole host of despicable bohemians who prattled of
free love; others who were obviously lazy bums, and would never
ever work, under any economic system, depression or no depression; and finally, a certain type . . . to whom no one but this weird
conglomeration of individuals would listen, if even they did . . . In
spite of Tom's unrestrained enthusiasm, the whole dreary crew
seemed to be a very futile threat to even the admittedly unsteady
economy of the United States in early 1933.

It may not be reaching too far to suggest that this sordid view
of the American Communist Party may have contributed to Gold's

acceptance of an espionage assignment. For, given the argument that the Soviet Union was striving to build a new society, that she needed help, contemplation of the misfits and outcasts who seemed her only allies in the United States may have convinced Gold that it was up to him—singlehandedly and in heroic pose—to lend a helping hand. But this was to come later—and much later than that he was to realize what a small cog he was in the apparatus. In September 1933, however, Gold was thinking in terms of the NRA, which had revitalized the Pennsylvania Sugar Company and brought him an offer from Dr. Reich to return to his job in the research laboratory. He accepted readily for two reasons: he would be reunited with his family, and he would escape the pressure to join a Communist movement he abhorred.

But this was not to be the case. Tom Black continued to visit him, still mingling humor and dialectics in his efforts to recruit Harry Gold. Then, in April 1934, he suddenly stopped propagandizing. During one of his visits to the Gold home, Tom Black took his friend aside.

"Harry," he said. "You've been stalling me. You've been trying to get out of joining the Communist Party. And possibly I don't blame you. You know, we are scientific men, and maybe we don't belong in." For Gold, there was an immediate sense of relief. He did not know that Black had been taken into the underground apparatus. Black immediately made this clear.

"But there is something you can do," he said. "There is something that would be very helpful to the Soviet Union and something in which you can take pride. The Pennsylvania Sugar Company has processes, processes on industrial solvents. There are materials of the type which are used in various finishes and lacquers. The people of the Soviet Union need these processes. If you will obtain as many of them as you can in complete detail and give them to me, I will see to it that those processes are turned over to the Soviet Union and that they will be utilized."

"And that," says Harry Gold, "is how I began it."

He was grateful to Tom Black for getting him a job. He had a "genuine sympathy for the people of the Soviet Union." But most of all, Gold had that attitude noted by Colonel Lansdale in his dealings with the MED scientists. "I got so that I could ignore authority if I thought I was right," Gold testified. "I have seen it repeated in other people, particularly those in the scientific fields . . . We get to know our own job, and most of us get to know it fairly well. And so we think that, 'Well, if we are right in this, we are right in all our other decisions.' . . . It seemed to me that I had the perfect right to take this authority into my hands to give information which the Soviet Union had no right to. I simply arrogated this right to myself."

And so, in his own words, the "stealing" began.

At this point, the case of the sad-eyed spy was also the case of the naïve spy. The formulas and blueprints which he took from the Pennsylvania Sugar Company's files were not turned over to a courier for microfilming—the usual procedure. Instead, Gold would copy them himself, working hours of the night at the drudging work, never realizing that there was an easier method. After about a year, as the laboratory branched out into other industrial fields, the mass of material became too great. Black and Gold turned to their Greenwich Village friend, Vera Kane, "in desperation"—and she seemed to be as naïve as they. She suggested that they have copies made by a commercial firm in downtown New York.

"The matter again arose," Gold recalled, "of how we were going to pay for this copying. The blueprints were very large. The blueprints for a chemical plant can be very detailed. And there were reports, and they were thick—fifty or sixty pages apiece—and to pay for that—I was making a little over thirty dollars a week and Black about fifty—we just didn't have the funds." It never occurred to any of them that the Soviets would be willing, in fact delighted, to do the copy work. Black took the problem to his Soviet contact and returned jubilantly with a solution.

"Harry," he said to Gold, "all our troubles are over. Now we can get all the information we want copied. I've got a wonderful setup. Furthermore, we have got some very good news about some of the processes you sent to the Soviet Union. They are very happy about them, and they've got them in operation. And there is a Russian who works for Amtorg who is very anxious to meet you. He is also the person who is going to arrange for the photocopying of any amount of material you want. And he can photocopy it and return it to you very quickly."

The man from Amtorg, first of a series of Russians Gold worked with, went under the cover name of "Paul" or "Paul Smith." Gold knew nothing else about him except that he was the organizer of an industrial espionage apparatus in the United States. The meeting took place near Pennsylvania Station in New York. Gold and Black were instructed to stroll along the west side of Seventh Avenue. "Paul" unobtrusively joined them and ". . . then the man mentioned very peremptorily to Black—he just sort of shoved him off with his hand and said something to the effect that Black could leave now, and Black left." This show of authority from the short, stocky man—blond, oval-faced, and with "a nose that flared somewhat at the bottom"—seemed to impress Gold.

As they walked along the dark, quiet streets, Gold was given his first orientation in espionage methods. He was asked for a detailed account of his life and his background, as well as those of his mother and father. He was told very precisely what kind of information the apparatus wanted. And he was given the routine arrangements for further meetings, providing for all contingencies. From that moment on, Gold was no longer a *novator* but a full-fledged agent. Thinking back at those early days, Gold said:

At this particular phase, the beginning, the question of doing it against the United States had not arisen. It was more a question of strengthening the Soviet Union. You see, this is also part of the pattern. I realized much later that these people operated with me in the very manner that a virtuoso would play the violin. They did a superb job on me . . . They knew what would appeal to me and what would repel me.

For instance, as we went along, I was not a paid agent, but I paid other people for their efforts, and they would continually commend me in very indirect fashion, of course, and would sort of low-rate the people who were accepting money from us. You see, they knew that I would feel good if I were told that I was doing this merely because I had a genuine desire to do it. They knew that money in itself would not appeal to me at all.

The agents assigned to work with Gold were not interested in theoretical formulas or in research that was still in the development stage. "I found," Gold noted, "that they were very, very slavishly addicted to processes as they worked, as they were in actual operation. In fact, they told me, 'If a process is good enough to make a profit in competition in the United States, then that is what we want.' " On several occasions, Gold learned of work being done which promised to lead to methods far superior to those then in existence. But his offer to procure the basic research was always brushed aside. "We would much rather have a process that works at 80 per-cent efficiency, but which makes a profit for the man who runs it, than one which works at 99 per-cent efficiency but which is merely in the theoretical stage," Gold was instructed. "We want things that work."

Harry Gold had run through "Steve"—a hulking dandy who wore spats—and "Fred"—a martinet who did not ask for material but demanded it—when the well began to run dry at the Pennsylvania Sugar Company. The choice of "Fred," who rubbed Gold the wrong way, was deliberate. The apparatus was preparing Gold for the major leagues, and it was necessary to know if he would take discipline. He was also being tested in another way. The apparatus took him off the job of stealing chemical data and assigned him to a make-work project: routine and unimportant spying on followers of Leon Trotsky. What Gold had to do was not significant. What counted, simply, was this: He was told that the spying was preparatory to an attempt on Trotsky's life. Gold accepted this and passed the test. By accepting a part, no matter how minor, in something that would lead to murder, Gold had demonstrated that he was fully committed to any assignment he was ordered to carry out. He was probably aware of this at the time, as he later explained:

Well, here is what happened over a period of a year. I got sick. I think it was part of the over-all pattern . . . We started off in a very innocuous fashion. What, after all, are chemical solvents? But then, step by step, they advanced the tempo. They advanced the level on which we worked, or rather, they degraded the level on which we worked . . . And you got used to it. It got to be a way of life with me.

It was a dreary, monotonous drudgery. If anyone has any idea that there is something glamorous or exciting about this, let them be disabused of it right now . . . You work for years trying to get information. Sometimes you are unsuccessful. You spend long hours waiting on street corners . . . And what became even more important, I was gradually losing my identity and my desire to be an individual. I was becoming someone who could be told what to do and who would do it . . . I didn't want to back out. Even if I wanted, I was set in this way.

But for a man of such deep alienation as Harry Gold, there were compensations in the work. The world of science was impersonal, antiseptic. In the apparatus, for all of the loss of identity, he was somebody. And he was able to develop a warm and deep friendship with one of the Russians who received the data he gathered from other agents or stole himself. The Russian went under the cover name of "Sam" (the name on his passport was Semen Markovich Semenov) and like Gold, he was a Jew. He was built more or less like Gold, though where the American ran to fat, the Russian was solidly built. Gold was struck by his black, dancing eyes and warm smile.

"Semenov was the only one of the Soviets who could have passed for an American," Gold has said, "in the manner in which he spoke, dressed, and acted—and especially in the way he wore his hat. For some reason or other, foreigners never put hats on their heads as Americans do." But "Sam" commended himself to Harry Gold in more important ways. He was erudite in the arts and in science, a mathematician and a mechanical engineer, with a master's degree from M.I.T. "He had read widely in English literature and was thoroughly familiar with the works of Charles Dickens, Fenimore Cooper, Somerset Maugham, Sinclair Lewis, and Thomas Wolfe—and the poets Wordsworth, Browning, Sandburg, Frost, and Edgar Lee Masters." In moments of fatigue or exhilaration, he would recite long passages from his favorite writers.

Basically, Semenov was an ebullient man, as so many Russians are, given to the boisterous joke and the personal anecdote. Again like many Russians, he had moody periods in which he deplored the kind of life he was leading—standing on street corners waiting for his "contacts" and dodging the FBI. During these times, he would talk nostalgically of his boyhood in Russia and his love of skiing, of his homesickness. He also worried about Gold and urged him not to overwork. Once, after Gold had to report an unsuccessful mission, Semenov exploded:

"Look at you," he said violently. "You not only look like a ghost, but you are one. You're positively dead on your feet and exhausted. What must your mother think? You goddam fool, I don't want to hear another word about coming to New York tomorrow"—Gold was still commuting from Philadelphia to make his contacts—"or for several weeks. Go home and spend some time with your family. This is an order. I'll bet you that son-of-a-bitch Brothman hasn't even started his report. The hell with this Buna-S and everything—even if it means Moscow will fall tomorrow."

Then, according to Gold, "Sam" calmed down. "Come," he said, "we'll go to the Ferris Wheel Bar and have a few double Canadian Clubs and some food, and then I'll put you in a cab personally and see that you get on the train to Philadelphia. I'll buy you a parlor-car seat and a couple of Corona-Coronas." Semenov was also concerned because espionage work prevented Gold from marrying and raising a family: "Don't think that our people fail to recognize the sacrifice you are making. You can't go on in this lousy business indefinitely. You have to get out and forget it completely. And then you can go ahead and run around with girls every night and pick out a nice one and get married and have children."

Perhaps this was part of the virtuoso performance that Gold would later mention, but he still believes it was sincere—and others who knew Semenov in the underground attest to this. Perhaps he really believed it when he told Gold, "The obtaining of information in this underhanded way will not always be necessary. You'll see. After the war is won, there will come a time of great cooperation between all nations. You will come freely to Moscow and will meet all of your friends, and we'll have a wonderful party, and I'll show you around the city. Oh, we'll have a great time." Gold was not the best judge of men, and he responded openly to those who showed signs of friendship or affection, and this eventually led to his downfall. But certainly the relationship with Semenov compensated for much that was barren in his life.

Before Harry Gold came to his strange and fatal interview with Klaus Fuchs, he had three major experiences in the underground. The first was with one Ben Smilg, who was described as "an important government official" to Gold. Smilg was connected with the air-development center at Wright Field near Dayton. Over the years, he had been carefully prepared for espionage work by the apparatus, which even helped pay his tuition at the Massachusetts Institute of Technology. But for two years, he refused to give Gold any information. When persuasion failed, Gold was instructed by the apparatus to attempt blackmail. The Center in Moscow forwarded to Gold photocopies of the receipts Smilg had signed during his college years—receipts for sums of three hundred and four hundred dollars which the apparatus had given him for his M.I.T. education. But this did not budge Smilg, and Gold was told to leave him alone.

The second experience was with Alfred Dean Slack. Like Gold, he had never joined the Communist Party and felt considerable antipathy to communism. The depression years, his struggle to put himself through college, and an unhappy first marriage, however, left him bitter and lost. His brother-in-law, a fellow worker at the Eastman Kodak Laboratories, began indoctrinating him on the evils of capitalism and the brave new world of the Soviets. When Gold was assigned to courier work with Slack, he was being paid as much as two hundred dollars for each report—a very big sum for the apparatus. Oddly enough, Semenov, who despised paid agents, had considerable respect for Slack and defended him. Slack's reports required a considerable amount of work to prepare, he said. Toward the end of his association with Gold, Slack began to show extreme reluctance. Contact was lost when Slack was transferred from a chemical plant in Kingsport, Tennessee, to Oak Ridge. But before then, he had given Gold the formula for the secret explosive RDX (which Professor Raymond Boyer had already passed to Colonel Zabotin's spy ring in Canada), for nylon, and for the manufacture of Kodachrome film and developers.*

* It is interesting that Gold considered the theft of this Kodachrome process, used for detecting camouflage, the most important to the Soviets:

"The material could not be duplicated anywhere else but in the files of Eastman Kodak ... But the plant ... that manufactured the emulsion for color photography was run in a different way from [that] in which other chemical plants are ordinarily run ... The man conducting the process merely carried it out in mechanical fashion and never knew what he was actually doing.

"The people who carried out the research on the various sensitizers and developers used in the production of these various types of color film, particularly the groups of film that are used in aerial photography for detecting camouflage, these people worked in separate departments ... from the men who actually carried out the work. Usually people take out patents ... But in this case, on certain critical materials, vital to these processes, I don't believe that Eastman took out patents.

"They tried to keep them as industrial secrets. This material was not

The third experience was with Abe Brothman, an expert chemist but a braggart, liar, and highly unreliable agent. In the meticulous notes which Gold prepared for the FBI, he wrote this of Brothman's contribution:

(1) Data on design of mixing equipment—essentially all Brothman's design. Obtained while Brothman worked for the Hendrick Co.

(2) Data on production of Buna-S, synthetic rubber. The information was probably given to the Hendrick Co. by either the United States Rubber Co. or Standard Oil of New Jersey.

(3) Data on manufacture of magnesium powder for flares and Aerosol spray and containers for insects. Both of these were developed while Abe was a partner at Chemurgy Design Corp.; the Aerosol spray composition, however, was a Department of Agriculture idea. Neither of these projects was ever turned over to Sam as he did not want them, because of his contempt for any of Brothman's own work.

Brothman, however, was not new to espionage. In 1940, he had met with Elizabeth Bentley and her superior, Jacob Golos—"John" to Brothman—in a Chinese restaurant on New York's West Thirty-third Street. During Brothman's trial, Betty Bentley was to testify in her almost prim manner: "Mr. Golos said in Mr. Brothman's presence that I was to be the representative of the Communist Party from whom he was to take directives." As a party member, he was expected to pay his dues to her, and to receive in turn a

---

available anywhere else in the world, and there was no way that the Soviet Union could duplicate this material except in one of two fashions: Either they had to steal it from Eastman Kodak or start an organization fully as large, if not larger, than Eastman's with any number of superbly trained organic chemists . . .

"This is something where there was no theory. It was just a matter of know-how—a matter of very, very specialized know-how on minutiae, very, very little things, but things which might take two or three years to find out. It might take a man two or three years to develop a particular sensitizer. Some of these photographic emulsions had six or seven layers . . ."

disquisition on the shifting party line. He was also to give her blueprints and technical data which she was told to take down in shorthand. Some of his data was industrial, some military. But Betty Bentley and Abe Brothman did not get along well. For one thing, he repeatedly violated one of the prime rules of espionage: he was not punctual. Sometimes he would be an hour late to a meeting with her—or he might not show up at all. He did not perform his "tasks" or was late with them. He also asked too many questions. Brothman, in turn, complained about Miss Bentley. She did not show the proper gratitude, he said. And she was unable to take down his formulas correctly. He demanded another contact.

Because he was a chemist, Gold was assigned to take over. At 10 P.M. on a Monday in September of 1941, he waited on a New York side street for a car with the license number 2N9088. Brothman, as usual, was fifteen minutes late. Gold slipped into the front seat alongside Brothman and said, "Hello, Abe, I bring regards from Helen." This was the identification signal. From that point on there were meetings at various cafeterias and automats, but Brothman continued to be late or to violate security. He also tended to be touchy.

His instructions were to gather any and all information on the manufacture of high-octane gasoline, on techniques for the manufacture of natural and synthetic rubber, organic chemicals, synthetic alcohol, colloidal graphite, and lubricants. Brothman resented being given orders and boasted that his services were of great value to the Soviet Union. He had given "Helen"—Miss Bentley—complete plans for the turbine airplane engine and for the Jeep, then new and one of the wonders of the war. He made very large promises about giving Gold "complete plans plus all the descriptive material for a military explosive plant" being constructed in Tennessee. This may have had something to do with Oak Ridge, but Brothman never delivered.

Nevertheless, Brothman and Gold got along reasonably well, to the point where the "contact's" persistent questioning forced

Gold, who used the name "Frank Kessler" to invent a story of a wife and two children, who were twins, of his married life, of the children's illnesses, and of his "wife's" infidelities. To keep Brothman happy and to feed his vanity, Gold arranged a meeting with a "very important Soviet official who wants to meet you"—with Semenov playing the part, flattering Brothman, and regaling him with descriptions of Moscow life. And Brothman had his good side, too. He knew that Gold was paying for the trips between New York and Philadelphia. Without making an issue of it, he would pick up dinner tabs or press a ten-dollar bill into Gold's hand from time to time.

But all of this was, in a sense, part of Gold's salad days in the *apparat*. Late in 1943, Semenov told him to drop Brothman and Slack. Gravely, "Sam" said: "Forget them. Forget everything you ever knew about them. You are never to see them or to meet them or have anything to do with them again." (Had Gold followed these instructions, he would never have been caught.) And Semenov went on: "Something has come up, and it is so tremendous that you have got to exert your complete efforts to carry it through successfully. You've got to concentrate on it completely. Before you make a single move in connection with this, you are to think, think twice, think three times. You cannot make any mistakes. It must be carried through."

Then, to Gold's surprise, he was asked: "Do you wish to accept this assignment? It will be extremely dangerous." This was the first time he had ever been given a choice. "Yes," he said proudly, "I'll accept this assignment."

. . . [Semenov] told me there was a man recently come to this country from England. He said he was going to work with a group of American scientists in the New York City area, that this man would have information on the construction of a new type of weapon. I don't think he called it an atom bomb, but he did say it was a new type of weapon and that I would meet with this man and would obtain information from him.

In late January or early February of 1944, Harry Gold received his instructions. He was to walk on an East Side street, near the Henry Street Settlement. He was to carry an extra pair of gloves in his hand and a book with a green binding. The man he was to meet would carry a tennis ball in his left hand. On a deserted street, alongside an excavation, Gold saw a slim, boyish-looking man, wearing horn-rimmed glasses. In his left hand, as he sauntered toward Gold, the man held a tennis ball. He was Klaus Fuchs.

X

Fuchs: The Compulsive Traitor

IT is an attribute of the psychologically successful spy to be able to turn his moral judgments against himself into moral judgments against society. In the case of Klaus Fuchs, this was an absolute necessity, for his entire political life, starting with his student days in Germany, was morally repugnant. A colleague on the British atomic project once described Fuchs as "a colorless, disembodied, methodical brain"—but this was a superficial diagnosis. Once having divorced himself from the moral imperatives which motivate most men, Fuchs divorced himself as well from the social preoccupations of men. He was methodical, but in a compulsive sense. In fact, compulsion was the most eminent factor in his life. His dedication to science was compulsive, for he would work all day, then withdraw to his room and work late into the night. He drank only on occasion and socially, but at such times, he felt compelled to down great quantities of liquor.

At first glance, the boyish, absent-minded look was deceptive. But behind the thick, horn-rimmed glasses, his eyes had a hard, unwavering fixity which should have been a clue to more than determination. From a very early age, he had decided that the tolerant humanism of his father—a minister of varying faiths—was a form of weakness. The eyes said that Klaus Fuchs had made his decision according to his own lights. It was no longer necessary to debate the point. He knew what was right, whatever the world might argue. Women found him appealing, and he made use of them. But he was bound by no laws of society, of brotherhood, or of love. Yet, though he prided himself on the rigor of his logic, spinning a rationale for every act, none of his explanations could survive the acid bath of examination. In short, he was a nihilist who used constructive achievement for destructive ends. It may be that like most nihilists he was a little mad.

In his student days in Germany, Klaus Fuchs was a Communist. But in the feverish activities of the pre-Hitler youth movements, he did not belong to that group of misty-eyed idealists who took up the hammer and sickle in the belief that it was their time's crucifix. From the very start he subscribed to the ruthless Nechaevist doctrine that evil was a weapon of the Revolution and must triumph before communism could succeed. Fuchs held, with the tougher and more sophisticated of his fellow conspirators, that a precondition to the defeat of Nazism was the destruction of all Social Democratic and liberal forces within the country. And so, like the Stalinized leadership, he was not only willing to, but actually did work with Nazi students against democratic and socialist elements. His first betrayals came when he headed a student group, presumably a "united front" of anti-Nazis, whose primary purpose was to suck in Social Democrats and expose them to Nazi vengeance. His later rationalizations for his espionage had a hollow ring, for he included among them the fact that the Nazis had beaten him and thrown him into the river on the day Hitler became *Reichschancellor*.

The Fuchs family remained in Germany, fighting Hitler, but Klaus escaped to France and then went on to England. There is some controversy as to whether he told the British immigration

authorities that he was a Communist. Rebecca West, a careful journalist, insists that he did. His counsel, when he was tried for
violation of the Official Secrets Act, stated that "in England,
Fuchs never pretended to be anything but a Communist." The
British government, Scotland Yard, and MI-5, which had motives
for obscuring the facts, have always argued that the only evidence
to any Communist associations was the allegation of the German
Foreign Office, based on a suspect Gestapo report. This report
was kicked back and forth, admittedly, by the British bureaucracy,
but it was never called to the attention of General Groves or the
Manhattan District security officers. Given the Groves hypothesis
that once a scientist was involved in secret atomic work it was
safer to keep him on than to fire him, the chances are that the
accusations of the Gestapo would not have barred Fuchs from
Los Alamos.

There is no record of any contacts between Fuchs and the open
Communist Party in Great Britain. He was a refugee, poor and
obligated to friends for food, shelter, and the cost of his education. However, those who provided for his physical and economic
needs in his early days as a student of mathematical physics were
far to the left of "liberalism." During his brief stay in Paris, en
route to Great Britain, Fuchs had been fed and clothed by the
French Communist underground, many of whose agents later
joined General Charles de Gaulle's hegira out of France. It is far
more than any extrapolation from known facts to assert that Fuchs
was under careful party observation from the moment that he
began to demonstrate his scientific brilliance.

When "enemy aliens" were transported to Canada, in part to
protect them from the consequences of a possible Nazi invasion,
Fuchs was sent with them. It is a matter of record that his closest
associate at the Sherbrooke internment camp near Quebec was
one Hans Kahle, a long-time Communist trained at the Lenin
School of revolution and subversion in Moscow, commander of a
unit in the International Brigades during the Spanish Civil War,

and an agent of the NKVD. When some of the refugees were recalled to England for special service, Fuchs and Kahle were among them. Kahle, a member of the central committee of the German Communist Party in exile, was attached to Professor J. B. S. Haldane at the Admiralty—a post which rejoiced his NKVD masters in Moscow. Fuchs returned to his research in mathematical physics at Edinburgh University. Kahle and Fuchs met several times in Great Britain after January 1941. It is a matter of record that they were seen together once at a Communist meeting in London.

At the time of this meeting, Fuchs was already working on the atomic bomb. He had been chosen for this by Professor Rudolf Peierls, an outstanding physicist who had read some of Fuchs's papers in scientific journals, who desperately needed someone who could do the elaborate calculations needed in nuclear research, and who had discovered that in wartime Britain a native physicist was hard to find. The security services took cognizance of the Gestapo report but advised that there was little else to go on in determining the reliability of Fuchs. They also noted that if he had espionage in his heart, he would unburden himself to the Soviets rather than to the Nazis. The atomic project, moreover, was under the Ministry of Aircraft Production, whose considered policy was that anyone who could help win the war should be called into service, no matter what his politics.

In May 1941, Klaus Fuchs began work on the atomic project. In October, British scientists had sufficiently advanced in their work on the gaseous diffusion method of separating uranium isotopes that they were given the dignity of a special organization with its secret code name, "Tube Alloys." In typical British fashion, "Tube Alloys" set up no elaborate front. It worked out of inconspicuous headquarters on Old Queen Street, Westminster, with a small staff which processed the reports from British universities engaged in atomic research. Of all those reporting, Fuchs was the most punctual, methodical, and quick to learn. As a result, he rose in the scientific hierarchy—and he was known for his ability to take on any problem, to solve it, and then to explain the results with unusual clarity.

Unfortunately, he was doing this explaining to others besides his colleagues and superiors at "Tube Alloys." Shortly after he began his secret work, Fuchs made contact with "Alexander"—secretary to the Military Attaché at the Soviet Embassy. "Alexander"—in his official duties—was Simon Davidovich Kremer. In his confession, Fuchs seems to indicate that the first step down the espionage road was his. He stated that he made the overture to "another member of the Communist Party," who in turn bore the glad tidings to the underground. But if Fuchs had approached Kahle, the "other member," and volunteered to supply information, the Center would have been more than somewhat leery. The chronology of events and the known facts clearly establish that Fuchs, who had been somewhat perturbed by the Hitler-Stalin Pact and the Soviet invasion of Finland, found all his doubts resolved when the Nazis broke the Kremlin's heart by invading Russian soil.

That this Hitlerian infamy coincided with Fuchs's involvement in atomic research was a fortuitous circumstance. From his confession, it is clear that he expressed consternation to Kahle over Soviet military difficulties, that he discussed his secret work, that this information was submitted to the Center, and that Fuchs was given his marching orders. In his confession, a document that is short on espionage background but redundant in rationalization, Fuchs said:

I have had continuous contact with persons who were completely unknown to me, except that I knew they would hand over whatever information I gave them to the Russian authorities. At this time, I had complete confidence in Russian policy, and I believed that the Western Allies deliberately allowed Russia and Germany to fight each other to the death, I therefore had no hesitation in giving all the information I had, even though occasionally I tried to concentrate mainly on giving information about the results of my own work.

This last clause is, of course, nonsense, for in any kind of complicated research it is often impossible to tell where one man's work ends and the next man's begins. But it had not taken Klaus Fuchs very long to realize that he was an important man on the project, a very important man, and from this point on it was easy enough to convince himself that the mathematical computations he made for Peierls were really his own. It became clear to those who interrogated him after his arrest that Fuchs believed that the secrets of atomic energy were peculiarly his, to bestow as and to whom he wished.

In 1941 and 1942, Fuchs met repeatedly with "Alexander" in London. This meant that to deliver the carbon copies of his own highly detailed reports to "Tube Alloys"—as well as manuscript material on the work of others—Fuchs had to travel several hours by train from Birmingham, where he was working with Professor Peierls. Accustomed to the double and triple betrayals of the German underground, Fuchs remained uncertain after his first meeting with "Alexander" as to his *bona fides*. Perhaps, he thought, it might be a plot. He therefore marched into the Soviet Embassy to find out for himself. The reaction of the Soviet officials with whom he spoke was one of absolute shock. An agent never visits an embassy or speaks openly of his work. Frantic inquiries immediately went to the Center in Moscow—and normally Fuchs would have been quietly told to "go private"—meaning, to cease and desist. But his *zapiska* in the Great Index was sufficiently detailed to indicate that he was the kind of man to violate the rules so blatantly.

"Alexander" left England before the arrest of Fuchs, which explains why the description of him in the confession was good enough to enable MI-5 to make an identification. The next agent assigned to Fuchs was a woman who met him in Banbury, a town some forty miles from Birmingham. Usually they met on a country lane, though once they risked being seen in a pub opposite the Banbury railroad station. Of her, Fuchs had little to say. She was British and would have been apprehended had he given MI-5 any kind of lead. But Fuchs was subject to frequent lapses of memory, even after he was professing an eagerness to co-operate with British authorities. Given Fuchs's fondness of women, there may have been other reasons for his reluctance to involve her. Whoever she was, she served as a courier for less than a year. Then Fuchs informed her that he was being transferred to the United States. At their next meeting, she brought precise instructions for a meeting with "Raymond," who would meet him on New York's lower East Side.

Had the politics of Klaus Fuchs suffered a sea change en route to the United States, the apparatus would still have owed him much. There have been some who minimize the information Fuchs gave to the Soviets. But Dr. Karl Cohen of Columbia University has unequivocally shown that even before Fuchs was exposed to the work being done on this side of the Atlantic, he was in a position to enrich vastly the Soviet store of knowledge:

Fuchs's name appeared on theoretical papers on the gaseous diffusion process to my certain knowledge in 1942, and I believe as early as 1941. Because of visits to this country of Peierls and others in 1942, when the relative merits of the Birmingham and Columbia versions of the diffusion process were discussed at length, and the . . . Anglo-American interchange of technical information, it is clear that before Fuchs' arrival he had good knowledge of the American plans for the gaseous diffusion plant. It is important to bear in mind that because of Fuchs' grasp of the theoretical principles involved, which interrelate the process variables so that the choice of a few determines the remainder within narrow limits, *he would be able to reconstitute our whole program from only scattered pieces of information.* [Emphasis added.]

Work on the control problem [of the gaseous diffusion method] was being carried out by the SAM laboratory under my direction and by a section of the Kellex Corporation . . . The future operating company [at Oak Ridge], the Carbide and Carbon Chemicals Corp., was also interested. Fuchs arrived in New York . . . and a series of meetings were set up, to be held at the Kellex Corporation and at the SAM laboratory wherein the two American groups and the British group [which included Fuchs] could compare results. After several meetings in December, a division of work was adopted, Fuchs' part of which was to calculate numerically for the [Oak Ridge plant] the effects of fluctuations on production rates.

All phases of the control problem depend on the intimate details of plant construction, and in the course of his assigned task, Fuchs obtained from the Kellex Corporation complete knowledge of the process design of the K-25 plant [at Oak Ridge].

At the first meeting between Fuchs and Harry Gold, there was little transfer of information. Fuchs simply discussed the general organization of the Manhattan Project work in New York and made arrangements for future meetings. Gold would later recall six or seven such in various parts of New York City and its environs. Sometimes the meetings would last but a minute—just long enough for Fuchs to hand Gold a bulky envelope. At others, they would walk together for long periods of time while Fuchs gave Gold an oral report. The written reports were on legal-size yellow pages, sometimes up to a hundred of them, in Fuchs's tiny, crabbed handwriting. The Joint Atomic Energy Committee has classified substantial portions of the Fuchs confession, but according to the British security officers who questioned Fuchs, he supplied careful plans for the design of the uranium bomb and almost everything about the gaseous diffusion process for separating U-235. This latter information gave the Soviets a vital shortcut, bypassing other, less effective, processes.

Harry Gold, who had sufficient scientific knowledge to grasp some of the importance of the data he got, said: "They contained everything, from what I could see by looking at it. They not only contained a tremendous amount of theoretical mathematics, but the practical setup. I think that as much as any one man knew about the progress of the atom bomb, except possibly those at the very top of the project, Fuchs knew, and was in a position to give. Possibly he knew even more than the top people, because he was in intimate contact with it, in daily contact with it, you see."

When Gold was assigned to serve as the go-between for Fuchs, the Center cut him off from Semen Semenov. The bomb was too important to entrust the delivery of data to a "legal" agent who might be under suspicion. A new agent, Anatoli A. Yakovlev, known to Gold as "John," took over. He was far more efficient, far more precise, than Semenov—and he timed a rendezvous so carefully that Gold would leave Fuchs, turn a corner, and find "John" waiting for him.

Then, in July of 1944, Fuchs suddenly disappeared. A series of alternate meeting places and times had been devised by Gold, but Fuchs was never there. Finally, in desperation, and at the prompting of Yakovlev, Gold went to Fuchs's apartment at 128 West Seventy-seventh Street in Manhattan. Neither the doorman nor the janitor could tell him anything more than that Fuchs had moved. The apparatus was aware that he might have been transferred suddenly, with no way of leaving word of his whereabouts. There was no real fear that he had defected. But by this time, the Center was pressing its agents everywhere to supply data on the atomic bomb, and Fuchs was a prime source. Violating all the rules, Yakovlev gave Gold the address of Fuchs's sister, Kristel, married and living in Cambridge.*

* How Yakovlev came to know of Fuchs's sister offers an interesting insight into the discipline of the underground. Gold described it in his testimony before the Senate Internal Security Subcommittee:
"Yakovlev obtained for me the name of Fuchs's sister. She had come into the matter once before—Mrs. Heinemann, Mrs. Kristel Heinemann.
"Q: How had she come into the matter?
"A: ... As part of the general pattern of which I spoke. On one occasion, Fuchs spoke to me, after we had met several times, and he told me that his sister was also living in the United States, in Cambridge, with her husband,

On a warm afternoon, Gold presented himself at Kristel's house, introduced himself as a close friend of Fuchs, and said that he had urgent business to transact with her brother. But Kristel knew nothing definite about his whereabouts, just that he was "somewhere in the Southwest." He had, however, said that he would spend a few days with her during the Christmas season. Gold gave Kristel a phone number in New York and departed. But before he did, he made one serious mistake. In an effort to ingratiate himself with Kristel, he talked about his two nonexistent children, Davie and Essie, repeating the story he had manufactured for Abe Brothman. (Years later, when the FBI visited Kristel, she remembered it. This small detail helped confirm a suspicion, for Brothman had casually mentioned the same two children to the FBI when, following Elizabeth Bentley's confession, they had visited him.)

When Fuchs arrived in Cambridge for the Christmas holidays, he was given Gold's message and dutifully phoned New York. Gold was hastily summoned from Philadelphia and sent packing once more to Kristel's house. There he was spirited into Fuchs's bedroom. The mathematical physicist seemed a little less eager to supply information, but he obediently agreed to put what he knew in writing. Several days later, on a Boston street corner, Fuchs presented Gold with a lengthy document. Again according to British sources—the Joint Atomic Energy Committee is still fearful that the Soviets may not know the value of what Fuchs gave them—it was treasure-trove. For now Fuchs could give, in his carefully annotated way, the details of MED work on the plutonium bomb, including the design and method of construction, on im-

---

and that there was a possibility that these two might separate, and he asked for permission, or rather asked me to ask for permission for him—that if his sister came to New York City that they could live together, that is, so that he could be with his sister. He was very fond of her ... He had to obtain permission ... from a Russian, Yakovlev."

In fact, Yakovlev did not have the authority to grant that permission. It came, after due deliberation, from the Center in Moscow.

plosion and the implosion lens, and on the atomic piles for the manufacture of plutonium at Hanford, Washington. For this information, Gold offered Fuchs $1,500 in cash—a gift from Yakovlev and "the Soviet people." It was haughtily refused—a gesture which should not have impressed Gold, since he had already spent well over four thousand dollars of his own money, saved from a fifty-dollars-a-week salary, in expenses directly attributable to his espionage work.

The meeting in Cambridge had one other consequence. The apparatus once more had Fuchs firmly between thumb and forefinger, and Gold insisted on arranging a rendezvous somewhere near Los Alamos. The date was set for 4 P.M. of June 2, 1945— some five months ahead—in Santa Fe at the Castillo Bridge. Fuchs agreed with some reluctance, for his months at Los Alamos, undogged by *apparatchiks,* had convinced him that he was free. Without the need for the very careful lying necessary to the working agent, Fuchs had for the first time since his student days in Germany shown signs of social adjustment. He bought a secondhand Buick which he drove with some abandon, he went to parties, and he suddenly seemed aware that people existed for purposes other than sex or intellectual drudgery.

Late in May, just before Harry Gold departed for Santa Fe, he was given new instructions by Yakovlev. The normally submissive Gold was tired and irritable from days of around-the-clock work at the Pennsylvania Sugar Company laboratory—work made necessary in order to get him the free time to take the long train trip to the Southwest. When he was told that after seeing Fuchs he was to travel to Albuquerque to receive information from another espionage contact, Gold objected strenuously.

"I protested very bitterly about this additional task," he was to recall. "I complained that I was jeopardizing the whole matter of the information I was getting from Fuchs. It represented an additional delay, an additional period or interval in which something could happen, and I just for once got up on my hindlegs and almost flatly refused to go to Albuquerque. But I was told that this was very important, extremely vital, that I had to get this information. There was no nonsense about it." Gold, however, was right. The side trip brought him into contact with David Greenglass, and in time, this would be the link to Ethel and Julius Rosenberg. For this breach of *apparat* security the Rosenbergs would pay with their lives.

Weary from the long train ride, Gold appeared on the Castillo Bridge in Santa Fe punctually at 4 P.M. As a precautionary measure, so that he would not have to ask directions, he had bought a street map. On time as usual, Fuchs met him in his Buick, and the two drove off. Fuchs silently handed Gold a thick sheaf of papers and then launched into his oral report. The work on actual construction of the atomic bomb was going along at a rapid rate, he said, and a bomb would be tested perhaps in a month at a desert site near Alamogordo. Fuchs expressed his surprise at the success of the MED in building the bomb. He had always felt that the war would long be over before all the problems were solved. But, he told Gold, he had not counted on American ingenuity and industrial potential. "I sadly underestimated it," he added. The next rendezvous was set for September 19, at 6 P.M., near a church on a road leading into Santa Fe.

And that was it. Gold took a bus to Albuquerque, where he met Greenglass—then boarded a train for the journey back to New York. On a deserted road near a cemetery in Queens, he handed Yakovlev two folders—one marked "Doctor" and the second marked "Other." The exchange between the two agents was very brief, and Gold returned to Philadelphia, glad that he would not be required to travel cross-country until September.

Then, once more, he was aboard a train, Santa Fe–bound, unaware that this would be his last espionage assignment. Between the two meetings, however, much had happened. The bomb had been tested at Alamogordo with Fuchs as a witness on July 16, 1945. On August 6, the bomb fell on Hiroshima, ushering in the era of the Great Mushroom, and on August 9, Nagasaki was devastated. On August 15 the war in the Pacific ended as suddenly as it had begun. Immediately, General Groves began arranging what he had all along desired—a bill of divorcement between the nuclear research of the United States and its British Empire allies. British scientists were almost abruptly edged out and began making preparations for their return to universities in England and Scotland.

On September 19, Fuchs volunteered to drive into Santa Fe in order to pick up the liquor for a farewell party the scientists and technicians at Los Alamos were planning. The meeting with Gold, scheduled for that evening, was one of the longest he had ever had. His written report was highly detailed and very important. For he not only delivered to the Soviets the dimensions of the bomb, he also included the sizes of the parts, how they were put together, what the bomb was made of and how, and what triggered the explosion. He also reported to Gold that the British and the Americans were coming to "a parting of the ways" and that he would be returning to his post at Birmingham. Neither Gold nor Fuchs knew that just two weeks before, Igor Gouzenko had defected with his incriminating documents, or that the Canadian government was in the process of translating cover names to real names in preparation for the highly secret investigation of a Royal Commission.

Fuchs had other problems to discuss, far more personal in nature, which he felt would make it difficult to continue his espionage work. This is how Gold recounts the conversation:

Fuchs told me that his father [who knew of his underground Communist activities in Germany] was getting a little foolish, and that was just what he was afraid of. He said:

"The British, in an effort to reward me and compensate me, have told me they are going to bring my father to England so that I can be with the old man in his remaining years." He said, "But if they do, he is bound to prattle about my activities in the student

Communist Party." He said, "And then people will begin to wonder about my background, and once they begin to pry, you know what will happen." He said, "So how in the world am I going to keep them from doing this presumed kindness to me without arousing suspicion?"

It was a bit of a quandary.

Nevertheless, Fuchs was still willing to maintain contact with the apparatus. Since there was no way to receive instructions from Yakovlev (and, of course, the Center), Fuchs himself worked out a plan for resuming his association once he returned to England. He would, he said, be at the entrance to one of London's underground stations on the first Saturday of every month. In one hand, he would be carrying five books held together by a string. In the other hand, he would carry two books. Whoever was to contact him would identify himself by holding a copy of Bennett Cerf's *Try and Stop Me*. Neither man knew that orders had already gone out to all resident directors—and to "legal" and "illegal" agents—putting espionage apparatuses in the United States and in Europe on ice until the Gouzenko investigation had been terminated and the Center knew just what men had been implicated.

Fuchs remained at Los Alamos, the last of the British scientists to go, until June 1946. He handled all the housekeeping details, wrote his final reports. In November 1945, he made an official trip to Montreal, where he was offered and accepted the position of chief of the Theoretical Physics Division at the Harwell Research Establishment, Britain's new nuclear-energy center. On June 28, 1946, he boarded a plane for England—the warm praise for his essential work and keen sense of security still echoing in his mind. At Harwell, he plunged into the work of building its massive atomic pile. From the £278 a year he had received as a professor at Birmingham, he was jumped in pay to £1,200—and this was quickly increased to £1,500. For a time, he made no effort to keep the appointments with Soviet agents at the Mornington Crescent

Station, but lived a normal and quiet life. Then, in 1947, after a visit to his Communist brother Gerhardt in Switzerland, Klaus Fuchs reached out for the espionage apron strings once more. Simon Kremer had gone to the Soviet Zone of Germany, but Fuchs was able to give his message to a woman Communist. The meetings with the elaborate recognition signals began once more for him. Though his old rationalization, hatred of Nazism, no longer prompted him, the old compulsion and the old arrogance had not been appeased.

After his arrest, Fuchs told security officers that he had met with his new Soviet contact eight times between 1947 and 1949. At the first encounter, he accepted £100, the first money he had not loftily brushed aside. What he might have told the apparatus is not really known. The British were building a plutonium pile at Windscale and another at Cumberland. Odds and ends of information about his activities in the United States crept into his reports. But the Soviets were now no longer passively listening and reading. They began urging him to divulge specific details of the hydrogen fusion bomb. They suspected that he was holding back and tried to force him to visit Paris, where he could discuss the British project with a scientist as highly placed as himself—presumably Joliot-Curie. But Fuchs refused.

Meanwhile at Harwell, the British had finally and with great diffidence decided to set up some kind of security system—in part impelled by the reluctance of the United States to share further data as a result of the Gouzenko disclosures. Wing Commander Henry Arnold was appointed Special Security Officer and began sifting the spotty files maintained at the time by the British government. He reported to MI-5 the scant details of Fuchs's past, relying mostly on the discredited Gestapo report. But there was no other evidence, and Fuchs remained in the clear. In the United States, however, atomic security had been turned over to the FBI with the passage of the Atomic Energy Act of 1946. Material which the Bureau had been unable to use against MED personnel was joined to Counter-Intelligence files and correlated with new information which the FBI began to unearth.

In the summer of 1949, the FBI made its first major break-through, identifying Fuchs as a Soviet agent. It has been said that the lead came from an address book, taken from Professor Israel Halperin by the Royal Canadian Mounted Police, which listed Fuchs's name. This is not so. It was a far more significant discovery, one of such importance that it is still highly classified.* The very bad news sped to England and to Wing Commander Arnold. He had the facts, but no evidence that would stand up in court. To confront Fuchs would be risky. The British plan, characteristically, was to seduce him into a confession.

As an alternative, security officials suggested that Fuchs be induced to resign. Obviously, they could no longer allow him to continue passing on the data of nuclear experimentation. But this was also difficult of achievement. With his usual conceit, Fuchs made no secret of the fact that he considered himself the most important man at Harwell (he was actually third-most-important) and of his conviction that the research center would shut down if he left for an academic post. Two events made matters easy for MI-5. The first was what may or may not have been a random shot at the windshield of a car in which Fuchs was being driven back to Harwell from a committee meeting at Wembley. A visibly panicked Fuchs slid to the floor of the car and would not proceed until he had protection. To him, this was a warning from his Soviet masters who he felt might be preparing to liquidate him to prevent any confession. Fuchs was wise enough in the ways of the apparatus to know that only by talking could he save his life if the Center had made a decision to end it.

The second event was a letter from his father telling him that

---

* Though the author knows the nature of this break-through, he must limit himself to this explanation: A highly secret intelligence group penetrated the communications system of an Iron Curtain country and discovered the names of Fuchs and other traitors. The group made its findings known to the FBI.

he was accepting a post at the University of Leipzig in East Germany. This, Fuchs knew, would raise eyebrows among the security officers and lead to a more stringent investigation of his past than had so far been conducted. He therefore volunteered the information to Wing Commander Arnold and suggested that it might be wise for him to leave Harwell since the Communists might attempt to put pressure on him by arresting his father. In the course of subsequent discussion, he adroitly mentioned a casual association with the Communists in his student days. When he had finished a full recital of his years in England and America—even mentioning the Communist he had known in the internment camp in Canada— he was asked by William J. Skardon, who had been selected to handle the Fuchs case:

"Were you not in touch with a Soviet official while you were in New York? Did you not pass on information to a Soviet representative about your work?"

"I don't think so," Fuchs answered, smiling at the preposterous notion.

"I am in possession of precise information that you have been guilty of espionage for the Soviet Union," Skardon insisted. Again Fuchs demurred, but in a manner which led Skardon to remark that the answer was hardly a categorical one.

"I don't understand," said Fuchs. "Perhaps you will tell me what evidence you have. I have done no such thing." But he suggested that though he was innocent, he should resign from Harwell if he were under suspicion.

This was on December 21, 1949. On January 10, 1950, Sir John Cockcroft, the director of Harwell, informed Fuchs that his father's presence in East Germany made it necessary for him to submit his resignation. There were other meetings with Skardon during which gentle pressures were put on Fuchs to speak. He began to feel that the authorities recognized his indispensability at Harwell and that, if he confessed, all would be forgiven. By a series of elaborate mental contortions, he convinced himself that having done wrong, he could wipe the slate clean by promising never again to sin. It would be a transaction between his conscience and Skardon.

On January 22, Fuchs told Arnold he would like to see Skardon again. Two days later, Skardon visited Fuchs at his small prefabricated house on the Harwell base. It should be noted that Skardon was still not fully convinced of Fuchs's guilt. At worst, he believed, the scientist had committed some minor indiscretions which had been magnified by the FBI into a serious crime. If he could shake Fuchs loose of the facts, that would end the matter— though MI-5 might take some convincing.

"You wanted to see me?" Skardon asked.

"Yes," said Fuchs, "it's rather up to me now."

But for several hours, he rambled on about his youth in Germany, his heroic battles against the Nazis, and his passion for science. Finally, he announced that, though he had a clear conscience, he was prepared to confess.

"When did it start?" Skardon asked—and got the jolt of his life.

"About the middle of 1942," Fuchs said quietly, "and it continued until about a year ago." And then, in a compulsive stream, he told the story of his treason, speaking rapidly but calmly. When Skardon left the Fuchs house, he had made no arrest. The case had now become one of high policy involving possible diplomatic repercussions. Fuchs, however, was in what bordered on a state of euphoria. He had confessed, and he fully expected that he would be allowed to remain at Harwell—in fact, that a more important post which had just opened up would be offered to him. The following day, Fuchs visited Arnold and urged speed in settling the business with Skardon. A meeting of British and American nuclear scientists was scheduled, Fuchs said, and it was important that he represent Harwell so that suspicions damaging to the British project would not be raised.

Punctilious to the end, the British did not bring Fuchs under guard to the War Office in London. He was invited to be present and eagerly made his appearance. "I ought to tell you," Skardon said, "that you are not obliged to make a statement, and you must not be induced to do so by any promise or threat which has been held out to you."

"I understand," Fuchs answered. "Carry on."

It was at this time that he dictated the famous statement, as revealing a document as any in criminal history, full of vanity and condescension and third-rate armchair analysis. It read, Rebecca West wrote, "like the ramblings of an exceptionally silly boy of sixteen." Its single contribution was the phrase "controlled schizophrenia" by which Fuchs explained his ability to live a double life. It had more meaning than he suspected, for Fuchs's schizophrenia consisted in being god and man simultaneously. His major concern was that Skardon get on with it, so that he would be able to get back to his work. But he had to return the following day because, by some perverted logic, he would not disclose to Skardon the technical details of the information he had stolen for the Soviets. He would speak of this only to someone cleared for secret information.

On February 10, 1950, Klaus Fuchs sat behind a cast-iron grille in the ancient Bow Street police court, calm, no paler than usual, and, as one observer remarked, "the most inconspicuous person in the room." His arraignment was brief and consisted mostly of Skardon's testimony. It was established that the information supplied by Fuchs had been "of the greatest possible value to a potential enemy." The trial, on March 1, 1950, was almost as brief, lasting one hour and twenty-seven minutes. Fuchs's face was blank when he heard his sentence, the maximum—fourteen years.

But though his defense counsel elicited from the prosecution that Fuchs had been completely co-operative, Fuchs remained tight-lipped when he was visited by two FBI agents who sought from him a description of the man he had known as "Raymond"— Harry Gold. Repeatedly, he was shown photographs of his former confederate, but Fuchs persisted in a denial that he could recognize him. Only after Gold had confessed did Fuchs find himself able to make an identification. After his release from prison, moreover, Klaus Fuchs forgot his long protestations of love for England and the democratic world. He slipped behind the Iron Curtain to East Germany to continue his nuclear research.

Much, however, had happened to Gold between the moment that he gave a last backward look at Klaus Fuchs and the day that he decided to confess.

For some fifteen months after his last trip to Santa Fe, the apparatus left Gold alone. There were several abortive stabs at meetings, but the summons always arrived too late for Gold to keep the appointment—until he felt that Yakovlev had dropped him. There had been no repercussions from the Gouzenko case, and Gold began to feel that he had escaped detection and could "go private." He had even gone into partnership with one of his former sources, Abe Brothman.

In December 1946, he received a phone call from Yakovlev. "This is John," the agent said. "Have you been well?" This was a code question. It meant: Was Gold under surveillance? Gold conceded that he was well. By code, Yakovlev set a time and a place for a meeting the following evening—at a theater in the Bronx. But it was not Yakovlev who appeared. Instead a "quite large and rather tough-looking character" approached him. "I am Paul," he said. "Give me what you have from the doctor." Gold had nothing and said so, and the large and "tigerish" man furiously directed him to Third Avenue and Forty-second Street, where Yakovlev was waiting. Gold was asked for news of Fuchs or for any papers from him he might not have delivered. The two men sat in a Third Avenue bar and chatted until Gold mentioned that he was in partnership with Brothman. Yakovlev jumped to his feet, threw some bills on the table, and said, "You fool, you have spoiled eleven years of preparation"—and he dashed out.

Yakovlev was right. For the association with Brothman was the major cause of Gold's downfall. Brothman had spied for Eliza-

beth Bentley and Jacob Golos. He also knew Gold's real name—
Gold had told him when they became partners—and that he
lived in Philadelphia (though he still believed the stories about
Gold's two mythical children and unfaithful wife). On May 29,
1947, two FBI agents visited Brothman. They showed him a photo
of Jacob Golos, the Soviet spy who had recruited him years
before. "Never saw him," Brothman said. Then they showed him
a photo of Elizabeth Bentley. Brothman, who was never very fast
on his feet, suddenly reversed himself. Somewhat shaken, he said
he knew Miss Bentley as "Helen"—the secretary of the man he had
not been able to identify. And he quickly explained that he had
lied about Golos because he thought the FBI was investigating an
espionage matter and "I didn't want to get involved." All he
wanted was to be protected from unfavorable publicity.

Brothman could have limited himself to a story about legitimate
business dealings with Golos. But for some reason, perhaps because he resented Gold's ability, he deliberately and unnecessarily
dragged him in.

"This man with the Russian name," he said disingenuously,
"he came to my office some time in 1938 and told me he had
some connection with the Russian government. He said he might
be able to get me some business with the Russian government . . .
I first loaned him blueprints for a vat or some machinery for a
chemical process. We became quite friendly. I used to have dinner
with Helen and him. Sometimes Helen came to my office for blueprints or plans. Then another party came instead of her, Harry
Gold. I got to like Harry Gold. He was a good man in chemistry.
Finally I asked him to come to work with me." Brothman admitted
that he had once been a member of the Young Communist League—
but that had been a long time ago, and now he had little time for
politics. No, he had never gotten any contracts from the Russians
or from Amtorg, but he had bid for them.

Having implicated Gold, Brothman called him in desperation to
think of some kind of story that would get them both off the hook.

He swore that he had mentioned Gold because the FBI had a picture of the two of them together—which was a lie. "Help me, Harry," he pleaded. Gold had no alternative. And so, when the FBI questioned him, he admitted readily that the man in the photo was a "Golush or Golish," a "real phoney-baloney" who had represented himself as a legitimate businessman. This "character" had asked him to deal with Abe Brothman on some chemical processes, since Gold was a chemist. Gold had been promised the world for his co-operation in this business deal, but nothing had ever come of it. Who had introduced him to Golos? One Carter Hoodless, a young man of some social standing (and, fortunately, for Gold, dead) had brought them together at a meeting of the American Chemical Society.

It was a good story, for Golos had misrepresented himself to loyal Americans in his work for the apparatus—and this the FBI knew. Gold and Brothman refined the story, coached each other thoroughly, and gave a good accounting of themselves when they appeared in 1947 before a federal grand jury investigating the Bentley charges. There is a wide gap between suspicion and knowledge, between knowledge and evidence, and so no indictments were handed up. Continued questioning by the Justice Department attorneys might have broken down the Brothman-Gold story. But suddenly, on orders from the White House, the espionage investigation at New York's Federal Courthouse was brusquely called off— among those questioned had been Alger Hiss and Harry Dexter White—and the government switched abruptly to the Smith Act cases of the twelve Communist Party leaders. Brothman breathed a sigh of relief, and Gold fervently prayed that he would have no more to do with the apparatus. (He was mistaken. A Soviet agent made a final contact with him to learn what he had told the grand jury.)

By this time, Gold had had his fill of Brothman. The two men did not get along, the business was not doing well—and Gold could not forget the gratuitous betrayal. He left New York and found a post as senior biochemist at the Heart Laboratory of the Philadelphia General Hospital.* For a while, it seemed that perhaps he might once again live a normal life. But from the moment that he read of Fuchs's arrest, he was certain that his days as a free man were done. He considered going to the FBI, but rejected the idea. He simply waited.

He had three months of waiting. For the FBI had very little to go on. Fuchs had described Gold as a man of about forty, five feet eight inches tall and weighing about 180 pounds,† with a round face and a Slavic look, possibly a scientist. The description given by Fuchs's sister was even less helpful, although she seemed to remember the name Davidson. The FBI found a New Yorker with the name who roughly fitted the description. When a photo was shown to Fuchs, he "identified" him immediately. Fuchs's sister was certain that the FBI had the wrong man. Carefully and methodically, the FBI gathered together a list of 1,500 suspects. One by one they were eliminated until there were one hundred, fifty, ten. Gold was among the ten. And then, two pieces fit together. Brothman's assistant, Miss Moskowitz, part of the apparatus, had casually mentioned that Gold had two children, Essie and David—the two mythical nonidentical twins. And Mrs. Heinemann, Fuchs's sister, recalled that the man who had visited Fuchs at Cambridge also had chatted of his children, Essie and David.

This, however, was hardly evidence to take into a court of law. The FBI decided that its one hope, unless Gold made a major slip, was to get a confession. The best account of what followed is Gold's, written down in a massive autobiography for the use of his lawyer, John Hamilton. The day was May 15, 1950, a Monday.

When Special Agents Miller and Brennan first walked into the Heart Station lab at three that afternoon, even before they showed me their identification, I knew who they were. And when Miller

---

* At the time of his arrest, he was chief research chemist.
† Gold was in fact five feet six inches tall and weighed 163 pounds.

said they would like to speak to me "about Abe Brothman—and some other matters," that last phrase sent a disturbing tremor through me . . . That night in the Bureau's offices in the Widener Building, for five hours I stubbornly repeated the story Abe and I had concocted in 1947 . . . I tried desperately to create the illusion that I was genuinely doing all in my power to cooperate . . . Questions such as "Were you west of the Mississippi" were, to put it mildly, very upsetting . . .

For the next few days, the FBI let Gold realize that he was under surveillance. Now and then a special agent would drop in casually at his place of work to ask a few innocuous questions. It was all very friendly, with no pressure of any kind except the psychological squeeze.

On Friday came further blows that jolted and badly shook me up . . . The special agents and I were together for nine hours, until 2 A.M., during which I submitted page after page of my handwriting and printing, calmly agreed to have motion pictures taken—"Sure, go ahead"—and went over and over the Brothman story. Then, about a half hour before we broke up, came the sharp stab of this question by Dick Brennan, "Did you ever tell Abe Brothman or Miriam Moskowitz that you were married and had two children?" And when I stoutly answered in the negative, "But Miss Moskowitz said you had. Why do you deny it? Why lie about something like this?"

I knew why, all right, because this was the story I had also told Mrs. Heinemann. So I kept desperately trying to veer the conversation away from this deadly reef. Then followed the pictures: "Do you know him? Him? Her? Ever see this person before?" . . . And then the shocker: "Do you know who he is?" The white, staring and somehow dully expressionless face, with those huge glasses—Klaus Fuchs.

"I do not know him," Gold said, but his voice was reedy. "I recognize him as Dr. Emil Fuchs, the Briton who got in trouble over there, but I don't know him. I've never been in England."

And the terrifying answer: "Oh, yes. You know him. You met him in Cambridge."

And the too casual answer: "Never been there in my life."

The two special agents gave up before Gold did, and they agreed to meet the following day. But Gold was busy until the evening with a heart patient—and then there was a half-hour session at FBI headquarters. Miller and Brennan were even more weary than Gold, for the adrenalin which kept the suspect alert was not shooting into their veins, and they called it a day. On Sunday, Gold was back at the hospital, doing an experimental gastrectomy on a dog, and then back to the Widener Building. The strangest aspect of these days of questioning and surveillance was Gold's inertia. He knew that in his cellar were blueprints from Brothman, notes and directions from his Soviet superiors—a kitchen middens of incriminating evidence which so many spies collect in violation of the rules and with no logic other than the subconscious wish to get caught. During the Sunday questioning, Gold reminded himself that he must destroy this material. But as he describes it, his attitude toward the FBI was wonderfully ambivalent:

I was literally walking on eggs. But somehow, as it seemed that Miller and Brennan began to droop with defeat, I strangely enough began to feel sorry for them; they had given it such a good try. Yes, I was almost in the clear. However, instead of going directly home and frenziedly cleaning out all those terribly damaging bits of evidence which I knew were there (though even I had no conception as to the prodigious extent of this bonanza), I went to see . . . the dog at the med school . . . I did not actually begin the search for the accusatory items until 5 A.M. on Monday . . . I had a dully fatalistic and apathetic approach toward the impending search; what would be would happen, and that was all. Possibly it was the sheer and utter exhaustion of that past week which had produced this reaction in me.

But when I started to look, in the depressing gray of the early

morning, I was horrified: Good Lord, here was a letter from Slack
dated February 1945; a stub of a plane ticket from Albuquerque to
Kansas City; a rough draft of a report on a visit to Cambridge;
a street map of Dayton, Ohio; a card containing instructions from
Sam relating to a procedure for approaching Ben Smilg; all this
was here and more—I tore it all up and flushed it down the toilet
(some I shoved down near the bottom of our rubbish can in the
cellar). Yes, I had taken care of everything.

On Monday morning, Miller and Brennan arrived to search
Gold's room, with his permission and almost at his request. They
went through school notes and laboratory notations and chemical
literature references. They examined every book, including mathematical textbooks and a large collection of paperbacks. Then, as
Gold wrote, it began:

First, a copy of Paul de Kruif's *Microbe Hunters* in a pocketbook edition turned up—and in the lower right-hand corner was
a tiny tag: "Sibley, Lindsay, and Carr."
"What's this?" said Dick [Brennan].
"Oh, I don't know," I replied. "Must have picked it up on a
used-book counter somewhere. Lord knows where they get them."
But I did know; it was the name of the Rochester department
store where I had purchased the book on one of my visits to Slack.
Then Scott [Miller] found a Pennsylvania Railroad train schedule: "Washington–Philadelphia–New York–Boston–Montreal," and
dated 1945. "How about this?"
"Goodness knows. I probably picked it up when I went (on a
trip) to New York." Again, the truth was that I had used the schedule on my trip to see Mrs. Heinemann.

None of this was evidence. None of it proved anything at all
except to Gold's guilt-ridden mind. The FBI men were asking
questions, but only by Gold's overelaborate casualness could they
get a clue—and they knew far better than he that their subjective

reactions were just that. No federal prosecutor would put any re-
liance on their value. But they continued to look, hoping to find
something which would shatter Gold's defenses. Like all well-
trained interrogators, they knew that what Gold feared and what
he knew would be of far greater importance in breaking him down
than legal evidence. They were right. It is not the bullet but the
crack of the rifle which frightens. Sound Jamesian psychology was
on their side. What broke Gold was Gold himself, though he described it as "the stunning blow."

From in back of my bulky, worn copy of . . . Principles of Chemical Engineering, Dick pulled a sickeningly familiar tan-colored
street map of Sante Fe. Oh, God. This I had overlooked. I knew
that it existed, but, in my hasty scrutiny that morning, could not
find it, and so had assumed that at some previous time it must
have been destroyed.

"So you were never west of the Mississippi," Brennan said.
"How about this, Harry?" There could have been a thousand explanations, but Gold saw the blood on his hands.

"Give me a minute," he said, slumping down in his chair. One
of the FBI men gave him a cigarette. He smoked it and then spoke
the words: "Yes, I am the man to whom Klaus Fuchs gave the
information on atomic energy." He had reached the end of the line.
It was now a matter of police routine. At first, Gold was determined to speak merely of Fuchs and to cover up for all the others.
But once the "fatal words" had been uttered, there was no stopping
the confession. Unlike Fuchs, who remained riveted to his compulsion, Gold found liberation by speaking out, by making his perfidy
plain. Some have called this "informing," but psychologically it is
far more complex than that.

The map of Santa Fe had been the needle's eye of truth through
which he could not clamber. And so he entered the gray world of
courtrooms, of testimony against Abe Brothman and Miriam Mos-

kowitz, against David Greenglass and the Rosenbergs. But more than anything else, he was a witness against himself. The gates of Lewisburg Penitentiary closed behind him finally, and he was safe in his laboratory. The evil he had done remained outside the prison walls.

X I

The Rosenbergs, Greenglass,
and a Will to Treason

ON the day that the Supreme Court, in all its majesty, met to consider for the seventh time the case of Ethel and Julius Rosenberg, one Willi Goettling, an unemployed laborer in East Berlin, was tried and summarily shot for committing a "disturbance." For seven years, the Rosenbergs had the benefit of every legal maneuver, every opportunity offered to the innocent and the guilty by American law and tradition. Yet Willi Goettling, executed for a misdemeanor and forgotten before his body had been tossed into an unmarked grave, caused no anguish to the world's conscience. But every device of propaganda and implication was employed in the defense of the Rosenbergs though their will to treason and their stony lack of humanity were apparent for all who would see.

The character of Ethel and Julius Rosenberg can best be exemplified by anticipating the unfolding of their story and offering up three pieces of evidence:

Item: "I decided a long while ago," Julius Rosenberg told Max Ellitcher, an engineer he tried to "develop" into an espionage agent, "that this was what I wanted to do. I made a point of getting close to one person after another until I reached a Russian who would listen to my proposition about getting information to the Soviet Union."

Item: At a time when Rosenberg was attempting to get his brother-in-law David Greenglass to flee, he suddenly asked: "Do you think we will beat the FBI?"

Greenglass answered, "I don't know."

"Well," Rosenberg said, "you know, if I get word that it is too hot, we'll just have to take off and leave the children and the women behind."

"We are going to leave them and go?" a startled Greenglass asked.

"Maybe yes, maybe no," Rosenberg said.

"How can you think that way?"

Rosenberg gave him a disgusted look. "The Russians will send in division after division against a position, and they will all be killed, and they won't bat an eyelash," Rosenberg answered, "as long as something is being done to gain their end."

Item: When Mrs. Tessie Greenglass, mother of David and of Ethel Rosenberg, visited her daughter at Sing Sing's Death Row to plead for a confession which would spare the lives of the convicted spies, she said: "Ethel, David is not lying. He is telling the truth. Why do you go on this way? If you don't believe in capitalism or free enterprise or anything else, if you believe in the Russians and feel they are right, think of your children. Think of what you are going to do to them."

"You are not my mother," Ethel said harshly. "Leave. I don't want to have anything more to do with you." And that night, she was singing arias in the voice she thought was made for grand opera.

This is the world that Ethel and Julius Rosenberg made for themselves—a world into which they dragged David Greenglass and his protesting wife Ruth, and many others whose names were part of the index to the case or remain in the FBI files, the doom they subscribed to neatly ticketed. A defecting Soviet engineer, who worked on data supplied by the Center, has described to American security officers the "thousands" of Signal Corps blueprints and documents his section handled. A good part of this data we know today, from confessions, partial confessions, and incriminating attempts to cover up, came from men and women recruited by the zealous Julius Rosenberg before, during, and after he had been admitted to the elite of atomic spies.*

The wreckage of lives—the bright young men from poor families, whose hard-won educations came to nothing as a result of Rosenberg's blandishments—makes a long catalogue. But Julius Rosenberg cozily offered the apple of espionage to his own family, and this ultimate perfidy led to his downfall. From the moment that Julius—a dark, bespectacled student with that drive and verbal assurance which are a product of New York's municipally owned City College—substituted for the placid faith of his fathers the combative Communist dogma, he was out to proselytize. At CCNY, he was not a leader of the Young Communist League, but an active member who gathered around him a group of young engineering students, later to be brought into his apparatus. He was also courting Ethel Greenglass, three years his senior, who shared Julius's Communist passion. Mrs. Tessie Greenglass had little use for Julius —"all that communism he talks about"—but David, Ethel's younger brother, was fair game. By a combination of lofty lectures on the merits of the Soviet system, by the pressure of derision for lacking the guts to accept "conversion," and by the skillful use of David's hero-worship for him—"he was my mentor," Greenglass would later testify—Julius was able to bring the sixteen-year-old boy into the YCL.

---

* The details of Rosenberg's activities in other areas of Soviet espionage are not germane to this account. But the record is there, though few outside the FBI and Army Counter-Intelligence have bothered to examine it or correlate the information.

But David Greenglass was not made for the solemn mumbo jumbo of communism's Junior Achievement. As he later put it, "It bored me. It held no interest for my type of personality. I couldn't subject myself to the discipline that was required. I would rather lie in bed on Sunday morning than be up at six o'clock shoving *Daily Worker*s under people's doors. And so I tapered off and stopped going." In 1940, when he was eighteen, he had simply dropped out. "But unwilling to subject myself to the discipline of the Young Communist League, I was not unwilling to believe in the principles behind it." What those principles were, Greenglass had only the vaguest idea. If asked to discuss the Marxist theories of surplus value or the mystical concept of dialectical materialism, he would have laughed, or as typically made a sarcastic remark.

Greenglass has said that "philosophically," he was a Communist. "Everything they stood for, I identified myself with. But my idea of what communism was, wasn't the actuality of communism. It was an idealized version of communism." But everything he knew, idealized or not, came from Julius Rosenberg. "He was the one who taught me about what communism was. It was his own version. Probably he lied to me, or maybe he even believed what he told me. I don't know. But in that way, he was my mentor."

Psychologically, this is of considerable importance. The young Greenglass not only respected a brother-in-law with a college education (David went to college for one semester, then was forced to drop out in order to go to work) and his intellectual conversation; he was also dominated by and to a degree afraid of him. Repeatedly in his conversation about Julius Rosenberg, Greenglass described his "persuasiveness." Rosenberg was a "salesman" who could "sell iceboxes to Eskimos"—a persistent phrase. (Greenglass has always tended to be a cliché expert, though, like many self-taught people, he often brought unconscious humor to these hackneyed expressions by misusing them.)

It was not until Greenglass was out of the Army and out of the apparatus that he developed the courage to stand up in opposition to the Rosenbergs. But it is also true that his lazy communism served a deeper purpose. Though on the surface he seemed the complete extrovert, ready always for the loud and inconsequential argument, he nourished a deep persecution feeling. This coupled to his ambivalence about Rosenberg—later transferred to the scientists he worked with on the Los Alamos project—demanded that in some way he strike back at those superior to him intellectually or in the scientific hierarchy. One of the people who observed him closely during the period between his arrest and trial had this to say of him:

From the outset of the investigation, Greenglass exhibited a friendly, easygoing, self-assured manner. He was extremely garrulous and expounded at great length on inconsequential matters. He was sometimes impatient and sarcastic, but usually was able to control his emotions. Greenglass appeared both courageous and honest. He was loyal to his family and friends [which explains why his first confession, though accurate about his own deeds, glossed over or evaded those of his co-conspirators] and was generous to the point of improvidence. Having a sense of humor and enjoying a joke, he took pleasure in attempting to startle others by his unexpected knowledge of facts and situations. He dressed in a sloppy manner and in rather poor taste, possibly because of color blindness. He did not like to shave regularly and had his hair cut infrequently.

Greenglass, who was a moderate cigarette smoker and did not care for alcoholic beverages, was extremely fond of food and tended to obesity. He enjoyed movies, chess, conversation, tampering with gadgets, and being better informed than his scholastic achievements would seem to indicate.

Had circumstances—financial difficulties and the tight-knit relations of the Greenglass family—not prevented it, David Greenglass would have shucked off his minimal Communist involvement and would by now be a well-paid research worker in an industrial laboratory. Many young men, far more committed to communism, were able during their military service to cut the social and political umbilical cord which held them to communism. When Greenglass married the girl he had known since early boyhood, Ruth Printz, he was only twenty. She might have tugged him away from the Rosenberg influence. But though she had no sympathy with communism, she felt that as an "obedient wife" she should go along with him, sharing his views and being in turn subject to the domineering of Ethel and Julius Rosenberg. This influence on the Greenglasses proved its value when the Rosenbergs plunged feet first into the espionage pit.

But this plunge was well prepared by the Center in Moscow. Julius firmly believed that he had by his own persistence brought himself to the attention of the apparatus. The contrary was true. For it was not until the Center decided that his connections could be of value that he was given the accolade he sought. At the beginning, he and Ethel were merely two hard-working members of the Communist Party. She was active, in an unimportant way, in the work of the Communist-controlled Local 65, United Retail and Wholesale Employees. (She also made repeated efforts to break into the fields of professional singing and acting, but she had more ambition than ability, and her small size, pinched features, and plump appearance did not exactly thrust her forward. It simply added to her sense of frustration, but oddly enough gave her that sense of importance so common among would-be performers.)

The Rosenbergs lived at Knickerbocker Village, a housing development in the lower East Side which streamlined slum-living by adding modern plumbing but reduced the organic community life of the tenements and the family shops to an antiseptic level. When, in September 1940, Rosenberg rose like the phoenix from a piddling private job to the position of junior civilian engineer with a Signal Corps Depot in Brooklyn, the Communist Party rewarded him by making him federal civil-service chief of the Federation of Architects, Engineers, Chemists, and Technicians— the same union of scientific workers which was employed to such good advantage in the infiltration of the Radiation Laboratory at the University of California in Berkeley and the SAM laboratory at Columbia. His Communist classmate of the City College days, Joel Barr—a talented engineer with a rich musical background— was part of the FAECT cell. So, too, was Mike Sidorovich, whose wife, along with Vivian Glassman (also in FAECT), became couriers for what eventually grew into the Rosenberg espionage apparatus.

Julius Rosenberg was very proud of his work with the FAECT and tried very hard to get David Greenglass to join. Once he insisted on taking Greenglass to a meeting, which was no more interesting to the young technician than attending the Young Communist League.

"While I was there [at FAECT headquarters] and going there and coming back," Greenglass would later recall, "he told me a little bit about the union. He said that most of the members were Communists or sympathizers, and that in the course of a jurisdictional dispute with the UAW over the engineers who were working in the Brewster Aeronautical Corporation that was in existence at the time in New York City, that he felt that the UAW was not being very fair, and they should have been, because at the time the UAW leadership was communistic. This is his words."

Just when Rosenberg was switched from party activity to spying is not clear. In the latter part of 1942, and until November 1943, he was reporting to Jacob Golos, spymaster of an apparatus in government which ranged from Assistant Treasury Secretary Harry Dexter White to William Remington—with way stations in every sensitive agency, including the Office of Strategic Services. Rosenberg would arrange a rendezvous with Golos by calling Elizabeth Bentley in the very early hours of the morning. His greeting would be, "This is Julius." She would get dressed and from a pay station relay the message to Golos. On one occasion, she drove with Golos to Knickerbocker Village—he was to meet "Julius, an engineer"––

where he got out of the car and conferred in the shadows with Rosenberg.

As late as February 1944, Julius Rosenberg was not yet a full-fledged member of the apparatus. Party records introduced by the prosecution at his trial showed that during that month he was shifted from Branch 16-B of the Industrial Division of the Communist party to the Eastern Branch of the First Assembly District under Transfer No. 12179. Had he already been in the apparatus, he would have severed all formal connection with the party. By June 1944, he was already active as an espionage agent. The Center in Moscow had tested his reliability and his willingness. If his probity is today questioned, it can only be said that he made one slip in making use of David Greenglass. But there is reason to believe that his relationship with Greenglass was the single most important factor in the Center's decision to allow Rosenberg his great desire to be a spy.

The June 1944 date can be set because of his visit to Max Ellitcher, a former City College classmate, shortly after D-day, the invasion of France by Allied troops. Rosenberg had risen in the civilian Signal Corps ranks to the post of inspector—which gave him free entry to industrial plants doing classified work as well as to military installations. He was on some kind of official business in Washington and took the opportunity to call on a college acquaintance. Ellitcher had never been particularly active in left-wing politics at City College. But he had with some reluctance allowed himself to be recruited into the Communist Party by his good friend Morton Sobell, already funneling classified information to Rosenberg. What recommended him most to the Center's attention was the fact that he worked for Navy Ordnance on fire control devices for ground-to-air rockets and other antiaircraft devices. His special field was computers.

Rosenberg exchanged some reminiscences and expressed his elation at the opening of the second front and then, rather importantly, asked Ellitcher if he could get his wife to leave the room. In 1951, Ellitcher testified of their conversation:

> He talked to me first about the job that the Soviet Union was doing in the war effort and how at present a good deal of military information was being denied them by some 'interests' in the United States, and because of that their effort was being impeded. He said that there were many people implementing aid to the Soviet Union by providing classified information about military equipment and so forth, and asked whether in my capacity at the Bureau of Ordnance would I have access to, and would I be able to get, such information and would I turn it over to him . . .
>
> Well, he asked about any plans or blueprints or anything that might be of value, and that all these things are needed, and that the choice would not be mine. If I had some such information, it should be turned over, and someone would evaluate it.

"If you agree to give me this information," Rosenberg said to Ellitcher, "I'll take it to New York myself and have it processed photographically and the material will be returned. It can all be done very safely in one night so that you can return everything before it is missed. There's really no danger. The microfilm will be carried in containers to protect it, and if anyone should tamper with it, any unauthorized person, the film will be exposed. It's very safe."

The normal reaction to a proposal of this kind would be to throw the seducer out of the house and to call the FBI. But in relatively few instances does it happen that way. Rosenberg was a very bad judge of people, but the apparatus has always made an evaluation of the "prospect" and knows that he will be thrilled, flattered, or frightened. In Ellitcher's case, moreover, he was a civilian employee of the Navy, and exposure of his Communist membership might mean dismissal or worse. It would not have been necessary to make the threat. A casual word dropped would be sufficient reminder. Ellitcher, however, showed no disposition to sound the alarm, though he was clearly not ready to submit himself to the apparatus. He said he would think it over. Rosenberg could report neither success nor failure—and for the next years he continued to try to lure Ellitcher a step at a time into the apparatus. He did not succeed and, in fact, chalked up one more witness against himself.

At a subsequent meeting in New York that summer, Rosenberg again tried to win over Ellitcher. This time, to grease the skids, he argued that their mutual friend Morton Sobell was in espionage for the Soviet Union. When Ellitcher repeated this to Sobell, there was an angry scene. "He should not have mentioned my name," Sobell shouted. "He should not have told you that." Ellitcher tried to explain that Rosenberg knew about their close friendship and therefore felt that it would not be dangerous, but Sobell would not be mollified: "It makes no difference," he said. "He should not have done it." This, however, did not prevent Sobell from adding Uncle-Joe-Needs-You arguments to those of Rosenberg—nor from asking Ellitcher to suggest likely prospects for the apparatus.

The relationship between Ellitcher and Rosenberg, however, was a seesaw. At some meetings, Rosenberg would press hard for information and urge Ellitcher not to leave the Navy Department for civilian employ. At other meetings, such as the one which took place in 1947, when Ellitcher seemed to be weakening, Rosenberg held him off by saying, "There's a leak somewhere, and I've got to take precautions. You better not see me again until this blows over—or until you are contacted." At this time, of course, the apparatus had become jittery over Elizabeth Bentley's defection and was waiting to discover just how much she had told the FBI, what people were under suspicion, how much could be proved.

The last significant episode involving Julius Rosenberg occurred in early August 1948. At that time, the newspapers were full of Elizabeth Bentley's testimony before Senate and House investigating committees. Ellitcher had finally quit his job with the Navy, packed his family in the car and driven to the Sobell home in Queens—planning, as they had agreed, to stay there until he found a place of his own.

> When I got there [Ellitcher testified at the Rosenberg trial] we put [our one] child to bed. I called Sobell aside and told him that I thought we had been followed by one or two cars from Washington to New York. At this point he became very angry and said I should not have come to the house under those circumstances. I told him that . . . whoever was following me would probably know about it. In any case it was our only destination. He was still angry and concerned. However, he didn't seem to believe that I had been followed. He told me to leave the house . . . I told him that it was not possible. I didn't know where to go . . .
>
> He finally agreed that I would stay. However, a short time later he came over to me and said he had some . . . information he should have given Julius Rosenberg some time ago . . . It was too valuable to be destroyed and yet too dangerous to keep around. He said he wanted to deliver it to Rosenberg that night.

Ellitcher argued that, under the circumstances, it was dangerous and silly to venture out. But Sobell insisted that it had to be done and asked Ellitcher to accompany him. As they left, Ellitcher noticed that Sobell had a small 35-millimeter film can in his pocket which he carefully locked in the glove compartment of his car. The two men drove to the lower East Side and parked a few blocks away from Knickerbocker Village. Sobell disappeared with the 35-millimeter film. Half an hour later, he returned, and he was in a more relaxed mood.

"Well, what does Julie think about this, my being followed?" Ellitcher asked.

"It's all right," Sobell said. "Don't be concerned about it. It's

O.K. Julie says he once talked to Elizabeth Bentley on the phone, but he's pretty sure she didn't know who he was. Everything is all right."

Everything, obviously, was not all right. For there was more building up against Julius Rosenberg than those after-midnight calls to signal a meeting with Jacob Golos. Harry Gold had already appeared before a federal grand jury, weaving the tangled web which later ensnared him. There was a road ahead for all of them, and a spoor on the path behind them. Ironically, had Yakovlev and Rosenberg and Gold strictly observed the etiquette of espionage, they might never have been discovered. It was a kind of tragic daisy chain. Elizabeth Bentley led to Abe Brothman, and he involved Harry Gold. Klaus Fuchs was tied to Harry Gold and Yakovlev—and Yakovlev had brought Gold and David Greenglass together. Greenglass was tied to Ethel and Julius Rosenberg—and they in turn completed the circle with Elizabeth Bentley. It was all very bad form.

Rosenberg could have had no premonition of this in the fall of 1944, when he and Ethel invited Ruth Greenglass to dinner. His Soviet contact had told him that David Greenglass, now in the Army, was working at Los Alamos on something called an atomic bomb, that the Soviet Union was very interested in any facts it could ascertain about this new device, and that David was to be recruited. The Center had all the facts about the relationship between Julius and David, the hold the older man had on his brother-in-law. It knew that David loved his wife and would be rashly tempted to do what Rosenberg asked if it meant that there would be enough money to allow Ruth to live in Albuquerque—close enough to Los Alamos so that he could spend the weekends with her. In similar circumstances, very many servicemen would have, with Greenglass, let heaven wait for this temporal and temporary joy.

Greenglass had sought military service, but his color blindness led to several rejections by the Navy. In April of 1943, he had been drafted into the Army. After a smattering of basic training, he was assigned to duty at the Aberdeen Proving Ground in Maryland. Then had begun for him that life of military gypsy which became the lot of soldiers who remained stateside. In November 1943, Ruth Greenglass joined the army of peripatetic wives who crowded trains and buses, joining David at the Pomona Air Forces Base in California. But what had been planned as a first wedding anniversary reunion became a little more permanent when she got a job at a hemp factory as a file clerk. When David was transferred again, she returned to New York. But the couple planned to be with each other again, if only during their second anniversary, on November 29, 1944. Meanwhile, however, David was pulled out of routine machinist duty and assigned to Oak Ridge, the Manhattan Engineer District.

For two weeks, Greenglass was given a thorough indoctrination in security, told he was now part of a highly secret project but given no idea what he would be doing. Then he was sent out to Los Alamos, to work in the "E" shop, machining highly secret parts for the nuclear experiments and the atomic bomb. He worked then under Dr. George Kistiakowsky of Harvard, later to become President Eisenhower's special assistant on scientific matters. The "E" shop was working on the high-explosive aspects of the bomb and on the special lens which turned the shattering force of the atom inward. By the time Greenglass was discharged from the service in February 1946, he had become foreman of the shop and wore a sergeant's stripes.

The dinner invitation which brought Ruth Greenglass to the Rosenberg apartment at 10 Monroe Street in mid-November 1944 could not have seemed significant when she rang the doorbell. Perhaps, she thought, Ethel and Julius planned to commiserate with her because the wedding anniversary trip would have to be called off; Ruth didn't have the money for it. The account of that dinner

has been thoroughly dramatized in a number of accounts, but this
is how Ruth gave it on the witness stand:

> Julius said that I might have noticed that for some time he
> and Ethel had not been actively pursuing any Communist Party
> activities, that they didn't buy the *Daily Worker* at the usual
> newsstand; that for two years he had been trying to get in touch
> with people who would assist him to help the Russian people
> more directly . . . and he went on to tell me that David was work-
> ing on the atomic bomb and I asked him how he knew because
> I had received an affidavit from the War Department telling me—

MR. E. H. BLOCH [counsel for the Rosenbergs]: I move to strike
out the "because."

THE COURT: All right, strike out "because."

Q: Just tell us what went on in the conversation.

A: I said that I had received an affidavit from the War Department
telling me that my mail to David would be censored and his to
me because he was working on a top secret project.

THE COURT: Madam, could you sit back?

THE WITNESS: Yes, I am sorry.

THE COURT: And just speak a little slower, please.

THE WITNESS: Yes.

A: [Continued] And he said—I wanted to know how he knew
what David was doing. He said that his friends had told him that
David was working on the atomic bomb, and he went on to
tell me that the bomb was the most destructive weapon used
so far, that it had dangerous radiation effects, that the United
States and Britain were working on this project jointly, and that
he felt that the information should be shared with Russia, who
was our ally at the time, because if all nations had the information then one nation wouldn't use the bomb as a threat against
another.

He said that he wanted me to tell my husband David that he
should give information to Julius to be passed to the Russians.

And at first I objected to this. I didn't think it was right. I said that the people who are in charge of the work on the bomb were in a better position to know whether the information should be shared or not.

Ethel Rosenberg said that I should at least tell it to David, that she felt that this was right for David, that he would want it, that I should give him the message and let him decide for himself . . . Julius and Ethel persuaded me to give my husband the message and they told me the information—

MR. E. H. BLOCH: I move to strike it out.

THE COURT: All right, strike out the word "persuaded." As a result of this conversation you decided to give your husband—

THE WITNESS: I decided to give my husband the message and Julius Rosenberg told me the things he wanted me to ask my husband.

Following routine practice, Rosenberg did not ask for any information that would have shocked Greenglass. It was of minor importance—the kind of thing that could be rationalized easily as not damaging to anyone: a description of the physical lay-out at Los Alamos, the names of the important scientists there (this, of course, was a closely guarded secret, since knowledge of their presence and their specialty would give away the nature of the work), what the security measures were, whether Los Alamos was camouflaged. Rosenberg also warned Ruth to tell David to be very circumspect, not to indulge in political conversation, not to remove any blueprints or sketches, and not to be obvious in asking questions. (The last point was a waste of breath. Before he had even considered espionage, Greenglass had irritated the scientists who came into the "E" or Theta shop by asking too many questions—simply out of unregenerate curiosity.) To clinch Ruth's participation in this first step, Rosenberg gave her the $150 she needed to make the trip to Albuquerque.

Ruth Greenglass arrived in Albuquerque and registered at the

Hotel Franciscan just before her wedding anniversary. David was able to get what she recalls as a "five-day" pass—probably three days and a weekend. She mentioned nothing to him until the third day, when they were walking along Route 66 on the outskirts of the city. At first, his reaction to Rosenberg's request was as negative as Ruth's. Then he learned that Julius had given her $150 and, past an initial anger that she had accepted it, Greenglass began to change his mind. The following morning, to Ruth's surprise and chagrin, he told her he would co-operate with the Rosenbergs. And so they were caught.

When Ruth Greenglass returned to New York, she brought back with her the answers to Rosenberg's questions, all carefully memorized. He was delighted and asked her to write it all down for him. He was even more pleased when she told him that David would be in New York on furlough in about a month. "How would you like to go to Albuquerque to live?" he said, offering the reward.

"I'd be very happy to be near David," Ruth answered.

"You are going to go there," he said. "You'll probably be able to find a job, but if you can't, just don't worry about the money. It will be taken care of." For those who experienced years of separation during the war, it is easy to understand—though not to condone—the effect of this declaration. When David Greenglass arrived in New York, Ruth was able to give him the news that, due to the generosity of Rosenberg's "friends," they would be able to be together in Albuquerque—at least on weekends, when David could leave Los Alamos. The bill was presented a few days later. Julius Rosenberg appeared one morning at 266 Stanton Street, where the Greenglasses lived.

"He asked me what I was doing out there, and I told him I was working on lenses, H.E. lens molds," Greenglass testified. This was an unexpected bonanza, though Rosenberg may not have known it. The apparatus had been prodding its agents for information on the implosion lens—Yakovlev had expressed considerable eagerness to get at least a schematic drawing of it from Harry Gold —and Greenglass could diagram it for Rosenberg, which he did.* That day, he also wrote a full report on everything he had picked up, either by questioning his associates or overhearing their shop

* During the trial, the Rosenberg defense conceded that Greenglass could have made this and other drawings. But it argued that they were neither important nor secret. This contention was torpedoed by the prosecution, which put on the stand Dr. Walter Koski of Johns Hopkins, who had done some of the implosion research at Los Alamos and taken his diagrams for translation into finished products to the Theta shop. Here is his testimony:

"Q: Do you recognize that exhibit [a copy made by Greenglass of the drawing he had given Rosenberg] as . . . a substantially accurate replica of a sketch that you made at or about the time which you have testified to at Los Alamos in connection with your experimentation?

"A: I do.

"Q: Is it a reasonably accurate portrayal of a sketch of a type of lens mold or lens that you required in the course of your experimental work at the time?

"A: It is . . .

"Q: What does it portray to you? [Another Greenglass drawing.]

"A: It is essentially—it is a sketch, a rough sketch of our experimental setup for studying cylindrical implosion . . .

"Q: Did you know [in 1944 and 1945] that the experiments which you were conducting and the effects as they were observed by you could have been of advantage to a foreign nation?

"A: To the best of my knowledge and all of my colleagues who were involved in this field, there was no information in text books or technical journals on this particular subject.

"Q: In other words, you were engaged in a new and original field?

"A: Correct.

"Q: And up to that point and continuing right up until this trial, has the information relating to the lens mold and the lens and the experimentation to which you have testified continued to be secret information?

"A: It still is.

"Q: . . . Is it not a fact that one expert could ascertain at that time, if shown Exhibits 2, 6, and 7, the nature and the object of the activity that was under way at Los Alamos in relation to the production of the atom bomb?

"A: He could."

This colloquy not only demonstrates the importance of Greenglass' contribution to the Soviet atomic bomb effort but, since an official of the Atomic Energy Commission sat in the courtroom declassifying documents needed in the trial (though not shown to the press) and then immediately classified them again, it destroys the later contention of the Rosenberg defense that Greenglass was coached by the FBI. The FBI had no access to the sketches for the implosion lens.

talk. Because his handwriting was not good, Ethel Rosenberg dutifully typed the material for Julius.

Several nights later, the Greenglasses were invited to dinner at the Rosenbergs'. Present that evening was Ann Sidorovich, whose husband Greenglass had known. The Sidoroviches had moved to Cleveland, but Ann had made a special trip to New York in order to be present. Before dinner, Mrs. Sidorovich left. It was at this point that Julius told the Greenglasses that "this woman" would be the courier who would receive information from him about the atomic bomb. During the dinner, Rosenberg outlined a plan for meeting with her. Either "this woman" or someone else would go to Denver. She would meet with Ruth in a motion-picture theater, and they would exchange pocketbooks in the dark. Ruth's pocketbook would contain David's data for the apparatus. Rosenberg said that Ann Sidorovich had been present "so that we would know what she looked like." Then the question was asked: Supposing the apparatus decided to send someone else?

"So Julius said to my wife," Greenglass testified, " 'Well, I'll give you something so that you will be able to identify the person that does come.' "

> Well, Rosenberg and my wife and Ethel went into the kitchen, and I was in the living room. And then a little while later, after they had been there for about five minutes or so, they came out and my wife had in her hand a Jello box side . . . And it had been cut, and Julius had the other part of it.

This recognition symbol was to cause much hilarity among those who professed to believe that Rosenberg was innocent. It was, however, one of the oldest devices—and perhaps the most reliable —in espionage work. For the side of the Jello box had been cut in a jagged pattern. When the courier presented his half to Ruth Greenglass, she could match it against her own. There was no possibility for a slip-up—although more sophisticated agents like

Hede Massing had once objected to so "old-fashioned" a method for making an "identity." David Greenglass, however, was impressed.

"That's very clever," he said.

"The simplest things are the cleverest," Rosenberg told him, as Ruth put her half in her wallet.

Before the Greenglasses left that night, Rosenberg told David that the apparatus wanted very much to discuss the implosion lens with him before he left New York. A rendezvous was arranged several nights later, to take place somewhere between Forty-second Street and Fifty-ninth Street on First Avenue, a grim neighborhood of warehouses and abattoirs before they were torn down for the United Nations, completely deserted after dark. Julius introduced David to a Russian. Greenglass and the Russian drove through empty streets, while the Russian, muffled in an overcoat, his hat pulled down over his eyes, asked searching questions about the lens, the formula for its curvature, the high-explosive used, and the means of detonation. He was obviously a man with scientific knowledge, which would indicate that he might have been Semen Semenov—but Greenglass was never able to identify him. The questions extended beyond what Greenglass then knew, so he was instructed to get more information to supply to the courier who visited him in Albuquerque or made contact with his wife in Denver.

Julius Rosenberg had made the introduction. When the Russian finished pumping Greenglass, the two returned to the corner where they had left Rosenberg. The Russian got out of the car, and Julius said to David: "Go home now. I'll stay with him." And Rosenberg and his Russian disappeared dramatically into the darkness.

It was early on a June 1945 Sunday that the doorbell rang at the small apartment the Greenglasses had taken in Albuquerque. "Mr. Greenglass?" asked a sad-eyed man. "I bring regards from Julius." He seemed startled and apprehensive that the man who let him in was a soldier. Greenglass walked to his wife's purse, took out the wallet, and produced her half of the Jello box. Harry Gold, his visitor, presented the other half, and they matched them. The fit was perfect.

"Do you have anything for me?" Gold asked.

"Yes," said Greenglass, "but I've got to write it up. If you come back in the afternoon, I'll give it to you." And he started to tell Gold about a number of people at Los Alamos who were, he believed, ready to be recruited. Gold, the professional, was horrified. He brushed aside Greenglass' explanation that he was only following Julius's orders. "I don't want to know about it," Gold said and departed hastily, refusing an offer of breakfast. This overlapping of espionage rings was a violation of the rules, but Yakovlev had insisted on it. Recruitment of agents by Greenglass would have been against the rules, too, but also a senseless risk.

When Gold returned that afternoon, Greenglass had filled several sheets of paper with more advanced designs of the lens mold as well as a description of the progress of the research in cylindrical implosion—the material which had been demanded of him by the Russian.* Gold accepted it and gave Greenglass an envelope with five hundred dollars. He departed with considerable misgivings, as well he might have. The trip to Albuquerque cost Ethel and Julius Rosenberg their lives and sent Greenglass to prison under a fifteen-year sentence, for Gold was the link in the investigative chain. "Will it be enough?" Gold asked when he gave Greenglass the money. "Well, it will be enough for the present," Greenglass answered him.

* "I showed," Greenglass testified, "a high-explosive lens mold. I showed the way it would look with this high-explosive in it with the detonators on, and I showed the steel tube in the middle which would be exploded by this lens mold." And describing this sketch to the jury, he said:

" 'A' is the light source which projects a light through this tube 'E,' which shows a camera set up to take a picture of this light source. Around the tube is a cross-section of the high-explosive lens 'C' and a detonator 'B' showing where it is detonated, and the course is that when the lens is detonated, it collapses the tube, implodes the tube, and the camera, through the lens 'B' and the film 'D,' shows a picture of the implosion."

All of this was corroborated by Dr. Koski.

In September 1945, Greenglass and his wife were back in New York on another furlough—and they had even bigger news. In January 1945, Julius had given him a very general description of the atomic bomb in order to brief him on what to look for. "There is fissionable material at one end of a tube," Rosenberg had said, "and at the other end of the tube there is a sliding member that is also fissionable, and when they are brought together under great pressure, a nuclear reaction takes place." This, in elementary terms, was the Hiroshima bomb. But Greenglass, during the September visit, had in his possession details of the more advanced Nagasaki bomb. Rosenberg asked him to "write it up" immediately and gave him two hundred dollars. That night, at the Rosenberg apartment, David handed his brother-in-law twelve pages of text and diagram. "This is very good," Rosenberg said. "We ought to have it typed up immediately." And Ruth Greenglass added, "We'll probably have to correct the grammar." Ethel Rosenberg set up a bridge table, put her typewriter on it, and the three clustered around her as she typed. That night, too, Rosenberg boasted that, as a Signal Corps inspector, he had seen a proximity fuse at a plant manufacturing it and had put it in his briefcase and walked out.

When the typing had been completed, Julius asked David what he intended to do, now that the war was over. "Get out of the Army," said Greenglass. Rosenberg argued that he should stay at Los Alamos, in a civilian capacity, in order to continue his espionage work. But though Greenglass was not yet ready to defy his brother-in-law, he wanted to break loose from the apparatus. He had gotten into it out of mixed motives—to impress Julius and to provide his wife with the means to be near him. Now the war was over. He wanted to earn a living, to continue his education. He had heard enough from Rosenberg to disillusion him thoroughly on the "idealism" of the Communist cause. He no longer needed the money the apparatus provided. It was almost a symbolic act when the originals of notes which Ethel Rosenberg had typed were burned in a frying pan and dumped down the drain.

When Greenglass was honorably discharged from the Army in February 1946, he had already been involved by his brother in a business partnership with Julius Rosenberg. At first, they bought and sold war surplus goods, then they set up a machine shop. But there was increasing friction between the two. David insisted that his brother-in-law treated him like an employee and that he did not attend to business. Rosenberg was still trying to woo David back into the apparatus, and the two argued about politics incessantly. Julius also held out what we have come to know as a prime lure. He urged Greenglass to return to school, particularly to one of those universities where he had friends from Los Alamos. It was his duty to maintain his relationship with these scientists and technicians, some of them still doing secret work.

"Well, how am I going to do all this?" Greenglass would say. He had a wife to support, and the GI Bill of Rights could hardly cover his expenses.

"So the Russians will send you to school," was Rosenberg's answer. "I do it all the time. I have a number of people that I send to school. I am the paymaster." When Greenglass refused, Rosenberg would show his annoyance, but he did not drop the subject.

During the postwar period, Rosenberg did not give up espionage activities. But he had a need to boast of his achievements, and the only person with whom he could speak frankly, other than his wife, was Greenglass. There was safety in this, for as a former co-conspirator, Greenglass was bound to silence. Late in 1947, Rosenberg told him that he had gotten information from "one of my boys" on a new scientific development—a "sky platform." *

---

* When Greenglass testified to this before the Senate Internal Security Subcommittee on April 27, 1956, he was accused by *The New York Times* and other newspapers of trying to capitalize on the American reaction to the Soviet sputnik by adding new spice to his story. The fact: He described the "sky platform" on March 12, 1951, during the Rosenberg trial, long before the Soviets had sent their first sputnik aloft—and long before United States scientists had the vaguest inkling of this Soviet project.

In a courtroom which thought he was talking in science-fiction terms, this exchange took place:

Q: Did he tell you just what information had been given to him by one of the boys concerning the sky platform project? Did he describe it to you at all?

A: Yes, he did. He described it in front of my brother, too.

Q: How did he describe it?

A: He said that it was some large vessel which would be suspended at a point of gravity between the moon and the earth and as a satellite it would spin around the earth . . .

Q: Let me ask you this. Did he mention any other projects, government projects, concerning which he had obtained information?

A: He once stated to me in the presence of a worker of ours that they had solved the problem of atomic energy for airplanes, and later on I asked him if this was true, and he said that he had gotten the mathematics of it, the mathematics was solved on this.

Q: Did he say where he had gotten this?

A: He said he got it from one of his contacts . . . meaning scientists in this country.

In 1949, the partnership between Greenglass and Rosenberg broke up. Julius owed David four thousand dollars at the time and attempted strenuously to evade the debt, causing still more dissension—and the two drifted apart. Occasionally they met at a Friday-night dinner, the command performances exacted by Mrs. Tessie Greenglass, but they were distant with each other. Then, on a morning in February 1950, Rosenberg went to Greenglass's apartment and awakened him. (Greenglass was working nights and slept late.) With no explanation, Rosenberg insisted that Greenglass get dressed and go for a walk, and the urgency in his voice was such that he got no argument. Walking along the East Side streets, Rosenberg said:

"You remember the man who came to see you in Albuquerque? Well, Klaus Fuchs was also one of his contacts." The Fuchs story had been on page one for several days. "The man who came to see you will undoubtedly be arrested now. You'll have to leave the country. Think it over, and we'll make plans."

Greenglass did not like the idea. He said he needed money to pay his debts, an argument which did not impress Rosenberg particularly, though he agreed to help him. "Why doesn't this other guy leave—the one who came to me in Albuquerque?" Greenglass asked. "That's something else again," Rosenberg answered cryptically. Greenglass, however, made no move to leave, and perhaps Rosenberg was given reassurances that Harry Gold would not talk. In any case, he did not press for immediate flight until May 22 or 23—shortly after Ruth Greenglass had left the hospital after giving birth to their first child. Rosenberg was now really excited, and he brandished a copy of the *New York Herald Tribune,* which carried a picture of Harry Gold and the story of his arrest.

"This is the man who saw you in Albuquerque," Rosenberg said. Greenglass was not quite sure, but Rosenberg insisted. "Don't worry, I'm telling you this is the man, and you'll have to leave the country." He had one thousand dollars for Greenglass and a promise of six thousand. Then he gave instructions: David was to go to the Mexican border and apply for a tourist card. In Mexico City, he was to write a letter to the Soviet ambassador on some innocuous matter, signing it "I. Jackson." Three days later, he was to stand on the Plaza Colon, at 5 P.M., holding a guidebook with his middle finger between the pages. He would be approached by a man and was to say, "That is a magnificent statue." The answering signal would be, "Oh, there are much more beautiful statues in Paris." The man would give him a passport to Sweden, where a similar rendezvous was arranged with an eventual destination of Czechoslovakia.

Rosenberg also said that he would probably have to leave the country. "I knew Jacob Golos and maybe Elizabeth Bentley knows me," he said. As a precaution, he advised Greenglass to get a lawyer and said that he was already in touch with his own. For Rosenberg, the pressure was building. He knew that with Greenglass out of the country, he would be relatively safe—at least from the charge of atomic espionage. But Greenglass continued to stall. Early in June, Rosenberg brought him four thousand dollars in a brown paper wrapper—the get-away money. (Ironically he used it to retain a lawyer when he was arrested.) Rosenberg had one question:

"Are you being followed?"

"Yes, I am," Greenglass said.

"What are you going to do now?" Rosenberg asked.

"I'm not going to do anything," Greenglass said. "I'm going to stay right here." Rosenberg left in a state of great agitation, ready now to make his own escape. But it was too late. Harry Gold had already tentatively identified a photo of Greenglass and, after searching his memory, recalled his name. On June 15, at 1:45 P.M., two FBI agents visited him at his apartment in Rivington Street. They advised him of his right not to make a statement and suggested that he might want a lawyer. Then they questioned him "regarding material which had been lost, strayed, or stolen from the Los Alamos atom-bomb project."

At 1:57, Greenglass, who was pleasant throughout his questioning, signed a waiver of search. In a footlocker, the FBI found some old photos of David and Ruth Greenglass taken in Albuquerque. These were rushed to Philadelphia for Harry Gold to examine. Meanwhile, Greenglass agreed voluntarily to accompany the FBI agents to the Federal Courthouse on Foley Square. He was questioned in Conference Room U on the 29th Floor where the Bureau is headquartered. At 8:30 P.M., word was received that Gold had made a positive identification. Greenglass was confronted with this and told of Gold's visit to Albuquerque on June 3, 1945 and of the transfer of classified information. He promptly confessed that he was guilty, signing a statement to that effect. But he insisted that he did not know who might have asked his wife to suggest espionage.

The Bureau, however, already knew of Rosenberg's involvement with Elizabeth Bentley. From Rosenberg's behavior, they also knew that his association with Greenglass was more than familial. Like Harry Gold, Greenglass attempted to shield his confederates. Like Gold, he finally began his long and earnest confession. That night, he slept at FBI headquarters. The following day, he was taken to a barber shop for a shave and the haircut he badly needed. Then, at 1:50 P.M., he was arraigned, his lawyer O. John Rogge at his side.

Julius Rosenberg should have known that the string had been played out. But he continued to go about his business. Ethel Rosenberg questioned Ruth Greenglass closely following David's arrest: Had he talked? she asked. Ruth said, "David is innocent. We're going to fight it." Sustained by the incredible conviction that they would remain untouched and that they could outsmart the FBI, the Rosenbergs began to relax. Then, on July 17, three FBI agents presented themselves at the Rosenberg apartment at 10 Monroe Street. Ethel was brash, almost flippant. She demanded a warrant before allowing the FBI to search the apartment—which was her right. The FBI men were startled by the manner in which the two Rosenberg children addressed their parents, using first names. The children—particularly the older boy, Michael, who was under the care of a psychiatrist—were completely undisciplined. (The Rosenbergs believed that a child should never be punished or restrained.) "Are you going to hang my daddy?" Michael asked gaily. So obstreperous did the children become that Ethel was asked to take them to the home of their grandparents, of course accompanied by an FBI agent. Julius was arrested that day, though he denied any complicity. On August 11, Ethel was taken into custody.

The trial of the Rosenbergs has been rehearsed in books and articles *ad infinitum.* But certain facts are of significance. The prosecution, expecting a long defense, had 102 witnesses ready to take the stand—most of them held back for rebuttal. But the entire Rosenberg defense consisted of a denial of the charges by Ethel and Julius when they took the stand. And even those denials were compromised by the frequent resort to the Fifth Amendment. (Morton Sobell, a co-defendant, did not even testify in his own defense.) Neither of the Rosenbergs showed any emotion as the government unveiled its evidence. Given the Rosenberg defense strategy, only a fraction of the prosecution witnesses were called. When the sentence of death was pronounced, Ethel and Julius Rosenberg were impassive, almost lethargic.

In the months that followed, as the case dragged through appeal after appeal, a vast propaganda campaign was mounted to prove that the Rosenbergs had not been given a fair trial, that Judge Irving Kaufman had shown bias, that anti-Semitism was the motive behind the arrest and prosecution, that it was all another Dreyfus or Sacco-Vanzetti case, and that the issue was "peace." The Rosenberg children were used as pawns to pump up sympathy for the condemned and exhibited at mass meetings. Pickets paraded in front of the White House, and there were riots in Europe. Eminent citizens proclaimed the innocence of the Rosenbergs and made unconscionable charges against the FBI, only to admit that they had never even read the trial record. Millions of dollars were collected, though where they went has never been determined. It was a Roman holiday for the Communists, for their dupes, and for the uninformed—and generous men who conceded the guilt but sought a commutation of the death sentence found themselves involved in a hysteria of which they wanted no part.

During the period of mass insanity, few remembered that at the conclusion of the trial, after Judge Kaufman had pronounced sentence, both defense lawyers had risen to their feet to thank the Court for its fairness and its courtesies, to praise the FBI for the co-operation it had given them. A study of the record shows no mystery. It is conclusive in its proof of guilt. But one question has plagued many who have not chased a legal or emotional will o' the wisp: Why did the Rosenbergs accept death rather than confess? At the very moment that they faced the electric chair, a word would have saved their lives. At Sing Sing prison, a line was kept open to the White House, just in case they decided to talk. But to the end, the Rosenbergs remained silent—sending back the last meal because it was not precisely what they had ordered, complaining that the execution should be postponed because they had "unfinished business." Julius Rosenberg showed fear only once, on the last day of his life, when he learned that the last possible appeal had been rejected.

A psychiatrist who followed the case had this answer to the enigma:

"Julius Rosenberg was an unimportant man until he became an espionage agent. Then in his own eyes—and to use a word he knew—he became a *Mensch,* a man, a significant part of a great cause. His ego was nourished by the importance of his treason. And the Soviets flattered and manipulated him. They gave him motivation. They made him feel that he was walking the stage of history. The great demonstrations, the appeals to the President, the request for clemency from the Pope—all these fed that feeling. And the same applied to Ethel Rosenberg. If she could not sing at the Metropolitan Opera House, she could speak to the world. To confess would have destroyed this. To themselves, they would have become two more defectors, two more informers. They would no longer be heroic. From their behavior after the trial, it is clear that they had lost all sense of reality. They were shielded by a mystical belief that somehow the power they worshiped would liberate them. By stealing America's atomic secrets, they had made America tremble. How could they die?"

This could be the answer. A simpler answer would be that they were Communists.

XII

"Peking Joan" and the House
on Harvard Street

THE story of Joan Chase Hinton, a brilliant atomic scientist who defected to Red China, made little stir in the United States. The Atomic Energy Commission did its utmost to suppress the simple fact that she had gone over to the Communists and exacted a pledge from the veteran newsman, Walter Trohan of the *Chicago Tribune,* not to publish any hint of what he had learned to be true. It was not until three years after Joan Hinton had defected—and two years after Trohan sought confirmation from the AEC—that reluctant admissions were made. By that time, Joan Hinton was filling the airwaves with violent anti-American propaganda, spreading the lie that the United States was conducting germ warfare in Korea, giving aid and comfort to an enemy engaged in killing American soldiers, and urging scientists to give up all atomic research.

This was in 1951. In 1954 and 1956, there was a mild flurry of interest when Joan's brother William Howard Hinton, who had remained in Communist China throughout most of the Korean war, was questioned by the Senate Internal Security Subcommittee. Bill Hinton was an unstable young man with too much "progressive" schooling, a conscientious objector during World War II until the "gallantry" of the Red Army and the boredom of a Quaker work farm had become too much for him. Then he volunteered for military service, was turned down, and landed on his feet as a propaganda analyst in China for the Office of War Information. Given his political predilections, he fell in easily with a group of State Department Foreign Service officers and Institute of Pacific Relations "researchers" in the Far East who could see no good in the anti-Communist Nationalist forces and all virtue in the Yenan Communists.

After a period with the United Nations Relief and Rehabilitation Administration (UNRRA), presumably administering aid to the Chinese people, he went on the Red Chinese payroll as an agricultural expert. His views of the world were expressed in a letter to Joan and their sister Jean, written from behind the Bamboo Curtain. "That great beast America," he said, "looks down upon the world and licks its lips . . . So far I have seen no evidence of the anti-American feeling that is supposed to be rampant here. This worries me a little, since it indicates the people have not yet learned who their enemies are." Having served the Communists during the Korean war, he returned to the United States to preach the glories of Red China and the iniquities of his own country. His journey back to the "great beast" was facilitated by a benevolent Soviet Union which paid his expenses, briefed him in Moscow, and sent him back to the West via Czechoslovakia.

But what of Joan Chase Hinton? No Congressional committee has given her any particular scrutiny. The AEC remains silent, except for a brief resumé of her activities at Los Alamos and the Argonne National Laboratories. The FBI, by law, cannot speak out. And yet she was an integral part of the great plot to loot America of its atomic secrets, to give Communist countries information they were economically incapable of developing, and of

feeding the vast propaganda machine which the Communist world
has employed to discredit her native country. Yet enough psychological and actual evidence is available to construct the story of
her role.

It is important to go back to her mother, Carmelita Hinton and
the Putney School which she founded and directed in that Vermont
town, to the ambient which created her character and guided her
actions. For Putney was one of those special communities which
spring up in the midst of New England's flinty conservatism. The
school was "progressive" and "experimental." Its faculty was rab-
idly left-wing, including at times notorious Communists. On its
board of trustees was Owen Lattimore, the nation's foremost apologist for the Chinese Communists and an expert political casuist.
Among Carmelita Hinton's close friends were Nathan Gregory
Silvermaster and his wife Helen. Silvermaster was busy then colo-
nizing the Washington bureaucracy with Communist Party members
and was a ranking member of Elizabeth Bentley's espionage apparatus. Around the Putney School, moreover, a group of interesting and persuasive people of Communist or fellow-traveling
orientation had gathered. Among them were Alger and Priscilla
Hiss and Harry Dexter White, the Assistant Secretary of the Treasury who doubled in brass as a Soviet agent.

It was in this atmosphere that Joan Chase Hinton grew up, a
precocious and in-turned child surrounded by people who saw
fascists under every bed and smelled reaction in every breeze. Her
sister, Jean, was more openly political. Joan was interested in
science from the time that she could turn the pages of a book and
read its print. Under healthier circumstances, this love of the beauty,
truth, and order in mathematics, physics, and chemistry might have
been an integrated part of her life. But from the "progressive"
acres of Putney, she was sent to Bennington College in Vermont.
There Joan was an oddball, whereas at Radcliffe she would have
been considered a talented and studious girl. Joan Hinton at Bennington had no interest in dates or in trips to New York to learn

about "life" and the great world. Though her politics were accept-
able, even unnoticed, her attitude toward education did not con-
form to the superficial concerns of her classmates. While they were
out dancing and necking, she was building a Wilson cloud-chamber
and studying advanced texts in nuclear physics. The only impression she left was of a girl who did not wear lipstick and confined
her beauty treatments to running a comb through her hair.

When she moved on to Cornell, for work at its cyclotron, she
often forgot to do even that. A skinny, tall, unkempt girl, she
deplored all the visible and emotional aspects of femininity. She
was simply interested in research—as if science were not a means
but an end in itself. What had once been considered talent in the
abstruse field she chose for herself was now being assessed as
genius—although this was an overstatement from male students
who were startled and somewhat overcome by so intense a female.
Since the world of science is, like the world of any specialized art
or craft, a small one, her reputation began to grow in academic
circles. When she transferred to the University of Wisconsin for
advanced studies, she was already known to her peers and superiors.

It was then that Joan Chase Hinton decided that she wanted to
take part in the accelerating researches of the Manhattan Engineer
District at Los Alamos. That she knew what this work was about
is an index to the lax security of the scientific community. That she
applied directly at Los Alamos should have raised a few eyebrows.
That she was hired is even more astonishing. No records exist
which give a clue to her assault on the MED's bastion. It is possible
that Dr. J. Robert Oppenheimer raised the portcullis. He was a
close enough friend of Carmelita Hinton to lend her his ranch,
Perro Caliente, in the Upper Pecos for the summer of 1945—and
Joan visited her there briefly. All that is known to date is that she
"pulled strings"—and this comes without further documentation
from a former Intelligence officer.

However it was done, Joan Hinton found herself at Los Alamos
in one of its most sensitive laboratories and wearing the "white

badge" assigned to those who had access to all information. Her title was "research assistant," but she was highly enough regarded to be one of those present and participating when the first atomic bomb was assembled. (As she would say dramatically in one of her "Peking Joan" broadcasts from Red China, "I held the bomb in my hands.")

Those entrusted with the security of Los Alamos and the entire MED project have never disclosed how she passed her investigation. Though her own life may have been bare of political activities, associations are of great importance in determining the risk involved in hiring a given person. And Joan Hinton was not only Carmelita's daughter; she was also Jean's sister, and very close to her. While Joan was preparing herself for a significant role in nuclear research, Jean had gone on to overt pro-Communist activity. Married to William Greene, a nonpolitical and somewhat bewildered businessman who eventually divorced her, Jean had moved to Washington and was deep in Communist works.

Her mother's friend, Silvermaster, got her a government job. She was extremely active in the affairs of the United Federal Workers Union, under strong Red domination. And the Greene home on Harvard Street was a meeting ground for a wide variety of fellow-travelers, Communists, espionage agents, and Soviet personnel. Rear Admiral Ellis M. Zacharias, once deputy chief of the Office of Naval Intelligence, describes the visitors to the House on Harvard Street—his information based on the reports of an ONI agent who was assigned to live next door to the Greenes and to report on their activities:

The people who visited them in that house represented a strange assortment of callers—Americans, Britons, Chinese—as well as Russians. Among the Americans were agitators of the most left-wing trade unions which have since been expelled from the CIO; young scientists and designers engaged in secret war work; a famous senator from New England who was especially loquacious with what appeared to us as classified information; the daughter of one of our top-ranking admirals in a key position of the Pacific war; and people who seemed to be engaged in recruiting members for the apparatus. Most of the Russian visitors were employees of the Soviet Purchasing Mission.

The members of the Soviet Purchasing Commission, as this account has already noted, had the double mission of prying loose as much Lend-Lease as possible and of serving as cover for espionage. But the two Soviet officials who most frequently were seen at the House on Harvard Street were Major General Ilya M. Sarayev, head of Red Army Intelligence's American division, and Colonel Pavel E. Berezin, a specialist on aircraft with NKVD status. General Sarayev's title, Assistant Military Attaché, did not hide the fact that he was one of the most important Soviet agents working out of the Embassy in Washington. The names of both men figure prominently in security reports on Soviet espionage in the United States.

From the vantage point of the house next door, agents of ONI and the FBI were able to observe Sarayev and Berezin as they entered and left. Peering through powerful binoculars, they were able to see, but not hear, Jean Hinton Greene and the two Soviet officers in earnest conversation. There seemed to be considerable traffic between the living room and the basement when Sarayev and Berezin were visiting—and it was discovered that the House on Harvard Street had an elaborate shop and darkroom, though Jean Hinton was not a photography enthusiast. Other frequent visitors were Silvermaster and William Ullmann, both members of the Bentley apparatus in Washington. In short, the House on Harvard Street was a magnet for every security agency in the United States, for it included in its polarity individuals known to Counter-Intelligence in a variety of guises. Only the MED's security group seemed to have neither knowledge of nor interest in the comings and goings of Joan Chase Hinton's sister.

The FBI and ONI were both restrained by Presidential directive from any interference in the atomic project. From time to time, as one Soviet apparatus overlapped the functions of another, the FBI would become privy to certain facts and submit them, from Director J. Edgar Hoover to General Groves, in the belief that action would be taken. (Both MED security and the FBI kept an eye on Steve Nelson, to cite an example, since he was supervising both atomic spies and their cousins in less spectacular areas of espionage endeavor.) And so it was with utter frustration that the ONI watched the postman deliver fat envelopes to Jean Hinton Greene, the return address corner inscribed "JCH/Box 1663/Sante Fe, Mexico." This was the Post Office box used by everyone at Los Alamos, whether of high rank or lowly, so that there would be no hint to mail handlers of the nature of the work being done there.

What Joan Hinton wrote to her sister—or how unconsciously or wittingly she was indiscreet—will never be known. Though the MED was warned of Joan Hinton's close relationship to a sister so surrounded by suspect characters, there is no record that any action was taken to investigate or to intercept the mail. Certainly when the Gray Board sifted through the security files of the Manhattan project, seeking evidence both favorable and unfavorable in the case of J. Robert Oppenheimer, there was not even a hint that he had been at any time linked with the Hintons. From Jean Hinton Greene's mysterious remarks to the ONI man who had insinuated himself into the Greene household, if only on a neighborly basis, it is clear that she was well aware of the work her sister was doing at Los Alamos—in itself a breach of security. And on the same day that the bomb was dropped on Hiroshima, Jean Greene burst out proudly that her sister was one of those who had manufactured the atomic weapon. She also boasted that one of her house guests had been a British atomic scientist working on the project. Admiral Zacharias has summarized the reaction of Naval Intelligence to these events:

The revelation shocked us. Here was a house frequented by two of Russia's secret agents in the United States, in which the untold secrets of the atomic weapon might be fully disclosed. We could not ascertain how much of this data was conveyed to General Sarayev and Colonel Berezin, or how much of it they could pick up themselves. But the mere connection between these two groups of people—the one group which had access to the information which the other group was most anxious to obtain—virtually scared the daylights out of us.

Naval Intelligence did not know that Joan Chase Hinton was particularly valuable as a source. Most of the Soviet espionage success at the MED had been in areas other than the physical manufacture of the bomb, though David Greenglass was important here. But ONI was sufficiently overwrought to violate the Presidential directive. A Navy representative was sent to Dr. Richard Tolman, one of the atomic scientists working with General Groves. Dr. Tolman, by coincidence, was in Washington and easily available—and ONI informed him of Joan Chase Hinton, her associations, and of the goings on at the House on Harvard Street. Presumably Dr. Tolman reported this conversation to General Groves. If he did, it made little impression, since Groves made no mention of Joan Hinton in discussing security problems in his book *Now It Can Be Told*.

With the fighting over, the staff at Los Alamos was reduced, and Joan Hinton, instead of going back to Putney, moved in with her sister Jean at Harvard Street. She claimed that she had resigned in shame and anger over the dropping of the bomb on Hiroshima and Nagasaki. And she vowed that she would devote herself to "peace" and to the outlawing of the bomb—in other words, to unilateral American nuclear disarmament. Once quiet and unaggressive, she became a crusader. But her zeal to change United States policy was frustrated by the stubborn and unreasonable men charged with the nation's safety—and her feelings were hurt. In almost childish terms, she described her experiences years later for

People's China, a magazine published by the Communist government:

After Hiroshima, I first joined the Association of Los Alamos Scientists and then participated in their mass migration to Washington. I spent some six weeks there working for the Federation of American Scientists [then attempting to frighten the American people and government into ceasing all nuclear research]. I was both enthusiastic and inexperienced. I will never forget my chagrin when I went to a certain senator's office to get some information and the secretary condescendingly looked up at me, asking: "Is this in connection with your school work?" Me, an atomic scientist, coming to Washington to fight for scientific freedom and world peace, the very nerve of her! Well, my heart was in the right place anyway.

And so, having been mistaken for a student by an overworked secretary, her importance not recognized at sight, Joan Hinton railed against the American system. At the Putney School or at Bennington College, the fact that she asked a question, that she "showed interest," would have won her praise and understanding, but in the "corrupt" United States Senate she was not overwhelmed with attention. Joan Hinton swore that she would never again work for the atomic project. Her Communist friends, however, had different ideas. Just as the apparatus had urged David Greenglass to remain at Los Alamos or to complete his education so that he would be more valuable to the Center in Moscow, Joan Hinton was told that it was her duty to return to the project and to rise with it. She sought out Dr. Enrico Fermi, one of the great nuclear physicists then assembling a staff for the Institute of Nuclear Studies at the University of Chicago, and asked that he accept her. Dr. Fermi agreed, and Joan Hinton happily told her friends at Harvard Street that she was to be his scientific secretary.

At the University of Chicago, she was given a fellowship in nuclear physics. Her major work was with the "heavy-water boilers"—declassified in 1951—but she was given access, according to the Atomic Energy Commission's belated admission, to secret data of considerable value to any nation seeking to develop its own atomic energy installations. "In the room where I studied," she later said in a letter to the Federation of American Scientists and in her propaganda writings, "there was only a little space in the corner for a desk. The rest of the room was piled high with cases of heavy water right up to the ceiling—for Argonne." And it was made known to her and to others that she was on the way up in the hierarchy of nuclear researchers.

Had she remained, it is probable that she would have risen very high. For some reason, two detailed reports on her by ONI and other security agencies were ignored by the Atomic Energy Commission, which blithely allowed her to continue at the Institute. She remained in constant touch with the Argonne scientists who were not inhibited by the fact that she no longer had top-security clearance.

But other forces were at work. Passage of the Atomic Energy Act, late in 1946, placed AEC security in the hands of the FBI. Methodically, it began to put together information about those who had been permitted to operate unmolested in the palmier days of the MED. Elizabeth Bentley had told her story to the Bureau, and in 1947 a grand jury began to hear evidence in New York of Soviet espionage. The Center in Moscow had pushed the panic button, and the implicated members of its "legal" apparatus were recalled. Harry Gold and Abe Brothman had been called before the federal grand jury. Though they talked their way out of an indictment, the professional espionage agents knew that it was a matter of time. One after another, Americans in the apparatus were being advised to leave the country. With the FBI methodically closing in, there was no course left to them except flight or exposure.

Joan Hinton's brother was in China, working for the Communist regime, so the pull for her was to him. Late in 1947, she received credentials from the China Welfare Fund, since cited by the Attorney General as subversive, to go to the mainland as a relief worker. In her application for a passport, she stated as her reason for leaving the United States: "I am going to China to work in welfare and to get married. My fiancé is waiting for me in Shanghai" —then still in Nationalist hands. On December 12, 1947, she was issued a passport. Among her effects when she sailed was a suitcase full of notes and other data on her work at Los Alamos and at the Argonne National Laboratories. In Shanghai, she married an American dairy-cattle expert. Then, with her new husband, her brother Bill, and his wife Bertha, she slipped behind the Bamboo Curtain.*

Joan Hinton's first destination in the Communist-controlled area of the mainland was a secret scientific installation in the Shensi Mountains. Counter-Intelligence lost track of her movements until she turned up near the Mongolian border, where the Chinese Communists and the Soviet Union were at work on a joint atomic energy project. In 1951, an escapee from behind the Iron Curtain who was interviewed in Austria stated that he had attended a meeting of atomic scientists in the Soviet Union. Among those present, he said, were "Bruno Pontecorvo and a woman named Hinton." Then, in September 1951, she appeared at a "peace" conference in Red China to deliver an impassioned speech against her fellow Americans in Korea and against her country. A series of propaganda broadcasts, which led Admiral Zacharias to call her "Peking Joan," followed. And in a letter to the Federation of American Scientists in the United States, she pleaded:

* It is of some significance that while Joan Hinton was preparing to defect to Red China, Carmelita Hinton and her daughter-in-law Bertha were attending a Communist "peace conference" in Prague and then voyaging to Moscow. It is also ironic that at the time Walter Trohan of the *Chicago Tribune* was being told by the AEC that to print the story of Joan's defection might endanger her life, Carmelita Hinton was sponsoring the so-called Waldorf Peace Conference in New York, described by Secretary of State Dean Acheson as a major Soviet propaganda effort.

Use your strength, use whatever you can, to work for peace and against war ... The American government drives for war abroad and attacks the democratic rights of American people at home ... The Chinese people have a will so strong that nothing America can do will ever stop them. The Chinese people are not afraid of America. If she must fight, China will show that she is made of steel.

Joan Hinton has gone a long way from the studious girl at Bennington, building a cloud-chamber. She is in an alien land, helping the enemy create the weapons to destroy her own country. On the witness stand, her brother Bill attempted to evade questions concerning her present activities. Finally he insisted that she was working on an "animal farm"—though he would not say what she was doing there. If he spoke the truth, he must have meant George Orwell's "animal farm," in which all pigs are equal, but some pigs are more equal than others. Her feed grain is treason, for she is nourishing the Behemoth. Or perhaps she has changed her field of endeavor on this "animal farm" and is developing cultures for the germ warfare she so cynically accused her countrymen of waging.

XIII

Pontecorvo, Burgess, and MacLean

FROM the same highly classified source that gave the FBI its lead to Klaus Fuchs in 1949, there came an equally disturbing piece of information. A nuclear physicist of considerable status was also supplying information to the Soviet Union. Neither his name nor his nationality was known, though there were indications that he was foreign born and possibly connected in some way with the British. This was all United States security agencies and MI-5 in Great Britain had to go on—so frustratingly little that it could be of no help. In the Gold case, the FBI had a rough description from Fuchs and his sister. They had a vague idea of his background. With this as a start, method and persistence could help them sift through 1,500 suspects. But here they had nothing more than the category "nuclear physicist." Was he theoretical or experimental? Did he work at Los Alamos or Chalk River or Harwell?

When it was too late, when the mysterious scientist was out of their reach, the FBI and MI-5 learned who he was. In effect, Dr. Bruno Pontecorvo told them himself by disappearing behind the Iron Curtain. And again, the British, who had uttered a *mea culpa* over the laxity of their check on Klaus Fuchs, struck palm to brow and said, "But of course. We should have known." Following which they argued, as they had in the Fuchs case, "Even knowing, we could have done nothing." The fact is that their suspicions had been aroused, on the basis of other information, before Bruno Pontecorvo fled, but they had "sat like patience on a monument," convinced that he would act like a pukka sahib. This, perhaps, is what makes England great.

Having let Pontecorvo slip through their fingers, they then allowed Guy Burgess and Donald MacLean to take the road to Moscow. Pontecorvo, Burgess, and MacLean were involved in atomic espionage. Pontecorvo, however, took far more with him to the Soviet Union than Western nuclear knowledge—his own brilliant and questing mind. Burgess and MacLean were not simply repositories of information—although what they told the Soviets did incalculable political harm. They too had the capacity for continuing treason. That the lives of the Burgess–MacLean duo and Pontecorvo had touched was probably as coincidental as any chain of events can be in the Communist conspiracy. The paths of the three men crossed on both personal and espionage terms, if the hints and less-than-candid utterances of British authorities are to be believed. But how brief or how crucial these tenuous contacts may have been, the world will not know until Pontecorvo, Burgess, and/or MacLean redefect—or MI-5 turns garrulous.

Here, then, are their stories:

It has been said that Pontecorvo's soul, like that of Klaus Fuchs, was bruised by World War I and the trauma of fascism. This, however, is far from the reality. Bruno Pontecorvo, one of eight children, was born to a prosperous family in Pisa. In the interbellum years, his Jewish origin did not bring him any religious or political discrimination. Until the late 1930s—and then reluctantly, under pressure from Hitler—Benito Mussolini had neither preached nor practiced anti-Semitism. Jews were part of the Fascist regime, and those in private life carried on their businesses without a hint of molestation. The number of Italian Jews who supported Mussolini—or who simply lived under his rule without giving too much thought to politics—was overwhelmingly in excess of those who joined the Socialist or Communist opposition. For the most part, Italians of all religions who were militantly against Mussolini fought him from the safety of France. It was not until 1938, when anti-Semitism became a Fascist policy, that Pontecorvo had cause to complain of the treatment accorded his family by the Mussolini regime. For it was not until then that his father's business began suffering, and by that time Bruno had been out of Italy for two years.

Like his seven brothers and sisters, Bruno was a brilliant student. After attending the *Ginnasio* and the *Liceo classico,* he entered the University of Pisa, getting his doctorate in physics with honors at the University of Rome in 1934. He was then twenty-one years old. Continuing at the University of Rome as teacher and researcher, Pontecorvo was part of a group of advanced physicists working under one of the great men in the field, Dr. Enrico Fermi. This group, under Fermi's tutelage, developed a process for creating radioactive elements by bombarding them with slow neutrons—a step in nuclear theory which led toward the atomic bomb. A patent for the process was the legal basis for a suit against the United States government by those responsible for it. They claimed one million dollars, but settled for $300,000. Pontecorvo's share was fifteen thousand dollars—but he never collected it. He was already behind the Iron Curtain when the litigation ended.

As a result of his reputation and achievement, Pontecorvo was awarded a national fellowship by the Italian government for further study in Paris at the Collège de France. He took with him to France, in February 1936, a predilection for bohemianism and communism. The two may have been of a common origin, for the party encourages social and sexual nonconformism among its intellectuals. And if Bruno Pontecorvo at that time did not hold a party card, he had certainly received a thorough indoctrination from other members of his family. His brother Gilberto had from his student days been actively involved in party activities. In 1939, he was forced to flee to France, where he was a leader in Communist youth movements, and he plunged into underground work as a courier. (In the postwar period, he returned to Italy as a party functionary. On November 19, 1950, he was of sufficient importance in the party to be tried and acquitted of sedition. This past did not prevent him from becoming one of Italy's most famous movie directors. In 1961, he won the Italian equivalent of the "Oscar.")

Bruno's sister Giuliana married Duccio Tabet, also a functionary of the Italian Communist Party. After the war, she was assigned by the party to work closely with, and encircle, Pietro Nenni, leader of the left-wing Socialist Party, which joined in a "united front" with the Communists. Pontecorvo's first cousin, Emilio Sereni, had the distinction of rising to one of the highest positions in the Italian Communist Party—member of the powerful Central Committee. In the confused days after liberation, Sereni held several ministries in the government and today represents a Communist constituency in the Chamber of Deputies.

The bohemianism took another form. During his Paris days, Bruno Pontecorvo worked with the Communist physicist, Joliot-Curie, at the Institute of Radium. At night, he frequented the Café de Floré on the Left Bank, and it was here—among the artists, eccentrics, and homosexuals—that, according to the Deuxième Bureau, he met Donald MacLean. It was here, too, that he met Helene Marianne Nordblom, a tall, slender platinum-blonde from Stockholm. Probably, she was already a Communist. She moved into Pontecorvo's rooms at 17 Place du Panthéon, and on July 30, 1938, bore him a son. He was named Gilberto, after Bruno's Communist brother. It was not until January 9, 1940 that the two were married. The Communists and bohemians who made up the Pontecorvo circle of friends accepted the irregular arrangement as a matter of course—and it did not hinder Pontecorvo's rise to the important post of research associate at the Laboratory of Nuclear Chemistry at the Collège de France. Espionage during that period was, of course, unnecessary. Joliot-Curie made certain that every scrap of knowledge in the nuclear field then residing in France was published.

Using Paris as a base, Pontecorvo traveled about Europe inspecting research centers and blowing his own horn. (Friends have since noted that he was an inveterate job-seeker, always on the hunt for better and more lucrative positions.) But the conflict between the West and the Axis powers kept inching up on him. Pontecorvo's only reaction to the Hitler-Stalin Pact seems to have been one of annoyance for the way in which it inhibited his movements and his possibilities for advance. He was not perturbed by the "phoney war" during which Germany and France faced each other across the Maginot Line. When the Nazi blitz made Paris untenable for an Italian of Jewish blood with Communist connections, Pontecorvo, his wife, and the child born out of wedlock but legitimatized, fled south from Paris. They joined his sister Giuliana and her husband, Duccio Tabet, in Lisbon. On August 9, 1940, the Pontecorvos and the Tabets boarded the Portuguese ship S.S. "Oranza" for the United States. The Pontecorvos were completely straightforward in the papers they signed, but the Tabets claimed first to be doctors and then business people.

In New York, Bruno Pontecorvo immediately called friends of friends in the academic field who knew him by reputation. His offers of service to the great universities were not accepted, but he was able to find a well-paying job with an Oklahoma firm as a consultant on radiographic oil-well logging. This was not precisely his field, but by applying himself he was able to work out new techniques for which he sought a patent. His presence in the United States was known, however, to the scientists who made up the first phalanx in the atomic energy project. His old mentor, Dr. Fermi, had been snatched from the jaws of the Axis by a careful and clever maneuver of a highly secret Intelligence group in this country. They had quietly pulled the strings in the scientific community to snatch a Nobel Prize for Dr. Fermi. The Mussolini regime had risen to the bait, allowing Fermi to leave Italy, where he was under guard, in order to accept the award. Once out, Fermi had refused to return to Rome, and his subtle liberators were able to bring him to the United States.

Fermi remembered Pontecorvo and the contribution he had made to nuclear physics in Rome. A recommendation to the British authorities led to an assignment with the Anglo-Canadian research group in Montreal. Neither the Atomic Energy Commission nor Scotland Yard has been prepared to name the scientist or scientists who suggested Pontecorvo—and there can be legitimate grounds for conjecture about this silence. Pontecorvo was still an Italian citizen, though he had filed first papers for United States naturalization. It would have been standard procedure, had the recommendation come from Fermi, for him to have gone to Los Alamos or to the Metallurgical Laboratory in Chicago. By one of those tantalizing coincidences, Pontecorvo arrived at the Canadian atomic energy installation at just about the same time as Nunn May, who in turn was a friend of both Donald MacLean and Guy Burgess when all three had been students at Cambridge and in London. (British Intelligence records indicate that the Nunn May–Burgess–MacLean association in London between 1940 and 1943 was very close.)

At Chalk River, the Canadian heavy-water pile, Nunn May and Pontecorvo were so casually aloof to each other that it caused some comment, but their associates ascribed it to a difference in personalities. Nunn May was extremely reserved, whereas Pontecorvo plunged into his work with the kind of gay *élan* he showed on the tennis courts, where he was an outstanding amateur. But Pontecorvo's six years at Chalk River were not uninterrupted. He made at least one trip to Washington, where, it is reported but not confirmed, he visited the House on Harvard Street. Hindsight would indicate that he was one of those mentioned under a cover name in the Gouzenko papers. But of the whole "G" group * in the table of organization removed from the Soviet Embassy in Ottawa by the code clerk, no person was ever satisfactorily identified.

Hindsight, again, raises a question about Pontecorvo's behavior in Canada between 1943 and 1949. In an extremely politicalized atmosphere, Pontecorvo refused to discuss politics. His colleagues, with a few notable exceptions, spoke out with great vigor about the course of the war, the performance of the Red Army, the strong points and the shortcomings of the Anglo-American leadership, the "second front," and the "stuffiness" of the military which demanded a modicum of security. After the war, many of them were equally vocal in condemning the United States for using the atomic bomb against Hiroshima and Nagasaki, in their horror over what their nimble brains had wrought, and in their ambivalence toward further experimentation in nuclear weapons of destruction. Pontecorvo, however, made it a point never to enter into these political bull sessions or into the shop talk of the nuclear fraternity. He limited himself to cheerful chatter and to innocuous flirtation at social gatherings. That he should have so acted proves nothing, except in the light of his later defection, but at the time his behavior was a great relief to security officials who were hard put to sort out the normally disgruntled from the dangerous.

In 1949, Bruno Pontecorvo again demonstrated a departure from the norm by requesting that he be retained at Chalk River. The British, however, had other plans and offered him an important post at Harwell, their newly established nuclear research center near Birmingham. He accepted, and there was no trouble over the transfer. In 1948, he had applied for and received British naturalization after a long interview with security officers to whom he blandly failed to comment on his Communist relatives or associations. The only reservations of Harwell's directors concerned Pontecorvo's weakness for women (his wife Marianne had left him in

---

* The cover names of each cluster of agents began with the same letter. The RCMP had to rely on internal evidence to break that cover.

1947 after one of his escapades, then reluctantly returned), and the farflung net he was continually casting out for employment in British, French, and American universities. But this was accepted as the mild instability of a genius. Since Pontecorvo loved money and was for sale to the highest academic bidder, however, it came as something of a surprise to his colleagues when he turned down tempting and highly lucrative offers from Cornell University and from the General Electric Company to accept a post at Harwell which, though important in the nuclear field, paid considerably less.

But whatever external force impelled Pontecorvo to go to Harwell—as we know today, it was the Soviet apparatus—he continued to seek the kind of income which he considered commensurate with his fame in scientific circles. He openly flirted with offers from the Anglo-Iranian Oil Company and from two Italian universities. But on arriving at Harwell, it was obvious that his personality had suffered a sea change. Pontecorvo seemed anxious to get out of the atomic energy program. He was no longer the life of the party. In fact, it was noted that something seemed to be preying on his mind, and his colleagues remarked that they saw signs of premature aging. Perhaps, very much like an addict, he was trying to kick the espionage habit. But the apparatus would not release him, and he was in no position to break loose. His Communist faith had always been osmotic, but he knew that his Soviet masters could destroy him simply by leaking a few bits of evidence which would incriminate him and destroy his career.

For Pontecorvo, the solution seemed simple. He would find some minor reason for losing his security clearance and accept a research and teaching post at Liverpool University. In this way, his reputation would remain unscathed—it might be given the added luster of martyrdom—and he would have a legitimate excuse to offer the apparatus for his departure from the green pastures of espionage at Harwell. When, early in 1950, the Fuchs confession had shaken England and the British Parliament, Pontecorvo thought he had found a way out. He suddenly appeared at the office of Wing Commander Arnold, the security officer who had handled the Fuchs case, with a "confession" of his own. In applying for British naturalization, Pontecorvo told Arnold, he had committed a sin of omission by not disclosing that his brother Gilberto was a Communist functionary. He did not mention his sister Giuliana, her husband Duccio Tabet, or his first cousin Emilio Sereni. Given the jittery state of British public opinion, this should have been enough to win him a polite request to resign from Harwell.

Arnold, like any good security officer, simply thanked Pontecorvo for his "frankness" and seemed to let the matter go. But two days later, he summoned Pontecorvo to ask him if it were not true that during a recent trip to a scientific meeting at Lake Como, he had conferred with Gilberto. Bruno admitted this, passing it off as a fraternal meeting, but his obvious agitation alerted Arnold. Nothing was said to Pontecorvo, but his conscience whispered that somehow he had betrayed himself. He did not know until some months later that he was under suspicion and that inquiries had been made to Stockholm by Scotland Yard. The information received was very damaging: The Swedish police reported that according to their record, both Bruno and Marianne Pontecorvo were members of the Communist Party.

The return in May 1950 of MacLean from a Cairo assignment which had been cut short after a riotous and scandalous drunken episode, brought the matter to a head. Technically, MacLean was back in England on sick leave, with no disciplinary implications. He therefore still maintained an easy social relationship with other Foreign Ministry officials, particularly those of the "Q," or security branch. And from them, he learned that his friend Pontecorvo was being watched. That much is known, though it has been suppressed by the British. It is also known that this information was conveyed to Pontecorvo, though there is no "hard" evidence that MacLean was the messenger of mercy. Since MacLean was in communication with the Soviet apparatus in England, it is conceivable that he did not himself warn Pontecorvo. A word to his superiors would have been transmitted to the Center in Moscow, which would have had no difficulty in relaying news of this dangerous state of affairs to Pontecorvo. It has been established that he knew and that he inadvertently gave away this knowledge in a number of cryptic remarks he made to friends in June and July of 1950. They were of an *ave atque vale* nature: "I hope we will someday play again," to a tennis partner, as if in farewell; his wife's behavior at a party shortly before they departed on July 26, 1950 for a "vacation" in Europe (she burst into tears when saying what should have been a casual *au revoir* to their hosts). But this was nothing to cause Scotland Yard to appear on the double or to do more than puzzle friends.

Optimist and extrovert, Bruno Pontecorvo believed that once out of England, he would be safe. He counted for protection on his well-founded reputation as western Europe's leading experimental nuclear physicist and on the British propensity to avoid scandal wherever possible. Universities in France or Italy, he believed, would not be shocked or intimidated by rumors that he was a Communist, and the British government was in no position to make a public announcement that he was an atom spy—a charge that would lay it open to cries of McCarthyism from the opposition and from the back benches. And so Bruno and Marianne Pontecorvo, with their three children, set out on a camping trip on the Continent. Offers from his friends to lend him equipment were surprisingly turned down, although Pontecorvo was a great borrower. One friend had some francs in Paris, which he offered to trade Pontecorvo for British pounds, the transaction to be completed on his return. But Bruno insisted on paying cash then and there. Wing Commander Arnold knew of the Pontecorvos' departure, but he made no effort to stop them. Later, British security pleaded that it had no right to prevent a British subject from leaving the island—but as any police officer can attest, a thousand excuses could have been found. It was simply assumed that he would return.

To do otherwise would not be cricket. The Pontecorvos contributed to that belief by leaving most of their possessions behind, including £165 in a British bank, £1,714 in Montreal, and no provisions for Bruno's share of the patent suit against the United States government.

Scotland Yard and its European counterparts have traced the erratic course of the Pontecorvos as they moved in Europe, southeast toward Italy. The details are of no real significance except to the dossier-makers. Of interest here are several observations. First, the family drove in Bruno's Vanguard Standard (license number NVC 744), a car of which he was inordinately proud. Second, they traveled very light. Third, he carried with him a brown zipper briefcase which he kept at his side at all times, with a zealousness noted by porters and by those few friends who have come forward to describe his actions. The Pontecorvos stopped briefly at Ladispoli, a resort town near Rome where Giuliana Tabet had taken a house for the summer, leaving their youngest child with her. Then they proceeded to Circeo, a coastal town south of Anzio, where Bruno intended to spend some time skin-diving among the submerged Roman ruins.

It was at Circeo, named after Circe, that Bruno Pontecorvo heard the siren call. On his thirty-seventh birthday, August 22, 1950, he was visited by Gilberto, his Communist functionary brother. The two men conferred long and seriously in what has been described as a "council of war." During this meeting Bruno Pontecorvo was either convinced or coerced into believing that the finger of exposure was about to be pointed at him, that he would not be safe anywhere in western Europe, and that his only recourse was to flee behind the Iron Curtain, where he would be welcomed, praised, and given an important post in the Soviet Union's nuclear research project. Those who have delved long and minutely into the events of those days are certain that the threat of Communist blackmail was waved delicately before his eyes should he decide to bluff it out by remaining in France or Italy.

Whether he was induced by the carrot or beaten by the stick, Pontecorvo agreed on that day to the plans the Center had made for him. That he was not happy about them is a matter of record. The evidence shows that from this point on, he seemed preoccupied and worried. His easygoing manner disappeared, and he became curt and irritable. The following day, he had a minor accident with his car and insisted on driving to Rome to have it repaired. The excuse was a thin one; the work on the car could have been done by any mechanic in a few hours. But Pontecorvo was needed in Rome for further planning of his flight. He returned to Circeo, gathered up his family and drove to Ladispoli to pick up his youngest child. Giuliana cut short her escape from the heat of Rome to return with him, and there were further conferences at her house on Via Gabi. Gilberto, too, was present at this gathering of the Communist side of the Pontecorvo clan.

Bruno had promised to meet his parents at Chamonix, in France, on his return trip—a visit which would combine pleasure with the business of inspecting a scientific laboratory with which Harwell was exchanging information on cosmic rays. But this side trip was abruptly, almost rudely, canceled in a letter to the elder Pontecorvos, which flatly stated that the children were not well. "It is not possible to come to Chamonix," he wrote "as we shall have no time, and it would tire the children." On August 29, he appeared with Marianne at the Rome office of the Scandinavian Airways System to book a one-way passage for himself (under his own name) and for his wife and three children (under the name of Nordblom-Pontecorvo). While he was talking to the airlines clerk, Marianne, thoroughly distraught and haggard, dragged him away from the counter, and the two were observed in a heated discussion. When he returned to the clerk, he asked that his own ticket be changed to include a return trip.

The transaction completed, Pontecorvo was unable to pay for the tickets in cash and asked that he be permitted to return the next day. But there was another hitch. The airline would not accept Italian currency. An angry Pontecorvo returned a few hours later with ten crisp one-hundred-dollar bills, somewhat startling the clerk, with which to pay the required $602. A careful investigation by British and Italian authorities shows that he neither cashed a check for that sum nor converted lire for American bills. On August 31, he wrote to his superiors in Harwell complaining of "plenty of car trouble," promising to be back in England by September 7, apologizing for his failure to make an appearance at Chamonix, and ending, "Good-by, everybody."

From the scene at the SAS office, it is reasonable to assume that Pontecorvo had not at that time told his wife that he was planning to defect. Obviously, he had said only that he was leaving her and the children with the Nordbloms in Stockholm and returning to Rome on business. On September 1, the Pontecorvos boarded a plane in Rome. When they put down in Munich, they remained on board. They arrived in Stockholm at 8:50 P.M., and Bruno made inquiries about hotel accommodations. The apparatus was, however, taking no chances that Marianne Nordblom-Pontecorvo might call family or friends. That night, the family was held virtually incommunicado at one of the party's "halfway houses," where agents in transit can hide out. On September 2, the Pontecorvo family flew from Stockholm to Helsinki. Since they had no visas, their passports were impounded. Bruno was asked to fill out routine forms in which he stated that the purpose of the trip was "tourism," that they expected to remain in Finland for one week, and that their passports could be returned to them at a local hotel. He refused coach service from the airport to the city, and the family luggage, eleven valises, were piled into a large black Buick sedan with diplomatic license plates. It was shortly after 3 P.M. that Bruno Pontecorvo, still clutching the bulging brown briefcase, helped his family into the car and climbed in.

The Buick took off in the direction of Porkkala, a Soviet enclave near Helsinki, which has its own landing strip for military planes. And that was the last time that Bruno Pontecorvo was seen west of the Iron Curtain. Later, passengers on the Stockholm-Helsinki flight told British Intelligence that the youngest Pontecorvo boy had loudly announced that he was on the way to see the Soviet Union and had repeatedly asked, "Is that Russia down there?" A British report quotes Pontecorvo as having blurted out to a friend, shortly before his disappearance, "I dare not go back." Every effort, however, was made to keep the defection quiet as long as possible and to confuse efforts to determine where and how Bruno Pontecorvo had gone. Though Pontecorvo had been expected at Harwell on the seventh, it was not until September 21 that the British authorities began to investigate his disappearance. Giuliana Tabet, when questioned, stated that the Pontecorvos had been living with her until September 6,—or for five days after they had boarded the plane for Stockholm. She added that on leaving Bruno told her he was driving back through France at a leisurely pace. But she contradicted her story by adding that she had later received a letter from him asking her to pay for the garaging of his Vanguard Standard and also to arrange for its shipment to England. (The car was later found by police in a Rome garage, stripped of its license plates and other identifying marks.)

It was not until October 20, 1950, that the British authorities finally made public a terse account of Pontecorvo's disappearance. The Soviet minister in Helsinki, Lieutenant General G. M. Savenenkov, immediately warned the Finnish government that any publicity about Pontecorvo would be "very unwelcome" to his government. By that time, Scotland Yard and MI-5, working with the police forces of Europe, had traced the movements of Bruno and his family to Malino airport in Helsinki and to the Buick which took them in the direction of Porkkala. But the government continued to argue that it had no idea of Pontecorvo's whereabouts, nor even that he had gone to the Soviet Union. Reports that he was behind the Iron Curtain gathering together a staff of nuclear scientists from the captive nations, that he was working on an atomic project in Sinkiang, and that he was seen at scientific gatherings in Moscow were brushed aside as rumor by British authorities determined to minimize their failure to keep a watch on Pontecorvo after he was under suspicion.

It was Bruno Pontecorvo, looking grim and emotionally weary, who eventually announced to the world from Moscow that he had defected to the Communists "because of Hiroshima." He did not explain why he would continue his nuclear researches in the Soviet Union or, on December 13, 1958, accept from his masters the Lenin Prize for constructing a ten-billion electron volt synchrophastron—an atomic particle accelerator. Nor would he comment on the information he bequeathed to the Communists—his highly expert knowledge of the Chalk River atomic installations, the solution to problems encountered by the United States in the construction of its plutonium pile at Hanford, or the theory and practice he had picked up at Harwell.

In a way, what he gave to the apparatus during his years in Canada and Great Britain, or what he put down on paper when he reached Moscow, was secondary to the gift of his brilliant and inventive mind. He was, according to his former colleagues, one of the greatest experimental physicists—and Dr. Fermi would note, in a devastating understatement, that Pontecorvo "might be very valuable to Russia" for "his general scientific competence."

But though the Pontecorvo defection, coming hard on the heels of the Fuchs confession, disturbed the British, they were to be truly rocked by what followed. The impact was so great that, for a few weeks, they ceased their barrage of sardonic remarks about America's fear of Communist treason. The cause of this traumatic experience was the disappearance behind the Iron Curtain of two young men, British-born and educated at the best schools, not tainted by the accident of foreign birth, and of good family. That subconscious disdain and suspicion of all those not born British had cushioned the shock of Fuchs and Pontecorvo. Nunn May had been bad enough, but he had taken his medicine and remained in England. The case of Guy Burgess and Donald MacLean opened for England, if only briefly, a view of the nature of Communist perfidy.

Guy Burgess figures in this account only tangentially. He was a spy, but there is no evidence that he ever had access to atomic secrets. He is mentioned only because of his political, personal, and sexual association with Donald MacLean. Beyond this, he is one more skeleton that the British regret did not remain in the closet. For he is living proof of the conviction among English intellectuals that the most conclusive evidence of a man's non-communism is his confession that he is a Communist. Cyril Connolly, the British author and critic, recounts that, in the days before World War II, a very close friend of Burgess was startled by an almost incredible conversation. "Guy had confided to him," Connolly wrote blandly, "that he was not only a member but a secret agent of the Communist Party, and he had then invited him to join this work." Nevertheless, when the war broke out, he was given a sensitive position in MI-6—the British equivalent of the Office of Strategic Services. After the war, he was posted to the United States as Second Secretary to the British Embassy. This appointment came after a severe reprimand for divulging "secret matters about which he had official knowledge." His cardinal sin, however, was in lending himself to anti-British talk. But before any action could be taken against him, he had disappeared with MacLean. To the very last, he was talking about "those horrible American purges." *

Donald MacLean had a somewhat similar, though more devastating, record. His father, Sir Donald MacLean, had been a distinguished statesman, respected by King George V and the Parliament until the day of his death. His son, therefore, could trade on that patrimony of honor. And to the very end, after his treason had been established, there were British leaders who sought

---

* The poet W. H. Auden, who knew Burgess for years, told a *London Daily Express* reporter *after* the defection: "Burgess was an open Communist in the 1930's . . . While he was at the Embassy in Washington he was still pro-Communist." Obviously, like a betrayed wife, Scotland Yard was the last to know.

ways to exculpate him—and themselves for tolerating his behavior. Despite his aggressive Communist activities at Cambridge—and his professed need for what he called an occasional drinking "orgy"— he was considered the "golden boy" of the Foreign Service. His very first assignment in 1938, to Paris, was a plum. He gravitated quickly to the Left Bank and to the Café de Floré, Bruno Pontecorvo's hangout, where the two became friends. It was at this emporium of liquor and phony art that he met Melinda Marling, an American heiress who was willing to marry and support him— and eventually to give up everything in order to join him in his Muscovite captivity. In 1944, he was assigned to the United States as First Secretary to the British Embassy.

Despite his heavy drinking and homosexuality—traits he shared with Burgess—and the irregularity of his family life (Melinda lived with her family in New York while he maintained "bachelor" quarters in Washington) he was given one of the most important and sensitive posts available to a British diplomat in wartime Washington—secretary of the Combined Policy Committee on Atomic Development, with a top-priority pass admitting him to all nuclear installations at any hour of the day or night. In this post, he was fully informed on all exchanges of atomic data between the United States and Great Britain. He happily forwarded what he knew to the Zubilin apparatus working out of the Soviet Embassy. What scientific data he was able to absorb is still being debated. But he was able to tell the Soviets, in the years after the Hiroshima explosion, how many atomic bombs the United States had in its arsenal, what the production rate and schedule of these bombs were, and how much uranium had been stockpiled—all matters of acute interest to the Center in Moscow.*

In 1948, MacLean was transferred to Cairo with a promotion

* The *Daily Express* stated, after MacLean's defection, that he was "head of Chancery in Washington, the man who decides who sees the telegrams: and head of the American desk in London, the man who sees and drafts the telegrams as they go." No wonder, the *Daily Express* commented, that Secretary of State Dean Acheson exclaimed, "My God, he knew everything."

to Counselor of the Embassy. The Egyptian police complained
that he associated with known Soviet espionage agents, but nothing was done. Then, in 1950, on one of his periodic "orgies," he
assaulted an armed watchman and broke the leg of a fellow British
diplomat. Two months later, he broke into the apartment of a
friend, drank up all the available liquor, smashed the furniture,
and wrecked the bathtub. For this bit of fun, he was sent home
on sick leave, and punished by being ordered to consult a psychiatrist. When he returned to the Foreign Office, after a week's
drinking, he was immediately appointed head of the American
Department. One day a friend called Cyril Connolly, the unmoved
repository of this kind of confidence, to say that, in his cups,
MacLean had blurted out, "What would you do if I told you I was
a Communist agent? Well, I am. Go on, report me." The friend
and Connolly agreed that the idea was "preposterous."

Again, in April 1951, MacLean pummeled an associate who
had spoken against Alger Hiss. "I'm the English Hiss," MacLean
said before he stalked off. The Foreign Office, which was then
seeking to discover who in its midst was giving the Soviets secret
information, did nothing. Even after it had narrowed the suspects
down to three men, including Burgess and MacLean, it refused to
act. On May 26, 1951, the two men disappeared. When the story
of their defection leaked to the British press, the stock excuse
was given: The British government had no right to detain either
man. As more than one irate member of Parliament remarked:
Two atom spies, MacLean and Pontecorvo, were allowed to escape
to the Soviet Union because a handful of civil servants had been
too timid to do their duty.

XIV

The AEC's Early War Against Security

AT the end of World War II, the United States had the most powerful Army, Navy and Air Force in history. No other country could match America in what came to be known as "conventional" weapons. In its military arsenal, moreover, was the atomic bomb. And on the drawing board, there were plans for the far more powerful hydrogen or "super" bomb. An arrogant or imperialist nation could have, with this tremendous power at its disposal, dictated the terms of victory. A wise nation would have imposed the kind of durable peace which could not be threatened by the Soviet Union. It is no twenty-twenty hindsight to note that had the nation's leaders bothered to read the signs, they would have known Stalin was already preparing to parlay the defeat of the Axis powers into the first steps toward Soviet hegemony.*

* Professor Philip E. Mosely, who served in the State Department and was an adviser at both the Moscow Conference in 1943 and the Potsdam Conference, has written of "the reversal of the Soviet 'party line' that had already been put into effect in November 1944. From that time on, Soviet propaganda . . . returned to the harsh insistence that while one enemy, Hitler, had been beaten, the main enemy, capitalism, had yet to be destroyed."

But the United States, succumbing to pressure from those who wanted a quick "return to normalcy," began immediately to scrap its Armed Forces. A small but vocal group sought to panic President Truman into making all nuclear secrets public, taking the world's most powerful weapon out of the hands that fashioned it. Simultaneously, there was a loud demand for "internationalization" of atomic energy by the delivery of American know-how and the Manhattan Project installations to the United Nations. President Truman was never fully convinced that the United States should divest itself of the advantage it held by a monopoly in atomic bombs. But the campaign was so persistent—and it reached up so high into his Administration—that Mr. Truman's freedom of action was inhibited and his thinking, for a time, confused.

As late as 1949, Representative Chet Holifield, vice chairman of the Joint Congressional Atomic Energy Committee, was still railing against "trigger-happy admirals and generals" who, he deplored, "want to take over the bomb, both as to production and custody." His cry of "wolf" was unnecessary, for the Atomic Energy Act had codified the surrender to civilians of Los Alamos, the Argonne National Laboratory, Hanford, and other former MED installations. The wisdom of this move can be endlessly debated. But on one aspect of the act, there can be general agreement. By taking Atomic Energy Commission security from Army bureaucrats who failed to understand the problem and turning it over to the Federal Bureau of Investigation, the nation had raised its guard appreciably. The voluminous security files of the MED were taken from the AEC, and the FBI was empowered to make a check on all the personnel who transferred from the older organization to the newly created civilian body.*

* Review of security cases was mandatory where derogatory information was found in the files. This, rather than any baleful influences, was responsible for the Oppenheimer hearings. The FBI presented to the AEC what it had gathered together after a study of Oppenheimer's file and a full field investigation. At this point, it would have been a clear violation of the Congressional intent to ignore the charges against Oppenheimer. The first

Due process and due deliberation were to be exercised in evaluating derogatory evidence concerning the AEC personnel. At the same time, the Atomic Energy Act firmly stated that no nuclear information was to be divulged until Congress had approved some adequate system of international control. In short, the House and Senate were seeking to lock the stable door before any new horses were stolen. Key members had been quietly informed by Bernard Baruch—America's representative on atomic matters at the United Nations—of a report he had made to President Truman: The Soviet Purchasing Commission had ordered $1.5 million worth of special equipment in this country, using blueprints and specifications which the experts recognized immediately as coming unmistakably from the MED. Some months after this disclosure, Isaac Don Levine, writing for *Plain Talk,* asserted: "It is no longer a secret that Mr. Baruch used his influence to stop the execution of this order, which made him the special target of the Soviet diplomats [at the U.N.] as well as of the pro-Soviet elements in our midst." *

(Baruch's discovery of the Soviet Union's wholesale pillaging of American atomic secrets confirmed the evidence adduced by Western scientists from their discussions with Soviet counterparts. As noted earlier in this account, Soviet nuclear science even employed the same technical neologisms that the men of Los Alamos, Oak Ridge, and Chalk River had invented and thought secret.)

Locking the stable door at this time was, of course, essential. Nuclear physics as applied to bomb technology was still an infant science. It was more than regrettable that the atomic scientists,

---

moves, therefore, were inaugurated by a Democratic Administration and came to a culmination in 1954, when the wheels could no longer be stopped. Even had Dr. Oppenheimer been among the stoutest proponents of the H-bomb—and he was just the opposite—it would have been impossible to avoid confronting him with what the files showed and then coming to a determination as to his fitness to retain a "Q" clearance.

* Levine, who has probably had more close contacts with former Soviet espionage agents than any other American journalist, estimates that during the MED period the NKVD had some one hundred agents scattered throughout the American-Canadian atomic project.

overriding common sense and seized by a kind of hysteria, had been able to catch President Truman off-balance and get his assent to the immediate release of the Smyth Report, *Atomic Energy for Military Purposes.* Why it was necessary to publish anything, before the world and the nation had recovered from its astonishment over the Hiroshima bombing, has never been fully explained. At the time—just four days after the advent of the Atomic Age— many scientists argued that this detailed and invaluable guidebook to the military uses of nuclear power told nothing that any physicist did not know. If this was so, then why the hurry? But it was not so. As David Lilienthal, one of the strongest "no-secrecy" advocates testified, the Smyth Report was "the principal breach of security since the beginning of the atomic energy enterprise." And the *Bulletin of the Atomic Scientists,* which propagandized for the elimination of secrecy, was constrained to admit that the "revelation that plutonium can be and was fabricated in large plants, that it can be and was used for filling bombs, was in no way urgent, and an invitation to engineers abroad to try to duplicate processes which they know to be successful." The Smyth Report did far more than that—as the Soviets themselves publicly acknowledged after the arrest of Allan Nunn May.

The Atomic Energy Act as finally written was designed to prevent repetitions of this sorry haste as the United States, now divorced from its British and Canadian junior partners, looked ahead. But no law is any better than the men who administer it. The first chairman of the Atomic Energy Commission was Lilienthal, recommended to that post by Undersecretary of State Dean Acheson and appointed without the knowledge (and to the consternation) of both Secretary James F. Byrnes and Bernard Baruch. Lilienthal was an excellent administrator and a most persuasive man. (Harold Ickes once described him as "the busiest propagandist the United States has ever produced.") But he was given to strong views and an inflexibility of mind. As coauthor with Acheson of a report on the international control of atomic energy, he had run head-on into Baruch, who demanded safeguards before the United States surrendered its monopoly in atomic weapons. The Baruch view prevailed with President Truman, but not before Lilienthal had delivered himself of this involuted piece of logic:

When the [Acheson-Lilienthal] plan is in full operation there will no longer be secrets about atomic energy. We believe that this is the firmest basis of security; for in the long term there can be no international control and no international cooperation which does not presuppose international community of knowledge.

Yet Lilienthal was chosen to administer law which in its language and intent insisted on continued secrecy and set up machinery for preserving it. If the United States was to maintain its lead and to checkmate Soviet espionage efforts to keep pace with new American discoveries and technologies—and if the FBI's counter-measures were to be successful—a man less antagonistic to these purposes should have been selected.

Much had already been accomplished simply by announcing that henceforward the FBI would be entrusted with the task of surveillance. The Center in Moscow, whose opinion of the Bureau has always been high, immediately called a temporary halt to the activities of its various apparatuses in this country. Soviet "diplomatic" officials, who had been doubling in brass as "legal" *apparatchiks,* were suddenly recalled, and the "illegals" were ordered to "go private" until the Center had surveyed the situation and regrouped its forces. Though there have been, since the passage of the Atomic Energy Act, several hundred minor infractions of security regulations and a number of major attempts at espionage, the FBI was able to prevent depredations on the previous scale. In 1951, the Joint Congressional Atomic Energy Committee reported:

Since mid-1946, when the law creating the joint committee and the Atomic Energy Commission was enacted, American espionage defenses, so far as is known, have not been breached. The Federal

Bureau of Investigation and other interested agencies have reported no successful act of atomic espionage committed against the United States from mid-1946 onward.

It was not for want of trying. For the Center in Moscow, which presumably "knew everything"—making further espionage unnecessary—devoted endless time and buckets of money (and incurred considerable risk) to penetrate the FBI shield. As of May 1, 1960, there were six hundred Soviet and Soviet-bloc officials in the United States, with 890 "dependents" to act as auxiliaries. A host of defectors from the Communist empire have documented their agreement that between 70 and 80 per cent of these "diplomats" had full or part-time Intelligence assignments. Since 1952, moreover, the Center in Moscow increasingly stressed the use of "illegals"—agents without diplomatic immunity—in conducting its "deep-cover" espionage affairs. Not all of them, of course, were assigned to nuclear work. But an FBI study of Soviet espionage, prepared early in 1960 to be used by Ambassador Henry Cabot Lodge in countering Soviet breast-beating over the U-2 incident, lifted the curtain briefly on the Center's continued onslaught:

For example, the prosecution of Judith Coplon, an employee of the Department of Justice in early 1950, was followed in October 1950 by a Soviet assignment to Boris Morros, an American motion-picture producer who was cooperating with the FBI, to revive his acquaintance with a member of the United States Atomic Energy Commission to obtain compromising information concerning this individual; and to carefully explore the possibility of placing a secretary in his office who could furnish information to the Russians . . .

From July 1955 through May 1956, [Assistant Soviet Military Attaché Ivan Aleksandrovich] Bubchikov maintained contact with a naturalized American citizen of Russian origin who was employed as a sales engineer. In July 1955, [Bubchikov] appeared at the sales engineer's residence late in the evening and sought his cooperation in securing data concerning jet fuel, atomic submarines, and aeronautical developments . . . This operation . . . was featured by clandestine meetings, complex recognition signals, and a variety of "drop areas" in which the source deposited [seemingly important material prepared by the FBI] for the Soviet . . .

In August of 1955, [Assistant Soviet Military Attaché Yuri Pavlovich] Krylov contacted an employee of the Atomic Energy Commission and attempted to obtain from him information concerning the technical aspects of nuclear power. In December 1955, he contacted a former commissioner of the Atomic Energy Commission in an effort to develop information concerning atomic energy for space heating. In February 1956, he attempted to purchase 26 unclassified films on peace-time atomic energy.*

The FBI's job was to protect the Atomic Energy Commission and its installations from spies. In the days of Lilienthal's hegemony, the Bureau's work was hardly facilitated by an attitude of aloofness amounting almost to hostility at the AEC. The administrators and many of the scientists took an even dimmer view of the FBI than they had of military security agencies. The AEC, moreover, by its curious reading of the Atomic Energy Act, suspended security procedures, took it upon itself to broadcast the products of nuclear research, and in general sought to act as a law unto itself. Lilienthal, appearing before the Joint Congressional Committee, defended these practices as in the national interest. And it might well be argued that behind these actions was nothing more than the stubborn belief on the part of Chairman Lilienthal that all secrets must be internationalized—but they hardly made the FBI's work easier.

In security matters, Lilienthal shared the views of many scientists that he knew better than the FBI—and in brushing aside one derogatory report, he resorted to the old chestnut that it was based

* The FBI could divulge this information because Morros had "surfaced" to become a government witness in several espionage trials. Krylov and Bubchikov had been declared *persona non grata* by the State Department for violation of their diplomatic status. Other, and similar, cases remain secret. It is preferable to keep a known agent under surveillance so that he may lead the FBI to his contacts and thereby expose them.

on information furnished by a "nine-year-old." (Though pressed, he never gave chapter-and-verse.) Lilienthal testified under oath in 1948, moreover, that the AEC in effect frequently bypassed the required FBI check of personnel by authorizing "emergency" clearances. In other instances, scientists and technicians were assigned to secret projects before the FBI check was completed. In practice, this AEC policy was no favor, and it worked real hardship on many of those concerned. They sold their homes, moved their families, and took up jobs which they considered permanent only to be told that clearance had been refused. If the accounts later published by the *Bulletin of Atomic Scientists* are to be believed, the AEC under Lilienthal refused to give them any explanation or the detailed statement of charges to which they were entitled. Blame was vaguely placed on the shoulders of the FBI, further increasing the antisecurity bias of the scientific community.

Though by 1947 the nature of the Communist conspiracy and its assault on United States atomic secrets had been well publicized and thoroughly documented by the Gouzenko documents, the Atomic Energy Commission, at Lilienthal's behest and according to his later testimony, gave clearance to Dr. Edward U. Condon (whose associations have been described in this narrative) and to Dr. Frank P. Graham, despite the adverse recommendation of the AEC's own director of security. Dr. Graham's file probably shows nothing more than several "front" associations and an embattled ignorance of the Communist threat. This determination on his part to think no ill of Communists was demonstrated in a speech he delivered in 1949, reported by the International News Service:

Senator Frank P. Graham declared today that it has not been proven that American Communists are disloyal to the United States. The former North Carolina University president explained that so-called liberal thinkers in this nation are not convinced that a Communist is necessarily un-American. He said the nation's "liberal" element is "groping" to discover if United States Communists really take direct and unquestioned orders from Moscow. As one of the gropers, Graham mentioned Atomic Energy Commission chairman David Lilienthal.

This antagonistic attitude toward counterespionage on Lilienthal's part was earlier demonstrated when, for the first eight months of his tenure as AEC chairman, he failed to appoint any director of security. The post was finally filled by a man who had no background in security matters or procedures, whatever his other merits. In evaluating AEC research fellows, the official in charge, when asked if he had passed on the Communist background of some of the applicants—a relevant factor in making any determination—stated: "I have no competence in that field."

In those critical and formative years, there was very little check of the truth of statements made on the standard Personnel Security Questionnaire. The employee in charge of the U-235 vault, it was later discovered, had been arrested for grand larceny but had failed to state this fact—a punishable offense. Instead of being summarily fired or disciplined, he was simply transferred to other duties. The general laxity was demonstrated by a May 10, 1949, AEC memorandum to all guards at the Argonne National Laboratory. Subject: "Persons allowed unlimited access to property." The memorandum stated:

The following persons *and their guests* will be allowed *unlimited access to all areas of the property at all times* upon identification of themselves. [Emphasis added.]

When security procedures were set up for the AEC, they were so cumbersome and complex that it required a Navy cartographer to put them into chart form. They were still incomprehensible— at least to Chairman Brien McMahon of the Joint Atomic Energy Committee—and required the attention of some twenty to thirty different offices, with no clear indication of final authority on the granting of clearances. As one senator, who studied the chart, said, "Well, you can figure that after going through the maze, if you're entitled to clearance, you'll come out. But if you're not entitled, you can keep going around in circles forever." Given this situation, it is a tribute to the FBI that no major espionage took place under the Lilienthal stewardship. When the Joint Atomic Energy Committee investigated charges by Senator Bourke Hickenlooper of "incredible mismanagement" of the AEC, it was also discovered that physical security at atomic installations was almost a joke.

Special investigators were sent to the various AEC sites. They wandered about, put machined parts and other classified materials in their pockets, and wandered out again with no search or check. One investigator carried out two uranium slugs in his pocket. When these facts were broadcast to the public, Merle E. Smith, president of the Guards' Union, Local 21, at Hanford, wrote in defense of his fellow guards, giving a startling picture of physical security procedures:

Various news items have accented the fact that two uranium slugs were carried by an individual through three guard posts with guards on duty. As a result, in the minds of many people, the Hanford guards are pictured as inefficient and guilty of failure in performance of their duty . . .

I do not believe that there is a single patrolman or patrol officer on the Hanford works guard who has not been appalled at the security laxness which has existed for some time and still exists. Unfortunately, patrol supervision is allowed little or no voice in the policies laid down for the security of this plant. These policies are drawn up by the Security Department . . .

How could a man walk through three guard posts carrying two slugs of uranium? At two of these posts, there are no orders calling for a search of persons entering or leaving. At only one of these posts may a superficial spot search be made. By superficial, I mean a pat search. Spot searching means the searching of perhaps one out of five individuals. For the past year, even this type of search has been practically discontinued . . .

Some weeks ago some 20 per cent of the Hanford patrol force was terminated by order of the security departments. As a consequence of these terminations, we are very short-handed and, of necessity, posts have been undermanned or not manned at all. Suggestions both verbal and written have been offered by both patrolmen and patrol officers, pointing out security weaknesses . . . *

But the biggest gap between the intent of Congress in setting up the Atomic Energy Commission and the performance under Lilienthal was found to be in the exchange of atomic information and the shipment of radioactive isotopes to foreign countries. It had been made legally clear in the Atomic Energy Act that there was to be "no exchange of information with other nations for industrial purposes." No radioactive isotopes were to be released by the AEC except for clearly determined medical purposes such as research and therapy. The AEC chairman, following his own personal beliefs, decided that there was no secrecy about isotopes and that nothing could be gained by not shipping them to other countries, even if the purpose was not the saving of human life. This became established policy, so that on April 28, 1949, a shipment of isotopes went to the Norwegian Defense Research Establishment, to be used for a study of steel and iron under high temperatures in jets, rockets, and artillery. (Prior to this, the AEC had allocated isotopes to Frédéric Joliot-Curie, the Communist physicist in France.)

This shipment to the Norwegian Defense Research Establishment, significantly enough, had been strongly opposed by the General Advisory Council of the AEC, a special group made up of Doctors Oppenheimer, Isadore Rabi, Conant, Fermi, and others with experience in the atomic energy project dating back to the pre-MED days. Lilienthal, when confronted with the facts, argued at first that

* Among the suggestions made by the patrol officers to the Security Department: a request that the men at guard posts be given some sort of briefing in order to know what they should search for. It was found that none of the guards had ever seen a uranium slug or had one described to him.

isotopes had only been shipped for medical research and then insisted that the Norwegians could have gotten them from European cyclotrons. His climaxing argument: a refusal to release the radio-active isotopes would have caused scientists overseas to "become disaffected in their attitude toward the United States." It was further noted that four of the five AEC commissioners voted for the shipment, with Lewis L. Strauss failing to concur on the ground that it "oversteps its (AEC's) statutory provisions."

But it was Dr. Oppenheimer who destroyed Lilienthal's argument that the isotopes for military purposes were as easily available from European cyclotrons. He pointed out that more than two hundred millicuries of Carbon 14 had been produced at Oak Ridge, or millions of times more than the amount available prior to that time. This Carbon 14 had cost the United States only ten thousand dollars, but it would take, Oppenheimer said, one thousand cyclotrons to equal this output—and the cost would be one hundred million dollars. Not noted in the debate was the danger of broadening the target area for Soviet agents. It was subsequently discovered that the Norwegian official who requested the isotopes had been forced to resign because he was a Communist agent.

The "why-take-precautions" attitude rampant among those entrusted with the husbanding of America's atomic resources—aided and abetted by the systematic campaign of those who simultaneously believed that the world's safety depended on sharing all nuclear data with the Soviet Union though there were no secrets left to share—may have accounted for the almost jaunty manner in which the still unsolved "Mystery of the Missing Uranium" was handled. The history of the world was not deflected from its course by the theft, loss, or problematical recovery of some forty-two grams of enriched uranium oxide. But the case posed some very serious questions which have yet to be answered. There are men in the United States Senate who hold to the view that the AEC's explanation, offered by a platoon of officials, was more ingenious than convincing. And if the AEC's tortured account was, in fact, accurate, it opened the lid to a Pandora's box of new charges which were never answered. The facts, as stated by Senator Hickenlooper, were these:

1. A container of about 9 or 10 ounces of uranium oxide enriched with 32 grams of uranium 235 was discovered missing at the Argonne National Laboratory, Chicago, on February 8, 1949.*

The AEC Chairman, David E. Lilienthal, has attempted to minimize this quantity. He has sneered at the nation's "four-gram jitters." The truth is that for research in the field of weapon development, this is a vast quantity of this precious material. Dr. Allan Nunn May, the British scientist, drew a ten-year prison sentence for stealing one one-thousandth of a gram of U-235; and we began building Hanford before we had as much as is still missing.

2. The AEC, in direct violation of its duty, did not notify the Federal Bureau of Investigation of this loss until March 28, 1949.

Mr. Lilienthal has declared that there was no suspicion of theft or espionage. This is completely untrue. The FBI was called in *only* because there was suspicion of theft and espionage; and though the trail was completely cold, the FBI made its investigation on the assumption of theft and espionage.

3. The AEC did not notify the chairman of the (Joint) Congressional Committee until April 27, 1949, though the law requires that such notification be made immediately.

4. When this loss was reported publicly on May 17, 1949, by the New York *Daily News,* Mr. Lilienthal replied that the loss was trivial and that it was being partially recovered from "waste." ... But there is no satisfactory evidence that what is now being reclaimed is, indeed, from the missing parcel.

We have no conclusive evidence that a theft has been committed;

---

* The AEC, in announcing the loss, stated that the uranium had been contained in "a brown bottle." Subsequently, it announced that the "brown bottle" had been found. But in its full report to the Joint Atomic Energy Committee, the AEC presented a clear Mason jar as the receptacle in question. Despite an FBI report that a majority of those questioned had stated that the container had been "a brown bottle," the AEC insisted that this was an error based on the fallible recollections of "eyewitnesses." This is one of the many puzzling aspects of the controversy.

but neither do we have conclusive evidence that a theft has not been committed.

The AEC's explanation, somewhat elusively stated by Dr. Walter Zinn, director of the Argonne Laboratory, presented a different picture. Dr. Zinn said that the bottle—whether brown or clear—had been locked in a storage vault. When orders were given to ship all uranium to a central deposit, an inventory was made of the materials in the vault. The inventory showed that the bottle of missing uranium was included and had been shipped. Zinn insisted that it was "fairly certain" that, despite the written evidence, the bottle had remained behind, but he could account for this lapse only by adding that "the young man who did the packing clearly was not capable at the time of understanding the figures well enough to know that he had left something out." It is a matter of record that no discrepancy was discovered at the receiving end. Zinn called this "a hole in the inventory system." He argued that no check had been made when the material was stored in the central deposit. He conceded that it had always been customary to make an inventory at the sending and receiving ends of other shipments—but not in this case.

The "transfer" from the original vault took place on September 16, 1948. The loss was not discovered until February 7, 1949, when a careful check of the contents of the central deposit was made. "Very thorough searches showed that the bottle itself, so to speak, did not seem to exist," Zinn said. "No bottle carrying the right label or any type of description did exist anywhere." It was recalled, however, that twelve galvanized iron cans, holding the waste of uranium machining operations, were awaiting shipment to a special plant which recovers the pure metal from the debris. It was "surmised" that the contents of the missing bottle had been inadvertently dumped into the waste receptacles. By a highly technical process, samplings from the twelve cans were analyzed. It was then learned that one of the cans had four times the amount of U-235 the AEC considered "normal." By dissolving all the material in this can, the Oak Ridge Laboratory was able to "recover" 27.31 grams of U-235. No explanation was offered for the inability to recover the other four-plus grams—a sizable amount of U-235.

Zinn's account of "what might have happened" was accepted as proof of "what did happen." The AEC assured the committee and the public that these lax procedures for the handling and inventory of U-235 and other uranium products had been tightened so that it could not happen again. But this left the Atomic Energy Commission planted firmly on the horns of a dilemma. If the uranium was not stolen by a spy but simply mislaid due to carelessness, the AEC stood self-condemned of the "incredible mismanagement" that Senator Hickenlooper charged.

In the shipment of radioactive isotopes to the Norwegian Military Research Establishment, the committee majority shared Dr. Oppenheimer's view that "you could use a bottle of beer for atomic energy—in fact, you do," and that the AEC had not violated the letter or spirit of the law. In the case of the missing uranium, the committee majority accepted the AEC's account but did not condemn the carelessness it laid bare. The majority report found much to praise, almost nothing to criticize in the management of the AEC under Lilienthal. The minority report, signed by six Republicans, was moderately critical. It cited the abuses in security—highlighted some months later when, on August 22, 1950, a former Los Alamos scientist was arrested for stealing a glass vial of plutonium "as a souvenir," which he buried beneath his house. (The theft had occurred years earlier, but was discovered due to FBI vigilance.)

But the crux of the minority report was in two brief paragraphs touching on matters which would occupy the nation's attention and lead to the controversy over Dr. Oppenheimer and the aversion he shared with some of his scientific colleagues for continued advances in nuclear weaponry:

Since the establishment of the Commission, almost three years ago, it has been aware, through authoritative recommendations, of the pressing urgency of putting into action certain programs that will strengthen our reserve of atomic materials and aid the objective of capturing and having available for effective use the largest practicable degree of the power of those atomic materials for weapon and other purposes.

The Commission's approach to this supreme task has been leisurely, has been characterized by indecision, and a number of the most important of these recommended projects have not developed into operating plants.

Among those projects was the development of the hydrogen bomb. The "why" of the AEC's indecision in time divided Americans, stirred up the scientific community, and led to serious charges against Dr. Oppenheimer. Much of the debate on both sides was complex, technical, and given to red-herring techniques. The missing factor in any understanding of the issues, however, remained as always the inability of many people to grasp a series of propositions:

(1) The Soviet onslaught on the American monopoly of the atomic bomb was two-pronged—first to steal the secret and second to immobilize further development by the United States—in the latter instances employing Pavlovian techniques.

(2) By the very nature of the secondary onslaught, the Soviet Union's most effective troops would be men and women whose dedication to American principles and abhorrence of tyranny could not be questioned.

X V

Phase Two: Soviet Atomic Judo

ON July 16, 1945—the day the first atomic device was tested at Alamogordo—"a group of nuclear scientists met around a conference table in a small, hushed room in the Metallurgy Building of the University of Chicago." So begins a horror tale told months afterward by Dr. Robert M. Hutchins, later to win fortune and fame of a sort as head of the Fund for the Republic. The purpose of this meeting, according to Dr. Hutchins, was to organize politically, to suppress knowledge of the atomic bomb, and to urge that it never be used against the Japanese. "These men knew that once the bomb was dropped, once the world learned that fission chain reaction could be accomplished, atomic bombs could be produced by any reasonably advanced nation on earth, and that the end result could be annihilation of all life on this planet."

This apocryphal tale fits none of the known facts. The record shows that the atomic scientists exhibited exhilaration at their success, congratulating themselves that they had probably saved the lives of American boys preparing to storm the beaches of the Japanese homeland.* From the moment that they knew the bomb experiment would be successful, moreover, they itched to tell the world about it. In fact, five weeks before the "meeting" described by Hutchins, a group of seven scientists from the same laboratory had stated to Secretary of War Henry Stimson that "it would be foolish to retain our leadership in nucleonics by secrecy." While Nazi Germany was still fighting, the atomic scientists had grudgingly tolerated what security General Groves and the MED were able to impose. Once the Hitler regime had collapsed, the attitude at Los Alamos was exemplified by the words of a leading physicist to his approving colleagues: "We will say the opposite of what General Groves says, no matter what it is."

Much earlier, Dr. Leo Szilard—one of those who urged the development of the bomb and sought Albert Einstein to intercede with Franklin D. Roosevelt in aid of this purpose—had shifted to the position later adopted by many in the scientific community. In March 1945, according to the *Bulletin of the Atomic Scientists,* Szilard wrote to President Roosevelt making two somewhat curious points: (1) the atomic bomb would weaken the United States in its relations with the Soviet Union, and (2) the fear among scientists was not what the Germans might have done with the bomb but "what the government of the United States might do to other countries."

It is always dangerous to suggest that men of high principle have been manipulated. It is even more dangerous to point out that the manipulators were conscious instruments of a conspiracy, for by a kind of perverse reasoning this is taken to mean that the men of high principle were Communists. It is precisely because so many of the eminent scientists were *not* Communists—and in an untutored way opposed to communism—that the manipulators

* Dr. Kistiakowsky, according to one account, "threw his arms around Dr. Oppenheimer and embraced him with shouts of glee" after the Alamogordo test.

could operate.* In the middle and lower ranks of the scientific world, as this account has demonstrated, were men who ranged from dedicated party members to intellectually unco-ordinated fellow-travelers. They served as the Typhoid Marys among scientists unconsciously susceptible to the virus. Phase One of the Kremlin's strategy was to steal all the atomic secrets it could. Phase Two was to make use of the "confusion potential" among scientists to turn America's atomic strength against it by applying the techniques of judo. This is what happened, according to plans carefully made and excellently executed by the Kremlin.

This atomic judo was described by Henry A. Kissinger in *Nuclear Weapons and Foreign Policy,* written well after the Soviet Union had exploded its own devices and had shifted to an attempted strategy of atomic blackmail:

The Communist campaign, finely attuned to prevailing fears, almost imperceptibly shifted the primary concern away from Soviet aggression—the real security problem—to the immorality of the use of nuclear weapons, which happened to represent the most effective means of resisting it. Because of its skill in exploiting the inhibitions of the non-Soviet world, the Soviet Union has discovered two forms of "atomic blackmail": The threat of its growing nuclear arsenal and an appeal to the West's moral inhibitions. In either case the consequence is a lowered will to resist.

Phase Two, in its early stages, consisted of a vast campaign to convince America and the world that Hiroshima and Nagasaki had been a crime against humanity (as opposed, of course, to Stalin's planned liquidation of millions of peasants—which was "social engineering"), that further development of more powerful nuclear weapons must be stopped, and that all the data thus far amassed must be turned over to the United Nations for dissemination to

---

* Since no one likes to be called a dupe, the scientists involved have taken umbrage at this analysis and charge those who make it of questioning their loyalty.

the world. This was a time in which the scientists who had so eagerly contemplated the first bombs toured the country describing the terrors of atomic war, expressed horror over the fate of "unborn generations," organized themselves into a semi-hysterical lobby which descended on Washington, became the self-elected guardians of American conscience, and posed as the ultimate authorities on Soviet intentions and geopolitical strategy.

Since many of these scientists had world-wide reputations and visitors' cards to the highest government circles, their influence was pervasive. According to notes kept by Secretary of Commerce Henry A. Wallace of the September 21, 1945, meeting of the Truman Cabinet, Secretary of War Stimson reported then that scientists were urging:

... the free interchange of scientific information between different members of the United Nations. [Stimson] said that the scientists told him ... that future bombs would be infinitely more destructive ... He said some were afraid they would be so powerful as to ignite the atmosphere and put an end to the world.

The Walter Millis summary of the James Forrestal diaries states:

According to Forrestal's notes, (Wallace) was "completely, everlastingly and wholeheartedly in favor of giving [all atomic secrets] to the Russians ... Failure to give them our knowledge would make an embittered and sour people."

In the Senate, the battle was continued by Senator Claude Pepper, fresh from his triumphs before Communist-front audiences, who called on the United States to "destroy every atomic bomb we have" and to plow under all American atomic installations. One of the few in high government circles at that time who took Stalin at his word and who pointed out that the Soviets still believed that "the capitalistic and communistic concepts could not live together in the same world," was Secretary Forrestal. His suspicion of Soviet intentions and his insistence that the atomic bomb "belongs to the

American people" and should not be given away without national consent brought him the unrelenting attacks of political gossip columnists like Drew Pearson, the scientific community, and the dupes of Soviet manipulation. Forrestal subscribed to General Eisenhower's formulation, uttered at high-level Administration meetings, that "any agreement about atomic weapons without enforceable methods of inspection would be most dangerous for the United States."

Those who sided with Forrestal were not acting out of paranoid fear of the Soviet Union. They were fully aware of Stalin's intentions in regard to the atomic bomb which, at that time, Soviet scientists were feverishly working to build. The Millis summary of the Forrestal diaries spelled it out clearly:

Forrestal entered in his diary the gist of an Intelligence report on Soviet atomic strategy. This represented Soviet policy as one of pressing for disarmament and outlawry of atomic weapons on the world stage while refusing to allow any inspection of Russia's own atomic activities. The result would be to create a world opinion that would force the Western powers to disarm and drop their atomic development, permitting the Soviet Union to continue its own atomic operations while the West slept.

On one level, there was the open conspiracy as exemplified by obviously Soviet-motivated propaganda efforts. The Scientific and Cultural Conference, held at the Waldorf Astoria Hotel in New York in 1949, was clearly in this category. It was part and parcel of a well-financed drive which included the Stockholm "Peace" Appeal, presumably signed by millions of people—though most of them were behind the Iron Curtain—the Partisans for Peace which sprang up in France and Italy, the organized pickets who paraded before American embassies, the riots and demonstrations against the atomic bomb, and the Belgrade Conference of recent memory which roasted the United States for not agreeing to "atomic disarmament" on Soviet terms (in the interests of mankind's future) but hardly murmured when the Communists resumed massive atomic tests in the atmosphere.

On another level, there was the unscientific chatter of men with access to mass communications. Modern man, it suddenly developed, was obsolete because he still clung to the primitive notion that aggression must not go unanswered—or because he refused to forget the lesson of the Rhineland and Munich that appeasement is the surest road to war. Men superlatively trained in the disciplines of science cast them aside for an emotionalism easy to comprehend but somewhat harder to forgive. An atomic scientist told a correspondent for one of the news magazines, when they were on their way to the first (and by today's standards small) tests on Bikini Atoll: "This nuclear explosion, or one like it, can split the earth into two parts which will then orbit independently." Warnings of a runaway chain reaction which would obliterate the entire solar system appeared *ad infinitum* in the popular press. Science-fiction writers turned out scare novels by the dozens. One of these, written by a fellow-traveler, described the end of the world in 1960, as a result of American nuclear tests. Though the scientists then—and now—had little more than guesswork to back their predictions of a deformed population, the fear of "fallout"—that detritus of nuclear blasts—was everywhere expressed.

The first victory of Phase Two was the defeat of the May-Johnson bill—a demonstration of the validity of Senator Brien Mc-Mahon's rueful remark that "the scientists participated in the formation of our international policy." In this case, the participation was negative. The bill—proposed by President Truman and drafted with the aid of such scientists and experts as Vannevar Bush, Karl T. Compton, James B. Conant, Enrico Fermi, Ernest O. Lawrence, and J. Robert Oppenheimer (though he later withdrew his support) —called for the orderly and expeditious development of military and peaceful uses of atomic energy by a joint Pentagon-civilian body. It was Dr. Szilard who sounded the tocsin against the measure. Scientists at atomic installations were suddenly reported to be in a state of "near revolt" over the May-Johnson bill. They denounced a "military conspiracy" and charged that they had been "forbidden to speak"—though they had done little else since Hiroshima. Secrecy, said four hundred of Los Alamos' finest, "will lead to an unending war, more savage than the last." *The Nation* criticized the bill because it considered atomic energy in the "narrow terms of national security."

The May-Johnson bill, once it had been garroted, was followed by S.1717, the product of Senator McMahon. S.1717 completely excluded the military from even the remotest association with any nuclear projects. It further stated that "basic scientific information" in the atomic energy field be "freely disseminated." And it gave a proposed Atomic Energy Commission the right to determine what information could be disclosed without violation of the Espionage Act, adding that in cases where no determination was made against disclosure, the punitive provisions of the act would be automatically suspended. In other words, all the wraps were off unless the AEC specifically laid down a prohibition.

When Senator Arthur Vandenberg introduced an amendment, eventually passed by the Congress, establishing a Military Liaison Committee to be kept informed of the work of the Atomic Energy Commission, the tocsin sounded again. McMahon charged that the Vandenberg amendment would allow the Pentagon to "look into every single phone call, every single file, every single action . . . anything from the hiring of janitors at atomic energy installations to the construction of atomic plants." Eighteen organizations immediately protested the amendment, and one propagandist left an indignant letter at the White House. In his diary, a somewhat puzzled Vandenberg wrote:

There is a perfectly legitimate demand in the country (especially among scientists and educators) that final peacetime control of atomic energy should rest in civilian hands . . . But! I do not agree that in the present state of world affairs the Army and the Navy should be totally excluded from consultation when they see the national security to be involved . . .

The trouble with those who have been most violently urging civilian control is that they all but ignore the national security factor. Of course, they are supported in this viewpoint by every Communist and every fellow-traveler and every parlor-pink in the country, because these latter groups would like to make the national security as insecure as possible.

The *Daily Worker* had its own response: "Atomic Fascism."

The House of Representatives, undaunted, amended the Atomic Energy Act to require at least a modicum of secrecy and security—though this was to a degree ignored by those who first administered it. But the real battle was joined over the hydrogen or fusion bomb, for which most of the theoretical work had been done by Dr. Edward Teller at the instigation of Oppenheimer before the Hiroshima bomb was exploded. According to John J. McCloy, the H-bomb could have been an actuality by 1947—except for the remarkable gyrations, feet-dragging, and general obstructionism of Oppenheimer and others of his colleagues who had been most zealous in beating the Nazis to the atomic, or fission, bomb.

In discussing Oppenheimer's role, there are great obstacles to any definitive statement of his position. He himself stated in 1954, and not facetiously, that "in the nine years we have been talking about these things, I have said almost everything on almost every side of every question." Oppenheimer was under oath and facing the loss of his security clearance, so this may have been a legal maneuver. But taking hyperbole into account, it was a fair statement of fact. What is significant in this context is not what he said at various occasions but the net effect of his personality and his sentiments on the scientific community. In its statement of charges, the Atomic Energy Commission attempted to synthesize what this effect had been. Disassociating the charge from its loyalty-security implications and evaluating it simply as a summary of Oppenheimer's point of view, it makes interesting reading:

It was reported that in 1945 you expressed the view that "there is a reasonable possibility that it [the hydrogen bomb] can be made," but that the feasibility of the hydrogen bomb did not appear, on theoretical grounds, as certain as the fission bomb appeared certain, on theoretical grounds when the Los Alamos Laboratory was started; and that in the autumn of 1949 the General Advisory Committee expressed the view that "an imaginative and concerted attack on the problem has a better than even chance of producing the weapon within five years." It was further reported that in the autumn of 1949, and subsequently, you strongly opposed the development of the hydrogen bomb: (1) on moral grounds, (2) by claiming that it was not feasible, (3) by claiming that there were insufficient facilities and scientific personnel to carry on the development, and (4) that it was not politically desirable. It was further reported that even after it was determined, as a matter of national policy, to proceed with the development of a hydrogen bomb, you continued to oppose the project and declined to co-operate fully in the project. It was further reported that you departed from your proper role as an adviser to the Commission by causing the distribution separately and in private to top personnel at Los Alamos of the majority and minority reports of the General Advisory Committee on the development of the hydrogen bomb, for the purpose of trying to turn such top personnel against the development of the hydrogen bomb. It was further reported that you were instrumental in persuading other outstanding scientists not to work on the hydrogen-bomb project, and that the opposition to the hydrogen bomb, of which you are the most experienced, most powerful, and most effective member, has definitely slowed down its development.

In view of the emotions and the controversy aroused by the Oppenheimer hearings—inflamed partly by his leaking to *The New York Times* of the bare charges and his written answer, without the evidence which might have allowed a dispassionate evaluation —it is necessary to note that it was certainly within Oppenheimer's right to oppose the hydrogen bomb. But it must also be added that this right did not include a corollary privilege of attempting to veto high government policy while he maintained his position as a member of the General Advisory Committee. Of the four reasons for his opposition, as ascribed to him by the AEC, only one was proper: that the facilities and the personnel to make the bomb were inadequate. Holding the other three, he should have resigned from the GAC and openly taken his case to the public and to the scientific community. As an adviser, his role was limited to the scientific and the technical; it did not extend to the moral and political. He himself stated that in the postwar years "our principal duty was to make our technical experience and judgment available . . . in a context and against a background of the official views of the government."

Of considerable importance is the next question: Were the AEC's charges well founded? Had they been made in a political debate rather than as the basis for a formal hearing, would Oppenheimer have denied them? And is there documentary evidence to sustain the AEC? On some aspects of the AEC's contention, there is sharply divided testimony. There are some who asserted that even after the hydrogen bomb had been ordered by President Truman, Oppenheimer and his colleagues carried on a campaign against participation by other scientists in the project. There is equally firm testimony that he did not. Oppenheimer's own testimony is hardly categorical, one way or another. In considering the subtle brainwashing which was a major end of Phase Two, the facts as they can be ascertained are of value to this account. They can be broken down into several categories.

1. *Did Dr. Oppenheimer believe in 1949 that the hydrogen, or the thermonuclear, or super bomb was not feasible? Or did he use that argument because he believed that the hydrogen bomb should not be made for moral reasons?*

On September 20, 1944—and after he had been informed by MED security officials that the Soviets had penetrated to an unspecified degree the secret of the atomic bomb—Oppenheimer wrote to Dr. Richard Tolman, urgently pressing for work on the super bomb.*

I should like, therefore, to put in writing at an early date the recommendation that the subject of *initiating violent thermonuclear reactions be pursued with vigor and diligence, and promptly.* In this connection I should like to point out that gadgets of reasonable efficiency and suitable design can almost certainly induct significant thermonuclear reaction in deuterium ... [Emphasis added.]
It is not at all clear whether we shall actually make this development during the present project, but it is of great importance that such (deletion) gadgets form an experimentally possible transition from a simple gadget to the super and thus open the possibility of a not purely theoretical approach to the latter. ...
At the present time, site Y [Los Alamos] does not contemplate undertaking this, but I believe that with a somewhat longer time scale than our present one, this line of investigation might prove profitable.
In general, not only for the scientific but for the political evaluation of the possibilities of our project, the critical, prompt, and effective exploration of the extent to which energy can be released by thermonuclear reactions is clearly of profound importance. Several members of this laboratory, notably Teller, Bethe, von Neumann, Rabi, and Fermi have expressed great interest in the problems outlined above ...

This was Oppenheimer in 1944, when the pressure of the scientific community—and the emotional drive—was to pile up armaments against the Nazis. Yet on October 29, 1949, as chairman of the General Advisory Committee, in a climate of opinion conditioned by a new kind of pressure against "warmongering" or exacerbating the Kremlin's sensibilities, Oppenheimer would write:

We believe a super bomb should never be produced. Mankind would be far better off not to have a demonstration of the feasi-

* The parts of this letter dealing with technical aspects are still classified.

bility of such a weapon until the present climate of world opinion changes.

2. *Did the argument that superiority in nuclear weapons would be a liability to the United States stem from scientific considerations, as Oppenheimer and the politicalized atomic scientists argued, or was it casuistry based on the change in the world situation?*

Writing to Dr. Tolman on October 4, 1944, Oppenheimer stated a view sharply at variance with the "logic" of 1949.

In transmitting to you the recommendations of workers at site Y on the technical and scientific developments which should be supported in the postwar period, it would seem unnecessary to provide a summary of our opinions. I should like, however, to emphasize a general point of view which I believe is shared by *most of the responsible members of this project*. [Emphasis added.]

Urging experimentation and development of the super bomb in a postwar era's more "scientifically sound manner," Oppenheimer argued:

The above considerations are all intended to focus attention to one point. Such technical hegemony as this country now possesses in the scientific and technical aspects of the problem of using nuclear reactors for explosive weapons is the result of a few years of intensive but inevitably poorly planned work. This hegemony can presumably be maintained only by continued development both on the technical and on the fundamental scientific aspects of the problem, for which the availability of the active materials and the participation of qualified scientists and engineers are equally indispensable. *No government can adequately fulfill its responsibilities as custodian if it rests upon the wartime achievements of this project, however great they may temporarily seem, to insure future mastery in this field.* [Emphasis added.]

Within two years, although the scientific facts had not changed, Oppenheimer would be taking a diametrically opposed line. All that had changed was the politics of the situation. No longer did Oppenheimer argue for steps to "insure the future mastery" of this country in nuclear weapons. Like the sponge he had always been in political matters, he absorbed and made his own the arguments of some of his colleagues, attempted to persuade men like Dr. Edward Teller to resign from the project, wisecracked that as far as he was concerned "you can give Los Alamos back to the Indians," and used his persuasive powers to argue against the very "hegemony" he had once sought. As those who have engaged in conversation with Dr. Oppenheimer will attest, he was a most persuasive man.

3. *Did Oppenheimer attempt to dissuade his fellow scientists from engaging in research on the super bomb?*

Oppenheimer has conceded that his lack of enthusiasm for continuing and accelerating work on the hydrogen bomb, even after the Soviets exploded their first atomic device in 1949, helped to discourage other scientists and militated against their participation in the vital work. (In point of fact, progress of the work at Los Alamos and the other atomic installations began grinding to a halt right after Hiroshima and did not move into gear until President Truman ordered a crash program on the super bomb.) Whether he actively campaigned against the new project is difficult to determine. The testimony of his friends contradicts that of other scientists—and Oppenheimer's self-admitted fallibility of memory does not aid in arriving at any conclusions.

It is not to impugn motives but to demonstrate the amazing success of Phase Two that the sole documentary evidence—a diary kept by Dr. Luis Alvarez—and the testimony of Dr. Teller, "father" of the H-bomb, are presented here. Alvarez began to keep this diary shortly after the Soviets had exploded their device in September of 1949, and he elaborated on its brief references in testimony before the Gray Board:

October 5, 1949. Latimer and I thought independently that the Russians could be working hard on the super and might get there ahead of us. The only thing to do seems to get there first . . .

October 8, 1949. Arrived Washington after lunch. Went to AEC and talked with Pitzer, Gen. McCormack, Latimer, and Paul Fine. Told them what we planned to do and got good response.

October 10, 1949 . . . Went to Capitol and had lunch with Senator McMahon and Representative Hinshaw. Told them of our plans and got good reactions.

(Testimony: "They said, 'We hope you can get something going.' ")

Back to AEC—saw Lilienthal. He was only lukewarm to proposition.

(Testimony: "I must confess that I was somewhat shocked by his behavior. He did not even seem to want to talk about the program. He turned his chair around and looked out the window and indicated that he did not want to even discuss the matter. He did not like the idea of thermonuclear weapons.")

October 11, 1949. In New York . . . we went to see Rabi and found him happy about our plans. He is worried, too.

(Testimony: "He agreed with us that the hydrogen bomb program was a very good program, and he was happy we were doing something to get it reactivated.")

October 16, 1949 . . . Drew Pearson's first mention of "H-bomb."

October 17, 1949. Talked with Hafstad, Zinn, and Pitzer this afternoon on phone. Things are going as well as possible . . . Zinn says he has ideas about how to do the job . . .

October 24, 1949. . . . Hafstad (at Oak Ridge Conference) says nothing has happened in the last week about our program. This is very disappointing in view of Hafstad's enthusiasm last week when he left . . . Apparently Zinn has thrown a lot of doubts in people's mind about the wisdom of our program . . . Talked with Teller . . . [I] felt Oppie was lukewarm to our project and Conant was definitely opposed.

Chicago meeting—then on to Washington—talked with all GAC and most of AEC Commissioners. Particularly interesting talk with

Oppie after he briefed Bradbury and Norstad at GAC meeting. Pretty foggy thinking.

(Testimony: "He [Oppenheimer] said that he did not think the United States should build the hydrogen bomb, and the main reason that he gave for this if my memory serves me correctly, and I think it does, was that if we built a hydrogen bomb, then the Russians would build a hydrogen bomb, whereas if we did not build a hydrogen bomb, then the Russians would not build a hydrogen bomb. I found this such an odd point of view that I don't understand it to this day. I told Dr. Oppenheimer that he might find that a reassuring point of view ... Dr. Serber * was present and agreed with Dr. Oppenheimer and this surprised me greatly in view of the fact that two or three days before he had gone to see Dr. Oppenheimer telling me that he would try to convert Dr. Oppenheimer's lukewarmness into some enthusiasm for our project.")

After the conversation with Oppenheimer, Alvarez felt that "the program was dead." It remained at least moribund, except for some lonely work still being done by Dr. Teller at Los Alamos, until the President revived it by ordering construction of the super bomb in January of 1950. Alvarez noted that though some experts had said the fission bomb was impossible, it had been built. "The technology [for the A-bomb] was developed because of the climate at Los Alamos, enthusiastic people [including Oppenheimer], who said we don't care what the experts say, we will make it work. This was the thing that was missing in the hydrogen-bomb program after the war, and the thing which came into being some while after the Presidential directive," Alvarez said. Then, in December 1950, almost a year after the President had ordered all-out work on the super, Alvarez was told by Oppenheimer: "We all agree that the hydrogen-bomb program should be stopped, but if we were to stop it or to suggest that it be stopped, this would cause so much disruption at Los Alamos and in other laboratories where they are doing instrumentation work that I feel we should let it go

* See testimony concerning Dr. Serber on pp. 74–75.

on, and it will die a natural death with the coming tests when those tests fail. That will be the natural time to chop the hydrogen-bomb program off." *

Edward Teller's account of Oppenheimer's activities—and of his influence on other scientists in support of his opposition to the hydrogen bomb—bolstered the Alvarez testimony and diary. Teller characterized Oppenheimer's effect on the program as one of "hindrance" which hurt the morale at Los Alamos until President Truman's directive. After that time, Oppenheimer was, in general, cold to the project—with one exception, in June 1951, when he warmly supported a new approach in research. And Teller added:

Prior to the [President's] announcement, preceding it perhaps by two or three days, I saw Dr. Oppenheimer at an atomic energy conference concerning another matter, and during this meeting it

* Alvarez testified that he was a member of a long-range planning committee on the hydrogen bomb to which he and Dr. C. C. Lauritsen were appointed by Oppenheimer. At the end of 1950, Alvarez was given evidence of the feelings of some of the scientists:

"I do know that Dr. Lauritsen apparently had strong reasons, probably some of a moral nature, for not wanting the hydrogen bomb. I do know that Dr. Lauritsen's closest associate, Dr. William Fowler, had been giving lectures on the radio against the hydrogen bomb. I was in Pasadena staying with Dr. Bacher one night when I was giving a lecture at Cal. Tech., and at a dinner party that night all I heard was stories about why you should not have hydrogen bombs, and the fact that the members of the staff at Cal. Tech. were giving public lectures and talking on the radio against the hydrogen bomb."

Alvarez also had the following colloquy with Roger Robb, counsel for the Gray Board:

"Q: You testified as others did that Dr. Oppenheimer did a splendid job at Los Alamos. Did it strike you as peculiar that one who had done such a splendid job at Los Alamos [on the atomic bomb] could entertain opinions which you considered so wrong in respect to the hydrogen bomb?

"A: I was very surprised when I found that he had these opinions since he had used the super as the primary incentive to get me to join the Manhattan District [during the war] . . . He had spent almost a solid afternoon telling me about the exciting possibilities of the super, and asked me to join and help with the building of such a device. So I was therefore very surprised when I found he had these objections [in 1949]."

became clear to me that in Dr. Oppenheimer's opinion a decision was impending and this would be a go-ahead decision.

At that time I asked Oppenheimer, if this is now the decision, would he then please really help us to work, recalling the very effective work during the war. Oppenheimer's answer to this was in the negative ... This negative reply gave me the feeling that I should not look to Oppenheimer for help under any circumstances.

A few months later, during the spring, I nevertheless called up Oppenheimer and I asked him not for direct help but for his support in recruiting people. Dr. Oppenheimer said then, "You know, in this matter, I am neutral. I would be glad, however, to recommend to you some very good people who are working here at the Institute" [of Advanced Studies in Princeton, headed by Oppenheimer] and he mentioned a few. I wrote to all of them and tried to persuade them to come to Los Alamos. None of them came.

Fortunately for the United States and the free world, Dr. Teller was able to recruit a group of scientists and to infuse them with his own drive to build the super. On November 1, 1952, the first fusion bomb was exploded at Eniwetok, and the United States maintained a lead which the Soviets were desperately trying to eliminate. It is now known that the Soviets, having gathered from their various apparatuses the know-how of the atomic bomb and the theoretical aspects of the hydrogen bomb, began work on both simultaneously. Given a more advanced technology and a firmer industrial base, they might have been able to explode their own fusion device before the Eniwetok test. Given its limitations, the Soviet Union's "success" can be explained in terms used by Jerome Wiesner: "All science and technology, in doing something the first time, is extremely difficult and takes a few strokes of genius and brilliance. Doing it the second time, once it has been demonstrated and the general outlines are there, is a good deal simpler."

The bemused attitude of many American scientists, and the two-way stretch of their political thinking, did not end with the explosion of the Soviet bomb or the increasingly apparent knowledge

that the Communists would use such nuclear weapons as they had
to bluff and blackmail the free world. Scientists and scholars remained convinced that any agreement between East and West
was a step forward—no matter who benefited by it. Men of otherwise reasonable judgment subscribed to the call of a series of
meetings which brought together Soviet and Western scientists in
what was to be a marriage of true minds. "Political disagreements
should not influence men of science in estimating what is probable,"
Bertrand Russell declared in launching the Pugwash Conferences
financed by the multimillionaire apologist for the Soviet Union,
Cyrus Eaton. "We have not yet found that the views of experts on
this question depend in any degree upon their politics or prejudices
... The abolition of war will demand distasteful limitations of
national sovereignty . . . Remember humanity and forget the rest."

The Pugwash Conferences helped to maintain the same kind of
blind optimism and blind fear that caused the delay in the work on
the hydrogen bomb. Lord Russell emerged from the first thinking
precisely what the secret conspirators wanted him to believe—
that the Communist countries would be "gradually improved by
public opinion from within if the fear of alien hostility were
removed." This hoary argument was garnished by Eaton's statement to Chairman J. William Fulbright of the Senate Foreign Relations Committee that he was "convinced that agreement can be
reached between East and West" and by his article in the *Foreign
Policy Bulletin* painting a cozy picture of Soviet integrity:

Each scientist there believed what the other scientists were saying . . . All of us were convinced that the Russians were being completely honest, completely frank. Therefore, it made for a remarkable community where the cards were all on the table, where
everyone was aboveboard with everyone else.

This description by Eaton—and even by others whose motives
cannot be questioned—has lived on in the attitude of those who
to this day insist that Soviet scientists are scientists first and only

incidentally tools of the Kremlin. But it was the Western scientists who placed their cards on the table. The Soviet scientists, whose commissar was Aleksandr Vasilevich Topchiev, simply repeated the Communist propaganda line on cessation of atomic testing and repeated *Pravda*'s charges against the United States. They were further bound by Topchiev's strictures on the uses of science:

Our scientists cannot and must not stand aside from ideological struggle between communism and capitalism. Some scientific work-
ers try mechanically to extend to the field of ideology the slogan of peaceful coexistence of states with different social and economic systems. A time has come, they say, when we can permit ourselves this coexistence of two ideologies. This is a profoundly mistaken conclusion . . . Any indefiniteness, neutrality, or an a-political stand, which V. I. Lenin constantly opposed, is now more than ever intolerable in our midst.*

Topchiev was, and is, the First Secretary of the Soviet Academy of Science, which Dr. Eugene Rabinowitch, editor of the *Bulletin of Atomic Scientists*—after his initial belief that Soviet scientists "share a common language [with those of the West] and approach problems in the same way"—described as "the general staff" of a "highly organized scientific army" utilizing "propaganda slogans." Topchiev clearly outmatched the scientists with whom he met and even convinced one Cornell professor that the answer to the problem of atomic testing and inspection would be a proviso in the treaty "making it a citizen's legal duty to report knowledge of secret testing to the International Control Commission."

It was by a combination of propaganda and confusion, of tugs at the heartstrings and punches at the terror zone, of fantasies and appeals to "reason," that the Center in Moscow and its masters in

* It is interesting to note that at these "cards-on-the-table" conferences, one of the Soviet delegates accompanying Topchiev was a Professor N. A. Talensky. Talensky, however, is a major general, Soviet Army General Staff, and is described in the *Biographical Dictionary of the U.S.S.R.* as "one of the most . . . influential military theoreticians on the general staff."

the Kremlin muddied the waters of American policy and weakened the will to resist. Among those from the West present at these conferences were members of the apparatus, one of whom defected to the Soviet Union. Were the open conspiracy and the manipulation of sincere and decent men more dangerous than the theft of atomic secrets? The history of Western wishful thinking during the past two decades may offer an answer.

XVI

The Unfinished Chapter

HISTORY is a jigsaw puzzle. From time to time, the impertinent researcher fits in a new piece, making the configuration clearer. But in the attrition of time, some pieces are lost. Others are willfully destroyed by those who have something to hide or something to gain. The puzzle is never completed. Yet each piece, as it is fitted into place, generates its own fascination. Take, for example, the conversation between veteran correspondent Frank Conniff and Marshal Zhukov, then the Soviet Union's most influential military man, in 1955. Conniff, with William Randolph Hearst Jr. and Bob Considine, was making a Pulitzer-Prize-winning investigation of the new men in the Kremlin—and of their hot-and-cold aggressions.

"If our intentions were to conquer the world," Zhukov stated, "we would have marched to the Channel in 1946 when your country had demobilized."

"But, marshal," Conniff answered, "it is generally believed that the reason you didn't march was because we had the atom bomb."

"Ah, yes," Zhukov said. *"But you only had five."*

In the context of this account, that remark assumes importance simply because Zhukov could so casually allude to what was considered in the early postwar era the free world's most strategic secret. For three American newspapermen to ask him how he knew would have been both futile and impolitic. Hearst, Conniff, and Considine, moreover, could have made some educated guesses. This single disclosure fits in neatly with two other pieces of the historical jigsaw—the first now forgotten, the second never generally known.

Piece 1. In December 1946, Dr. Robert Bacher, who had headed the bomb physics division of the MED, made an inspection of Los Alamos. By that time, production of atomic bombs had slowed down almost to a halt. Many scientists had departed from Los Alamos, trailing moral indignation, for lucrative positions and the luxury of demanding that the United States share the new and more sophisticated secrets of nuclear research with the Soviet Union.* Walter Lippmann was excoriating Bernard Baruch for failing to trust the Kremlin. And David Lilienthal was proposing that this country build atomic energy plants in the Soviet Union as a token of good faith. Only the more dedicated scientists continued to work in the depleted laboratories of Los Alamos. Testifying with some horror in 1949 to the crumbling state of America's defenses apparent three years earlier, Bacher said:

I spent two days as a representative of the [Atomic Energy] Commission going over what we had. I was very deeply shocked to find out how few atomic weapons we had at that time. This came as rather a considerable surprise to me in spite of the fact that I had been rather intimately associated with the work of the Los Alamos project—roughly a year before. Judging by the consternation which appeared on some of the faces around there,

* Those who argued that there could be no such thing as a "scientific secret" changed their approach after the Fuchs disclosures. "Why bother hiding what the Soviet Union already knows?" they argued. In 1953, Medford Evans, a former official of the AEC, answered them in *The Secret War for the A-Bomb:* "The case of Klaus Fuchs dramatized the lie that there was no secret of the atomic bomb. There were many secrets, and there still are. A complex scientific and industrial project generates new secrets daily."

I concluded that this must have been the first detailed inventory that had been made.

Piece 2. Though the American people were told in 1949 by the Joint Atomic Energy Committee's majority members that David Lilienthal had found a shambles at Los Alamos but brought order and efficiency to the bomb project—and again in 1954 by Dr. Oppenheimer that he had opposed the hydrogen bomb because he wanted all effort to be focused on perfecting the fission bomb —the facts were somewhat at variance. For in 1948, shortly before the Soviet blockade of Berlin, another inventory was made at Los Alamos by the AEC. A check of A-bomb components showed that most, if not all, of America's nuclear arsenal was probably worthless. An essential ingredient of the stored bombs, it was discovered, had deteriorated and could not be counted on to bring about the necessary chain reaction.

President Truman has been roundly criticized for resorting to an airlift when the Red Army interposed its forces between West Germany and Berlin by closing the corridor. But knowing that America's major deterrent had been tragically compromised—and suspecting that the Kremlin risked war because it knew of America's impotence—he could not do otherwise. Hasty demobilization and the policies of Defense Secretary Louis Johnson had left United States Armed Forces a shell, as the world discovered when the North Koreans marched across the 38th Parallel in 1950. In the light of that knowledge, the President made do with what he had, and only the healthy respect for America's ability to rearm rapidly prevented the Soviet Union from embarking on a new military adventure in 1948.

This view of the atomic project—decimated by scientists whose tragic flaw was an arrogant belief that they knew better than "ordinary men" and could therefore impose their will on the body politic —contrasts sadly with J. Robert Oppenheimer's description of Los Alamos when Nazism was the enemy. "There was a community of aim and effort that's very hard to reproduce," he told John Dos Passos in 1952. "The work went on in an atmosphere of intellectual cordiality. People took pleasure in fitting their minds into other people's minds. That's what made it a community." It was the purpose of Phase Two, in the Kremlin's assault on America's nuclear defenses, to destroy that community—and in the crucial years, it succeeded.

But Phase One, or espionage, and Phase Two are interrelated. Therefore, it is still asked by those who consider the random political pronouncements of scientists as more valid than those of experts trained in cold war strategy: "Did the Soviets really steal the secrets of nuclear energy and its military application?" The question has been exhaustively answered, but it continues to be repeated because what it really asks is something else again: "Do spies and traitors exist?" Protesting the purity of their craft and the brotherhood of the test-tube, the scientists in effect denied this. In the West, it is almost an article of faith that a scientist is by definition a free soul seeking data unadulterated by political bias. Is Bertrand Russell's *Materia Mathematica* less valid because he would rather be Red than dead?

To those who shun logic's assessment in favor of a curbstone opinion, it is possible to reject the Center's vast researches in Western nuclear strongboxes as an aberrative manifestation of the time's plague. For them no consequence impinges on this "truth." Science, like love, conquers all. Hence the next—and already answered—question: "Wouldn't Soviet science have eventually arrived at the theoretical, experimental, and technological data of portable nuclear fission independently of the Center's efforts?" At this point, science and observable phenomena part company. For a fact, to have meaning, must lie snugly in its context. What Soviet science might have done begs the question. Far more important is what Soviet science did do, given the state of postwar technology and Russia's shattered industrial plant.

Knowing that controlled fission in a small package had been

achieved by the United States, Soviet scientists could, once the
state allocated money and materials, have duplicated the theoretical
labors which preceded the development of American nuclear
weapons and, in time, have also repeated the preliminary laboratory experiments of Fermi, Teller, Bacher, and their colleagues.
But this work would simply deposit them at the locked door of the
Atomic Age. Even the Smyth Report, which according to Senator
McMahon "brought other countries from one and a-half to two
years closer to their achievement of our own knowledge of atomic
secrets," would not have sufficed to unlock that door—for all of the
book's wealth of detail.

Without the aid of the Center's spies and its far-ranging apparatus—and at a cost which might have thoroughly disrupted the shaky
Soviet economy—the Kremlin's scientists would probably have
built the nuclear devices now in their possession. But there is more
than a possibility that without the certainty of success—a certainty
which could come only from categorical knowledge that the blueprint was theirs and could not fail to be made three-dimensional—
Stalin would have delayed while he took stock of the wreckage
about him. He was a cautious and dubious man, and it was in his
nature to look suspiciously at what had not been, in our contem-
porary gobbledygook, "concretized." Imagination and the venture
spirit entered the Kremlin with Nikita Khrushchev.

In 1951, the Joint Congressional Atomic Energy Committee was
ready to concede that had the Soviets started from scratch, it might
have extended the "nuclear gap" by up to ten years. Other experts
have set the figure higher. It took four years for the massed industrial might and accumulated efficiency of such industrial giants as
du Pont, General Electric, Tennessee Eastman, the Bell System,
and a host of other corporations—working with the greatest con-
vention in history of scientific minds and mobilizing existent
resources of trained labor and raw materials—to produce the primitive bomb which fell on Hiroshima.

Even with the mass of data supplied by Fuchs, Nunn May, Hiskey, and other agents to ease the Soviet way (and the millions of dollars in scarce metals and strategic supplies, specifically designed for atomic development and graciously donated by the Lend-Lease Administration), the U.S.S.R. took four years to explode its first atomic device. It will never be known whether this was, in fact, a bomb—but we have President Truman's word that it was not. We have no one's word that it was. Whether the fissionable materials used in the Soviet test of 1949 were manufactured behind the Iron Curtain or stolen from the United States is also a moot point. Medford Evans has made a convincing case for the possibility of theft, and his argument is bolstered by the admission of Dr. Bacher, head of the Los Alamos bomb physics division, that no inventory of America's uranium stockpile was made until July 1950.

Certainly, the Soviets continued to reach out for the product of the decadent United States right up until the zero hour of their test. Hardly noticed among the piled-up sensations of the Judith Coplon espionage trial was the testimony of FBI Special Agent Robert Lamphere on June 7, 1949. Lamphere was called to identify a report he had written which had found its way into Miss Coplon's hands. It disclosed that the Atomic Energy Commission, presumably standing guard over all materials and equipment pertaining to nuclear energy, had allowed Amtorg, a cover for Soviet espionage, to thwart the clearly stated intent of the McMahon Act —by means as yet unexplained. According to *The New York Times,* Lamphere's report stated that

... no export license had been issued for the shipment of atomic equipment that reached Soviet Russia aboard the steamship Mikhail Kutuzov in August 1947. It said a shipment of similar secret instruments was found aboard the steamship Murmansk in New York harbor Sept. 2, 1948, but American authorities removed the shipment because it had not been authorized. Then a third shipment was found on a dock in Claremont, N.J., Jan. 14, 1949, and this was also confiscated.

To understand the greatness of America's contribution to the Soviet atomic project, it is necessary simply to recapitulate in brief some of the facts, figures, and problems solved by Western inventive and engineering genius under the driving leadership of General Groves. The major point is not that the atomic bombs which ended the Pacific war cost x billions of dollars,* but rather how those bombs were made. The scientists and engineers had no guidelines, no technological precedents. They took raw theory, sometimes imperfect or tentative, and almost by trial and error began to construct the tremendously complex plants at Hanford, Oak Ridge, and Los Alamos. No one really knew what would work and what would not. Everything was tried. Since time was an essential factor, Groves and his associates could not afford to worry about duplication or waste motion if this would advance the work. There was no certain knowledge that one process might be superior to another—the scientists often differed—so different methods were simultaneously employed, at a justifiable cost in money and man-hours.

No other country in the world could have sustained this push.

Yet it took the United States, Britain, and Canada four years.

It took the Soviet Union four years.

Q.E.D.

Before the bomb could be built, means had to be found for the mass separation of fissionable U-235 from U-238 which contained it in very small quantities. To this end, the green light was given to three different methods: the gaseous diffusion process, the electromagnetic process, and the thermal diffusion process. Eventually, the gaseous diffusion process proved to be the most effective. And it was this process, which Klaus Fuchs helped develop, to which the Soviets became heir. Had the U.S.S.R. been compelled by sound security at the MED to duplicate this three-pronged assault, the story of the last decade would have been differently written.

* Even the AEC cannot estimate with any degree of certainty an approximate cost.

The bad quality of Soviet workmanship, to which any visitor to the U.S.S.R. can attest, would have led to serious failures. But with the knowledge that they were moving down an already blazed trail, Soviet scientists proceeded with confidence.

The electromagnetic process plant cost close to four hundred million dollars. Electric power, of which the Soviet Union had a drastic shortage, alone counted for ten million dollars. Earmarked by the Treasury for the MED's industrial use were 86,000 tons of silver. General Groves has written of the "fabulous" amounts of special equipment needed—"the enormous oval-shaped electromagnets, the process bins and the units enclosed in them, the control cubicles, motor generator sets, vacuum systems, chemical recovery equipment and thousands of smaller parts." To give a small idea of these requirements, Groves notes that 128 carloads of electrical equipment arrived at Oak Ridge in one two-week period. (It was the severe shortages in the Soviet Union of the materials to manufacture this equipment during the postwar years that led President Truman and others to conclude that the atomic explosions detected after 1949 were caused by laboratory-created devices rather than production-line bombs.) In building the plant and beginning operations, 24,000 skilled men were needed—and the MED was compelled to send many of them to school to learn their new and unprecedented tasks. The electromagnets, 20'x20'x20', had to be rebuilt because of unforeseen bugs. One building in the complex of structures was put out of action when a bird perched on a high-tension wire and shorted it.

Groves drove ahead at a breakneck pace, refusing to allow the perversity of inanimate objects or a more nagging human obtuseness to deter him. "The task of whipping the bugs out of equipment, overcoming failures, low efficiencies and losses, with untrained personnel, while surrounded by the dirt and din of construction work, was a prodigious one," he has stated—and this was an understatement. Often equipment would be installed at one end of a plant while construction work was still going on at the other—

and this in handling equipment where tolerances were microscopic. Yet by mid-July 1944, the electromagnetic plant at Oak Ridge was delivering required amounts of fissionable materials to Los Alamos. Could this "miracle of the MED" have been repeated in the chaos of postwar Russia without precise blueprints?

The gaseous diffusion process, according to General Groves's statement, was "completely novel." * It was one, moreover, which required the ultimate in engineering and technological sophistication. Its purpose was to separate U-235 from U-238. The method, Groves wrote in *Now It Can Be Told:*

was based on the theory that if uranium gas was pumped against a porous barrier, the lighter molecules of the gas, containing U-235, would pass through more rapidly than the heavier U-238 molecules. The heart of the process was, therefore, the barrier, a porous thin metal sheet or membrane with millions of submicroscopic openings per square inch . . . However, there is so little difference in mass between the hexafluorides of U-235 and U-238 that it was impossible to gain much separation in a single diffusion step. This is why there had to be several thousand successive stages.

Despite a crash program to develop the necessary barriers, it was not until the entire K-25 plant at Oak Ridge had been constructed (at a cost of two hundred million dollars and covering close to forty-five acres of space) that the problem was solved. Then came a new problem: how to mass-produce the barriers. Union Carbide found the answer. Special gas pumps to propel the uranium gas

* The Groves characterization is somewhat over-enthusiastic. Some years prior to the launching of the great American experiment in 1939, Dr. Gustav Ludwig Hertz of the N. V. Philips Gloeilampenfabrieken company in Holland had discovered the basic theoretical principles of the gaseous diffusion process. Dr. Hertz, a winner of the Nobel Prize in Physics, had also begun the practical application of his theories. Using his work as a starting point, MED scientists perfected it and took the long leap forward to its application on a mass production basis. The Philips Laboratories, which had ties with Dr. Fermi and collaborated in planning his escape from Italy, successfully hid its patents from the invading Nazis.

were devised by Allis Chalmers. In designing the plant, the engineers suggested that solid nickel be used for the hundreds of miles of piping, in order to prevent corrosion—an excellent idea except that it would have required more than the world's total nickel output. A revolutionary new method of nickel-plating had to be devised —and was. New instruments, new methods of welding (and men sent to school to learn it), means of keeping equipment clinically clean—these were the order of the day. Another 25,000 skilled workers and technicians had to be found for K-25.

It is not necessary to describe the construction of the thermal diffusion plant or the plutonium installation at Hanford to make the point. Every inch of the road which led to the Alamogordo test was dangerous and uncharted. Like the pioneers, the scientists and engineers had to cut through virgin forests, blunder into impassable terrain and retrace their steps, forge new implements in the wilderness. All the massed scientific and technological might of three nations had to be mobilized. A whole new world was created at Hanford, Oak Ridge, and Los Alamos. Yet such is the nature of science that Dr. Walter Zinn, director of the Argonne National Laboratory, would remark that these new discoveries could sometimes be reduced, for transmission to a hostile nation, to "just a number."

The Soviet Union received far more than a number from the traitors, the dupes, and the professional agents. Thousands of words in the precise handwriting of Klaus Fuchs, sketches from David Greenglass, applied theory from the Communist cell at Berkeley, data from Clarence Hiskey, experimental techniques from Pontecorvo, bomb technology from Joan Hinton, invaluable materials from Nunn May, blueprints that funneled through Great Falls—this was the ball game. Every piece of information which reached the Center in Moscow for distribution to teams of Soviet and German scientists saved Stalin and his successors thousands of man-hours in laboratories and over drawing boards. Every piece of information sped the Soviet traveler down the road hacked out by Western scientific genius. Given this help, the wonder is not that the Soviet Union developed a nuclear device of its own in four years but that it took so long.

And what of the super bomb, which Oppenheimer had in 1944 urged as essential to America's postwar arsenal? What of the "community of aim and effort" which abruptly ended with World War II, when the Soviet Union, rather than Nazi Germany, became the potential enemy? This, too, has been discussed. But armchair analysis aside, the flat and incontrovertible fact has been stated by Joseph Alsop and the scientist Ralph Lapp: "Between July 1945 and January 1950, there was no serious or concerted American effort to make the hydrogen bomb." Neither the scientific community (as a whole) nor the Atomic Energy Commission was really willing or ready to push ahead in a manner comparable to the earlier Los Alamos effort.

This, then, is the unfinished chapter. For the full story will not be closed by history. All the pieces of the jigsaw puzzle will never be fitted into place. But most of the blank places can be filled when those who now refuse to observe the emerging pattern cease to deny the facts of Soviet espionage, to belabor those who expose it, and to hamper those who must detect it. The spies, when discovered, flee the country or go to prison. But the spies do not act alone. They are aided and abetted by an underground conspiracy which gives them cover and supplies them with a constant stream of new recruits. Phase One of the greatest plot in history would not have succeeded had communism been understood and rejected by all honorable men in the 1930s and 1940s. It would not have succeeded had the scientific community not been poisoned in its thinking by *apparatchiks* and friends of *apparatchiks* who convinced it that security, FBI vigilance, and a concern over subversion were an abomination.

Phase Two would have failed had not the intellectual community absorbed, almost with the air it breathed, the notion that the world's most vicious tyranny was an occasionally misguided but essentially idealistic experiment in social engineering. It would have failed had it realized that the uncertain verities of science do not apply to a battlefield where secret armies clash. Scientists construct, but the Communists, in Harold Laski's phrase, are dedicated to "the organization of catastrophe." Science and communism are mutually antagonistic.

Until the Communists have told their last lie, betrayed their last friend, and conquered their last enemy, Phase Two will continue. Voices will continue to plead that the Kremlin be given still another chance to demonstrate its good intentions. Only when Communist perfidy has been forever ground into the dust can this chapter be ended.

Index

A-bomb; *see* Atomic bomb, U.S.

Acheson, Dean, 246n, 251

Adams, Arthur Alexandrovitch, 3–4, 5–7, 8, 10–11, 12–14, 15, 18, 39, 43–44, 81–94, 128

Addis, Thomas, 76n

Aerosol bomb, 158

Alameda County, Calif., 16, 56, 64

Alamogordo, N.M., bomb test, 34, 44, 46–47, 136, 173, 264, 293

Albuquerque, N.M., 201, 204–5, 208–9, 213

Allis Chalmers Co., 293

Alsop, Joseph, quoted, 294

Alvarez, Luis, 276–79, 279n

Amo, U.S.S.R. automobile plant, 7

Amtorg Trading Corporation, New York, 9, 11, 101, 152, 182, 289

Angelov, Lieutenant ("Baxter"), 133, 134

Appell, Donald T., 113–14, 116–18

Argonne National Laboratory (AEC), 81, 95, 134, 135, 219, 293; theft of uranium from, 260–62

Arnold, Wing Commander Henry, 176, 177, 178, 179, 238

Aronoff, Jacob B., 13, 43

Association of Los Alamos Scientists, 226

Atomic bomb, Soviet, 20n, 46, 289, 291

Atomic bomb, U.S., 34, 46–47, 173, 201–10 *passim,* 221, 222, 224, 263, 285–86; Soviet theft of information on, Phase One (Espionage), 20–247, Phase Two, 4, 264–83, summary, 287–95; processes, 290–91; summary of program, 290–93; *see also* Hydrogen bomb

Atomic energy, international control of, 26n

Atomic Energy Act (U.S.), 176, 227, 250, 251, 258; amendments, 271

Atomic Energy Commission, U.S. (AEC), 20, 248–63 *passim;* Oppenheimer testimony before Security Board, 62, 64, 75n, 271–73; security (FBI), 176, 227, 249–52; May-Johnson Bill, 269–70; Military Liaison Committee, 270; General Advisory Committee, 272–76 *passim*

Atomic Energy for Military Purposes (Smythe report), 137n, 142, 251, 288

Atomic espionage, Soviet, 4–5; Great Index, 22, 123–24, 167; Moscow Center, 22, 28–29, 192, 195, 293,